Valley for Dreams

Valley for Dreams

Life and Landscape in the Sacramento Valley

SUSAN WILEY HARDWICK
DONALD G. HOLTGRIEVE

ROWMAN & LITTLEFIELD PUBLISHERS, INC.
Lanham • Boulder • New York • London

ROWMAN & LITTLEFIELD PUBLISHERS, INC.

Published in the United States of America
by Rowman & Littlefield Publishers, Inc.
4720 Boston Way, Lanham, Maryland 20706

3 Henrietta Street
London WC2E 8LU, England

Copyright © 1996 by Rowman & Littlefield Publishers, Inc.

British Cataloging in Publication Information Available

Library of Congress Cataloging-in-Publication Data

Hardwick, Susan Wiley.
    Valley for dreams : life and landscape in the Sacramento Valley /
Susan Wiley Hardwick, Donald G. Holtgrieve.
        p.   cm.
    Includes bibliographical references and index.
    ISBN 0-8476-8285-4 (alk. paper). — ISBN 0-8476-8286-2 (alk.
paper)
    1. Sacramento Valley (Calif.)—Geography. 2. Human geography—
California—Sacramento Valley. 3. Landscape—California—
Sacramento Valley. I. Holtgrieve, Donald G. II. Title.
F868.S13H37   1996
979.4'5—dc20   96-29243
                                                             CIP

ISBN 0–8476–8285-4 (cloth : alk. paper)
ISBN 0–8476–8286-2 (pbk. : alk. paper)

Printed in the United States of America

To Paige Christine,
our youngest "Valley Girl"—
born during the flood of 1995

Contents

Figures

Tables

Preface

In our teaching and in our travels in the Sacramento Valley, we discovered that many of our students along with many other residents of the region originally came from somewhere else. It also seemed that most of our friends, relatives, and professional colleagues who lived outside the "North State" had little or no knowledge or conception of the "Valley" as a geographic entity. The immense and diverse area was, in fact, almost *terra incognita* to everyone who lived elsewhere. The story of life and landscape in this "Forgotten California" clearly needed to be told.

But we soon found that the most difficult dilemma facing any writer of regional geography is what *not* to write (rather than *what* to include). Time and space limitations pressured us to seek a concise way to introduce the Sacramento Valley to newcomers and visitors and yet add interesting information for those who have lived here for a long time.

To delve into the geography of the real "North State," you will note that we have minimized our discussion of the city of Sacramento. This largest of Valley cities has its own literature. Our focus, instead, is centered on the region's other smaller cities and towns, its rural areas, and its natural environment. Most importantly, we have chosen to focus on the people who live in the region. Their stories and their impacts on the land form the heart of the Valley and thus are the lifeblood of this book. In tribute to pioneer residents of the region, and as a theme for our focus on historical geography, we have entitled this work *Valley for Dreams*. After more than twenty-five years of research on the land and people of the Sacramento Valley, we believe the dream is still alive.

Acknowledgments

The narrative and maps for this book were prepared with enthusiasm but also some trepidation because everyone we discussed the project with was passionately concerned with his or her own topic within the vast region not being overlooked. We hope we have presented the essence of life and landscape in the Valley as sensitively and completely as did each informant and each reviewer who so generously shared their story with us.

Research for the book would not have been possible without the financial support of the Office of Sponsored Projects at California State University, Chico. Thanks to this help, we were able to enlist the excellent research assistance of graduate students Jennifer Helzer, Laura Mainwaring, Matthew Bokemeier, Kris Kackert, Kamela Blas Polo, and Jeanette Gardner Betts. Most of their data gathering effort took place in Special Collections in Meriam Library at California State University, Chico. They were guided there by the able and talented Director of Special Collections, William Jones, and his enthusiastic and knowledgeable staff, Mary Ellen Bailey and Pam Herman Bush. The vast majority of the data presented in the chapters that follow were gleaned from their substantive experience assisting scholars and students with research on the Valley and their remarkable archival collections. Materials gathered from this rich repository were supplemented by historical information gathered at Bancroft Library at the University of California, Berkeley; Shields Library at the University of California, Davis; the California State Library in Sacramento; and the Library of Congress in Washington, D.C.

Cartography for *Valley for Dreams* was expertly handled by Jennifer Helzer, doctoral student in geography at the University of Texas and Steve Stewart, graduate student in geography at California State University, Chico. We owe both these talented professional cartographers our warmest appreciation. Also deeply appreciated is the elegant (yet simple) art provided by Elizabeth Polivka of Paradise, California. Her vision of life and landscape in the Valley enhanced our efforts significantly. Completion of the final manuscript would not have been possible without the talent and expertise of Anne Russell. We owe her an immense debt of gratitude.

Reviewers for various sections and chapters of the book made helpful comments and added a great deal of useful information to the narrative, especially to the ethnic histories. These reviewers were invaluable in making the book readable and accurate and we deeply appreciate their important contribution. They include Irene Helzer for reviewing the chapters that focused on equity immigrants and on the evolution of the city of Redding; Parveen Pamma and Seema Raikhy who reviewed the section on the Sikhs in Yuba City; Maribel Medina, Guadelupe Rivera, and Jesus Moreno who commented on the Latino chapter; May Yang and Jennifer Helzer who read the section on Southeast Asians; Angela Morris who critiqued the chapter on Midwesterners; and, last but definitely not least, William Jones and Chester Hendrix who reviewed the section on Latter Day Saints in Gridley. In addition to these content reviewers, William Dreyer's excellent commentary on Native Americans added a great deal of new information to Chapter 3, especially pertaining to the theme of human-environmental interaction of this important group of people in the Valley.

We would be remiss not to extend our deepest appreciation to the faculty and students in the CSU, Chico *Department of Geography and Planning* for sharing their ideas about what a regional historical geography of the Sacramento Valley should contain. Their constant support and belief in the importance of completing this book made it all possible. We especially appreciate the more than twenty years of support provided by Professors Margaret Trussell, David Lantis, and Bruce Bechtol. Without their belief in both of us all along the way, none of this would have been possible.

Finally, both of us are deeply indebted to Chico poet Amy Runge Gaffney for sharing her moving perceptions of the Sacramento Valley with us as a powerful opening for the first chapter of the book. "Sacramento Valley Summer" was first published in "The New Voice" as "North Valley Summer" and is reprinted here with permission.

Susan Wiley Hardwick
Donald G. Holtgrieve
Matsu-Ya, Forest Ranch, California, 1996

Written by an Indiana poet after her first summer in the Sacramento Valley . . .

Sacramento Valley Summer

It's brazen,
this clarity of light—

this immediacy of objects,
this transparency of air.

Here no gauze of moisture
softens
or protects the waking eye,
the guarded heart,
from what will not be denied.

No supple green
lies between us
and bone
of rock, of limb.

Only the meadowlark's song
arcs
supple as spring leaves
across the sunstruck sky,

the sweet scent of dried grasses
whispering.

—Amy Runge Gaffney

Chapter 1

Early Images

On a topographic map, the Sacramento Valley appears as a wide, green swath up the center of northern California. From a commercial aircraft at 30,000 feet, its rice fields and orchards are emerald green and interlaced with silvery waterways. The scene rushing by a car or bus window at ground level reveals a region of extreme regularity and pragmatic efficiency. Landscapes seem almost redundant. But this narrow angle of vision surely obscures both the magnitude and diversity of the Valley's life and landscape. These views, in fact, are much too limiting for geographic analysis.

Up, Up and Away: A Hot Air Balloon Flight

Imagine instead that you are relaxing in a hot air balloon at 200 feet, carried by a southerly wind, enroute north from Sacramento to Redding. From this vantage point, barriers to observation such as road cuts, river levees, and vegetation are eliminated. Imagine a clear, summer day with a superb view. Passengers in our balloon glimpse breathtaking views of the Sierra Nevadas off to the east, the Coast Ranges to the west, and the Sacramento Airport surrounded by rice fields below. Another way of looking at the Valley from above is shown on the air photograph in Figure 1.1. This view shows the Sutter Buttes and a portion of Yuba City.

In the far distance, snow-capped Mt. Shasta rises 14,162 feet above sea level and to the northeast Mt. Lassen reaches 10,457 feet in altitude. Our balloon glides silently between the mountain ranges. As you strain to see every detail, you look down and see that the land below appears as a flat patchwork quilt of patterns and forms. Everything looks somehow familiar but yet different from ways we may have imagined them in our minds from the usual ground-level vantage points.

Figure 1.1. The Sacramento Valley.

Our relaxing flight continues north along the meandering 327 miles of the Sacramento River and its complex network of slough and channels. We note that the free flow of the river's water is constrained by an intricate and controlling system of dams, levees, field crops, and flooded rice fields on both sides. Canals bring in irrigation water and remove field drainage. Everywhere we look, the warm glow of sunlight is reflected not only from the river but also from innumerable sloughs and farm ponds that provide nourishment for diverse forms of life below.

Another web of connections linking Valley life and landscape come into full view. Railroads, roads, highways, and freeways connect urban nodes which are scattered strategically and somewhat regularly in front of the balloon. The only noticeable vertical features on the landscape are high voltage electric towers, grain elevators, and the somewhat surprising Sutter Buttes.

At mid-Valley, the river appears comfortable in its meanders, leaving oxbow lakes, sloughs, and riparian forests in its historic bed. Orchards with their attendant ranch houses, more vivid green rice fields and grain fields form the most expansive uses of the land. Towns that carry the names of the Valley's earliest occupants, such as Colusa and Tehama, resist change like lingering historic monuments.

A barrier to the full flow of the river is observable near the town of Red Bluff. Immediately north of this diversion dam, the river hastens its pace as it squeezes through rugged Iron Canyon. Here the Valley ceases to be a flat plain. The river now transects a more topographically diverse system of creeks and low hills. Where it has not been cleared for grazing and field crops, the natural ground cover is now dominated by foothill pine, live oak, and thick manzanita. Suburban tract homes and ranchettes surround Red Bluff, Anderson, and Redding seen just ahead.

Commerce and industry are mixed with the subdivisions at the rural-urban interface near Redding, the largest city in the Sacramento Valley north of the state's capitol. Shasta and Keswick Dams, north of Redding, provide visual signposts marking the end of the Valley and the beginning of the rugged Siskiyou and Klamath Mountains that lead into Oregon. A much more urbanized landscape fills the far reaches of the North Valley around Redding. This view provides a somewhat startling contrast to more rural images common to the mid-Valley.

At last we must return to Earth and come back to reality. Unless you are fortunate enough to take such a trip several hundred feet above the landscape, however, these glimpses of real life in the Valley are more often completely hidden from view. No wonder tourists who never leave Interstate 5 or Highway 99 enroute from Los Angeles to Portland or Seattle miss much of what the Valley has to offer. These travelers often choose California's coastal route to avoid the region altogether since popular images of the flat Sacramento Valley do not compete favorably with those of coastal and Southern California or the San Francisco Bay Area for most of the state's residents. The Valley remains a place for everyday living much more than a place for the romance of tourist travel. But the region is now, and always has been, a place for dreamers and for dreams.

And the dreamers continue to come. The 1990 census listed 480,000 more people in the counties that make up the Sacramento Valley than were recorded in 1980, a 30 percent increase. Most of this growth occurred because of in-migration. The vast majority of these new arrivals came to the region from other parts of the state, nation, and world because they wanted to improve their lives and improve future opportunities for their children. This book tells their story and the stories of those who came before them.

Early Perceptions

Dreams of life in the Valley took many forms over the past decades of settlement in the region. In Cunningham's (1993) study of boosterism in the Sacramento Valley, this dreamlike image is captured in the words of aggressive land speculators and others. The following quotations from various publications promoting settlement in the Valley are indicative of this urge to paint the little known region in very positive, almost surreal, terms:

> With such soil, such climate, and the pure, clear water of the mighty Sacramento flowing from Shasta's mountains of perpetual snow, the balmy and wholesome climate and peerless soil, the establishment of such a paradise needs but the people to occupy it.
> —Sacramento Valley Land Company, The Agricultural Dream, 1912

> The Valley itself is a magnificent domain capable of sustaining hundreds of thousands more people, and of developing an industrial system second to none.
> —Immigration Association of California, The Industrial Dream, 1883

> The river, as it passes through Sacramento County, is a broad stream with a smooth surface, mirroring in quiet places, the trees upon the low, level banks. . . . All along its course, the fringe of soft foliage stands out against the blue

sky and over the placid stream, forming a picture of . . . idyllic repose.
—H.S. Crocker Company, Sacramento, The Dream of Nature's Perfection, 1894

The area drained by the Sacramento is an area of opportunity, mainly because of the advantages of this river system. Water is wealth in all the arid West. Nowhere else does it mean such wealth as in California, where the growing season never ends. The Sacramento River and its tributaries, the waters of which for the most part flow unused to the sea will in time yield millions to those who see and grasp the opportunities which they afford.
—*Sacramento Valley Monthly*, The Dream of Controlling Nature, 1915

Many of those who first came to the Sacramento Valley quickly found a sense of community here. Others found economic opportunities. The vast area ultimately became a homeland for people from many parts of the world. For more than 150 years, people of all ethnic backgrounds and belief systems have resettled in the Sacramento Valley in search of their own version of the good life. Shared perceptions of a relaxed lifestyle; a comfortable and warm climate; minimal traffic, pollution, crime, and other urban problems; and the availability of affordable land continue to lure people into the region.

Despite lingering images of an all-white, ethnically homogeneous region dominated by a *cowboy culture* with conservative, Midwestern values, the Sacramento Valley has long been home to a diverse population with a rich and varied cultural and ethnic heritage. Indeed, the region today is one of the most multicultural and rapidly growing rural environments in the nation.

Even the earliest residents of the area were diverse. People of the Yana, Maidu, Miwok, Wintu, and other groups of Native Americans occupied the Sacramento Valley until the arrival of other immigrant groups after the mid-nineteenth century. Although the descendants of these original Californians are increasing in number in the 1990s, Native Americans remain one of the most invisible of the region's ethnic groups today. Tens of thousands of these aboriginal people lived in the area when the earliest white explorers first witnessed their settlements and varied lifeways. They preferred living along streams where fish were abundant or in surrounding foothills where temperatures were cooler in the summer and wildlife plentiful. The Valley ultimately became home to one of the largest populations of Native Americans anywhere in North America. Their vision of the region as *home place* and their attachment to images of the river itself are captured in the Maidu legend summarized in Box 1.A.

As the Sacramento Valley filled with newcomers from other places, its economy changed and expanded and the ethnic and racial makeup of its population

---

Box 1.A
Birth of the Sacramento
(Maidu Story)

The Maidu who used to live around here were happy and rich. But then a whole lot of water came down here and the whole Sacramento Valley was turned into an ocean. Most of the people were drowned. Some tried to swim away but the frogs and salmon caught them and ate them. Only two people got safely away into the Sierras.

Great Man blessed these Maidu with many children, and all the tribes arose. One wise old chief ruled all of them. This chief went to the Coast Range but was disconsolate because the Sacramento Valley was still under water. He stayed there for nine days without any food, thinking about the water that covered the plains of the world.

This thinking and fasting changed him. He was not like a man. No arrow could hurt him. He could never be killed after that. He called out to great Man and told him to get rid of flood waters. Great Man tore open the Coast Range and made the waters flow down to the ocean. This flow of water was how the Sacramento River began.

Source: Haslam and Houston, 197, p. 8

---

diversified. Anglo and German farmers who dreamed of owning their own land and raising crops in a climate where the growing season never seemed to end came from the American East Coast, the Midwest, the South, and beyond. Chinese miners came in search of gold and to work on the railroads. Irish, French, Portuguese, Basque, and Italian laborers and farmers came to find a new life in a new land as farmers or laborers. Religious groups such as Latter Day Saints, Mennonites, and Jewish settlers came to work the land and to open thriving businesses that supported the Valley's urban economy, supplying early settlers with needed goods and services. The Japanese came to grow vegetables and strawberries. Swedes and other northern Europeans came to work the land as part of emerging water district colonies, successfully developing the rice industry so important to the region's economy today. Sikhs came from the vast plains of the Punjab of north central India because the Valley's flat landscape reminded them of home. Eventually, these enterprising farmers became some of the region's most successful orchardists. African-Americans came to work in the lumber mills of Oroville, attracted to the slow-paced, semi-rural environment they had known and treasured in the American South. Anglos, Irish, and Germans from the Midwest and South came in the 1930s—driven out of their homes in Missouri, Arkansas, northwest Oklahoma, and Texas by drought, dust, depleted soil, and impatient bankers. Latinos came to work the fields, encouraged by the attractive offer of the U.S. governmen's World War II-era *Bracero Program*, many becoming residents of the region's urban communities within one generation after their arrival here. And, like other newcomers, immigrants continue to come. Southeast Asians from Vietnam, Cambodia, and Laos, along with families from the many republics of the former Soviet Union who are searching for religious and economic freedom, are settling in towns and cities in the Sacramento Valley in the 1990s. The graph shown in Figure 1.2 summarizes the settlement histories of some of the immigrant groups discussed in the chapters that follow.

The Sacramento Valley is now home to people from all these diverse groups—and many more. Urban "escapees," *equity immigrants*, retirees, and *alternative lifestylers* are finding their way to the region from the bulging cities of southern California and the San Francisco Bay Area. Because of this daily influx of newcomers, the great Sacramento Valley is now growing at a rate two and half times the state average. Some local residents fear the worst, viewing these new arrivals as threats to a way of life they have known for decades.Whatever their motives, these new arrivals came to the Valley to find new opportunities for realizing their dreams. One person's dream, however, may be another's disappointment. Visions of prosperity through the harvest of resources such as gold, timber, fish, water, and crops from the soil often created conflict among the users and degradation of natural resources. Logging caused erosion and deforestation. Mining caused siltation. Both aggravated flooding. These stories of economic growth and the region's prosperity are discussed in this book along with related stories of waste, environmental mismanagement, and loss of the very qualities that originally attracted newcomers to the Valley.

Valley for Dreams focuses on the interrelationship between people and place, settlement and economic development, and natural and altered environments. It also takes a close look at the sometimes volatile growth issues in the Sacramento Valley today. But along with the challenges of growth, there is also a great deal of good news to report about recent efforts to conserve and protect resources in the region through the restoration and conservation of those very resources that were threatened in the boom years. This delicate balancing act has become as challenging to today's decision makers as the challenges that faced explorers and pioneer settlers in the first half of the nineteenth century. Within editorial space constraints, the pages that follow attempt to reconstruct past landscapes, analyze current conditions, and very tentatively predict the future of this very special place called the Sacramento Valley.

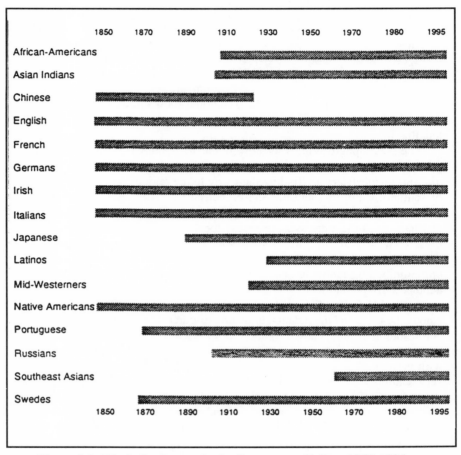

Figure 1.2. Ethnic Settlement in the Sacramento Valley, 1850-1995.
Source: United States Census of Population, 1850-1990.

Previous Studies

Several complete histories of this important region of California have already been written. Best known is Joseph McGowan's *A History of the Sacramento Valley* (1961). Even earlier, Woolridge published *History of the Sacramento Valley* in 1931. Numerous local histories have also been published about various places in the Valley by such organizations as ANCRR (Association for California Records and Research) and the local branch of the National League of American Penwomen. These publications are treasures that spotlight various topics, counties, or other sub-regions within the larger Sacramento Valley.

But *Valley for Dreams* is not another history. It provides, instead, a geographic interpretation of past, present, and future landscapes in the Sacramento Valley. First, we discuss the physical geography of the region. We then overlay human impacts affecting the region onto this natural setting. We discuss the locational, environmental, social, and economic factors that helped shape today's Valley landscapes. Present day patterns and processes are explained in the context of historic precedents, current conditions, and contemporary issues.

Other major studies of California's Central Valley have been accomplished by Gerald Haslam, Stephen Johnson, James Houston, and Robert Dawson (1993, 1990, 1978). Their interpretations lean toward the artistic, photographic, and literary. Their most recent contribution, *The Great Central Valley: California's Heartland* (1993) is a photo montage of the San Joaquin and Sacramento Valleys that focuses on the area south of Sacramento. It is highly recommended for those interested in San Joaquin Valley landscapes.

Method

Valley for Dreams is a spatial and environmental interpretation of people and place through time. As such, the book depends on a number of visuals to help readers really picture the geography of the study area. These include maps, graphs, tables, sketches, and historic and contemporary photographs. Map analysis and map comparison are effective methods to identify changes on the land over time. The use of selected photographs also provides opportunities for visual comparisons of places and times. These allow the reader to better understand and compare the character of places past and present.

Key statistical information is presented throughout to amplify our narrative. Census data on counties is also used, although minimally. It is important to remember, however, that large portions of some of the counties included in this study are located in adjacent mountains and foothill regions and so lie outside the limits of the Sacramento Valley.

Defining the Study Area

Which brings us to our final point in this chapter. What exactly is the region known as the "Sacramento Valley"? Defining and delimiting this large and complex region have been accomplished in a number of different ways by different scholars and writers. For example, the map shown in Figure 1.3 was drawn by Sacramento Valley boosters in 1915 to attract immigrants into the region. The boundaries of the Valley on this map are obviously not topographic since they include all of Shasta, Placer, and El Dorado Counties, most of which are mountainous. Boosters writing for the *Sacramento Valley Monthly* also placed dozens of town names on this map, where, in fact, no structure existed in 1915 or today. This cartographic optimism provides yet another example of the Valley as a place for dreams.

For the purposes of this book, we have drawn the perimeter of the Valley at the break in slope of the surrounding foothills (see Figure 1.3). At the southern end of the study area, we include all of Sacramento, Yolo, and Solano Counties in our analysis. Most of the emphasis in *Valley for Dreams*, however, lies in areas north of California's capitol city because the city of Sacramento deserves its own histories and geographies. We recommend McGowan and Willis's *Sacramento: Heart of the Golden State* (1983); Hardwick's *Ethnic Residential and Commercial Patterns in Sacramento with Special Reference to the Russian-American Experience* (1986); and a forthcoming book co-authored by Dennis Dingemans and Robin Datel of the University of California, Davis. References to the city of Sacramento in this book, therefore, are always mentioned in the context of its regional importance and its connections to places and people to the north.

There is, likewise, no visible or invisible line separating the Sacramento Valley and the delta country. For purposes of this book, we have drawn a boundary to exclude anything south of West Sacramento. Again, several excellent sources on the history and geography of the Sacramento/San Joaquin Delta have already been published and so lie beyond the scope of this analysis.

Themes

Valley for Dreams is structured around four key geographic themes in an effort to make a broad overview of this complex region possible. They include:

Figure 1.3. Promotional Map of the Sacramento Valley, 1915.

- Environment
- People
- Economy
- Landscape

The first theme, *Environment*, focuses attention on the natural features of the landscape as they existed in aboriginal times. This investigation includes a discussion of landforms, climate, soils, vegetation, and wildlife. We are particularly interested in the interrelationships between these physical systems and the human activities that have been influenced by them over the past two centuries. Concerns for maintaining or restoring the ecological integrity of the region guide our discussion of this important theme. Issues of "sustainable development," "growth impacts," and environmental consciousness frame the discussion of past and present environments.

In the second theme, *People*, our approach is not biographical. These are abundant in the historical literature. Writing from a geographical perspective instead, we concentrate on a broad sweep of human history in the region, emphasizing the migration and settlement of various immigrant groups who were held together by virtue of their culture, religion, ethnicity, or race. Groups discussed in detail include Native Americans, Germans, Anglos, Irish, French, Italians, Portuguese, Basques, Japanese, Chinese, Sikhs, Swedes, Latter Day Saints, African-Americans, Midwesterners, Southeast Asians, Alternative Lifestylers, Equity Immigrants, and Retirees.

The third theme of this book, *Economy*, is tied closely to interaction between the first two themes. People creating their own livelihood utilized natural resources of the area to build the regional economy. Economic development influenced the location and settlement patterns of communities and explains many if not most of the human-created patterns recorded on maps. Concerns with economic development began with John Sutter's arrival and continue in today's chambers of commerce and real estate offices.

The Valley's economy long has been based on its natural wealth. Among these, we focus on mining and agriculture and their impacts on local ecosystems. Secondary economic activities, including transportation, commercial development, government, education, and residential living, are all discussed in the chapters that follow. All have modified the natural environment, sometimes creating problems not yet solved in the 1990s. These include flood control, water redistribution, wildlife degradation, air pollution, urban sprawl, and changes in the quality of life.

The theme of *Landscape* examines features viewed on a map as well as those experienced on the ground. A composite of human activity in a particular physical environment creates a region's distinctive landscape. The landscape, in turn, evokes emotion and feeling which help define the Sacramento Valley's unique "sense of place." The best way to capture this sense of place, of course, is to actually be there. We, therefore, enthusiastically recommend visiting the places mentioned in the pages that follow and meeting and talking with some of the people who live in those places.

Chapter Summaries

Following this introductory chapter, Chapter 2 begins with an overview of the physical environment of the Sacramento Valley as it existed for centuries before human impact. Topography, climatic patterns, soils, hydrology, and ecologic communities are described and interactions between these elements of the physical environment are stressed. Impressions of the Valley's natural setting written by early explorers provide fascinating insights into their visions of the potential for future settlement in the area.

Chapter 3 focuses on Native American life and landscape in the Sacramento Valley. It describes and analyzes the experiences of these earliest Valley residents, emphasizing issues of *human-environment interaction*. Lifestyle, languages, and other cultural characteristics of the many different groups of Native Americans in the region are mapped, discussed, and compared. Conflict between aboriginal people and incoming groups are presented along with the current status and cultural landscape of these earliest Valley residents.

Chapter 4 narrates the travels, observations, and opinions of the earliest Euro-Americans who came upon the "pristine" Valley in the early nineteenth century. Their journals and letters home describe a region rich in promise and potential for development. Chapter 4 also describes the pre-Gold Rush settlement process from Sutter's Fort in the south to Shasta City in the north. Linkages between these early settlement nodes by water and land are mapped and analyzed.

Chapter 5 presents social and locational histories of the migration and settlement of immigrants occupying the Valley in the latter half of the nineteenth century. The experiences of Germans, Anglos, Irish, French, Portuguese, Italians, Basques, and Chinese are compared and analyzed. The far reaching effects of the Gold Rush upon the Valley's economy and population growth are presented along with a discussion of the early development of its agricultural base. Even in this early era of the region's development, water plays a pivotal role.

Chapter 6 focuses on economic development and urbanization in the Sacramento Valley in the decades of the nineteenth century after 1848. Agricultural development and mining impacts are explained in more detail and information is presented on the Valley's concurrent development of towns, cities, and transportation routes. A case study of one religio-ethnic group, the Jews, also is discussed. Chapter 7 examines the settlement patterns of immigrant groups who arrived in the early years of the twentieth century including Swedes, Latter Day Saints, and Japanese. The development of early irrigation colonies in West Sacramento, Orange Vale, Corning, Oroville, and Durham are also discussed in the context of agricultural development and other land use in rapidly evolving parts of the Valley. Challenges to be faced during the decades of the 1920s and 1930s are evidenced by the arrival of new people from the troubled midwestern states during the Dust Bowl years. Other incoming groups, such as Sikhs and African-Americans, also find life in the Valley challenging during these years, but ultimately better than the land and life they left behind. In response to the Great Depression, public works projects such as the Central Valley Project, various road and highway improvement projects, and the creation of recreation areas enhance economic and lifestyle opportunities in the Valley. These topics are discussed in Chapter 8.

Chapter 9 presents some of the post-World War II experiences of such groups as Latinos and Mennonites in various places in the Sacramento Valley. The growth economy of the post-war years, encouraged by the completion of the California Water Project, significant urban expansion and suburbanization, and improved transportation accessibility are all discussed within the context of this chapter as well. The price of economic growth during this period was paid for by increased water and air pollution and an increasing concern for limiting growth among local residents.

Chapter 10 continues our discussion of environmental and social issues as newcomers such as *alternative lifestylers*, *equity immigrants*, retirees, and people from various places and cultures in Southeast Asia arrive on the scene. Growth issues dominate the storyline of this chapter as thousands of newcomers arrive on the scene.

The final chapter of *Valley for Dreams* explores issues that will face decision makers at the beginning of the twenty-first century and also makes a few predictions about the future geography of the Sacramento Valley. Proper management of resources, limits on population growth, reduction of ethnic conflict, and sound environmental and urban planning priorities head the list of problems and potentials to be addressed in the years ahead.

As background for your exploration of the life and landscape of the

Sacramento Valley, whether in your car, in a hot air balloon, on a speeding bicycle or motorcycle, on a river raft or fishing boat, or on foot, we invite you to further your understanding of its past, present, and future landscapes by reading the chapters that follow.

Chapter 2

Nature's Gift

Spanish, French, and English explorers who first visited western North America had rare opportunities to see places virtually unchanged for over ten thousand years. No one knows exactly what most of these soldiers, trappers, and opportunists thought or said. A few, however, did keep diaries or journals. From these written observations and from a century of scientific investigation we now can more than speculate about what the explorers most likely saw and experienced (see Thompson 1961).

Many thousands of people lived in the Sacramento Valley at the time of the arrival of the earliest Europeans. The story of these only real "native" Californians is offered in the next chapter of this book. Although the natural environment of the Valley was somewhat modified by the effect of Native American hunting, harvesting and burning, most of their landscape was in ecologic balance throughout their years of settlement here. The region had evolved into a somewhat unique biome over a quarter of million years, remaining minimally changed until the arrival of large numbers of Euro-American, African-American, Latin American, European, and Asian settlers after the Gold Rush in 1848. Later chapters of this book depict impacts resulting from their activities primarily in massive elimination or alteration of the "pristine" conditions described here.

The prehistoric Sacramento Valley was the evolutionary product of a unique combination of landforms, soils, hydrology, climate and ecosystems. The Valley contains only about seven percent of the state's total land area. An analysis of this map reveals that the 5000 square miles defined as the Valley proper are really part of a much larger geologic system made up of the Coast Ranges, the Sacramento-San Joaquin delta, the Sierra Nevada and the San Joaquin Valley. This chapter describes this large and complex bioregion according to its geomorphology, soils, climate, hydrology, and ecology.

Landforms and Geologic Background

Two major forces of nature created the Sacramento Valley; tectonic uplift of two parallel mountain ranges and millions of years of precipitation and flooding that filled it with transported clay, silt, sand and gravel. This evolved into a structural depression or trough between the uplifted Sierra Nevada/Cascades and the Coast Ranges. Around 140 million years ago, the Valley was a submerged arm of the sea. Having been uplifted and filled since that time it is now marked in the north with its connection to the foot of the Klamath Mountains north of Redding. There is no well defined southern boundary to the region because it extends into the San Francisco Bay delta and on into the San Joaquin Valley. Some studies and government reports define the Sacramento Valley as the flat land lying south of Red Bluff rather than including the drainage basin south of Redding. This may be a more accurate geomorphological definition but for purposes of understanding the historical geography of the area, the Valley should not be subdivided. We have arbitrarily drawn the southern boundary along a rough line between Roseville/Sacramento and Vacaville. Note that the Delta region is not included because it has already been studied in depth by other scholars and also because it is, in many respects, a distinctive region as compared with the heartland of the massive Sacramento Valley north of the state's capital city.

A State Lands Commission report describes the channel of the river in four distinctive sections (1994, 131). From Redding to Red Bluff, the river channel is naturally constrained by resistant geologic formations on both banks. From Red Bluff to Hamilton City, the channel freely meanders, flanked by a broad flood plain. Between Hamilton City and Colusa, the river meandered between natural levees but is now constrained by constructed levees and bank protection. Downstream from Colusa, the Sacramento River is completely constrained by flood control levees.

The trough created by uplifted mountains surrounding the Sacramento Valley is filled with thousands of feet of material, first deposited on the sea bottom then washed down by yearly rains, particularly from the Sierra Nevada/Cascades. This layered gravel, soil and mud, in some places more than a mile deep, produced natural gas to be extracted later and underground aquifers for retention of millions of acre feet of water. A cross section of the Valley showing these features is presented in Figure 2.1.

Unlike many long valleys transected by rivers, the Sacramento Valley is a product of deposition rather than erosional down cutting. It was built rather than carved. The 170 mile long and 30 to 50 mile wide floor of the Valley obtained

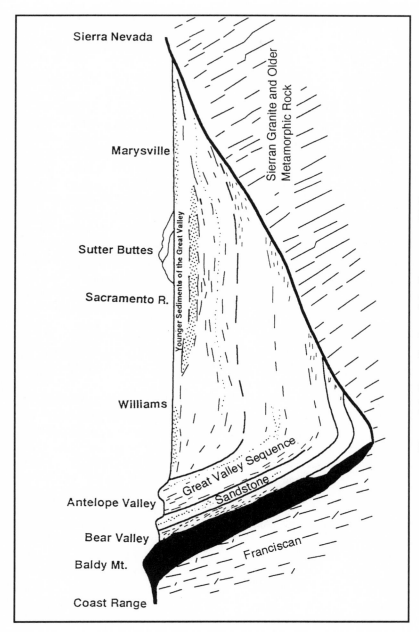

Figure 2.1. Cross Section of the Sacramento Valley.
Source: Alt and Hyndman 1975, 178.

its topographic detail from the deposits of local streams and shallow lakes over the last million years. Its slight gradient from north to south ranges from 550 feet above mean sea level, to 200 feet at Chico in the center, to sea level in the delta.

One early study defined several natural divisions of the Valley based on topography (see Bryan, 1923). The first was called *Red Lands*, named for its typical soil color bordering the edges of the Valley above the flood plain. These ancient stream deposits have been uplifted and eroded creating its present rolling terrain. The second category, *Low Plains,* consists of very gentle alluvial slopes on opposite sides of the Valley. They owe their form to the process of deposition during flooding from tributary creeks. The third type of Valley landform is termed *River Lands.* These consist of very wide natural river levees and old channel ridges caused by the constantly shifting meanders of stream courses. These levees rose from five to twenty feet above the streambed and ranged in width from one to ten miles (Sands 1980, 1). Some natural levees blocked outlets for runoff and created flood basins, the fourth landform type. *Flood basins* are broad shallow low spots where surface drainage outlets are minimal. These basins are dry most of the year but fill and retain flood waters during wet seasons. In high flood years they resemble vast inland seas. It has been estimated that before reclamation 60 percent of the Valley or over three quarters of a million acres were subject to such overflow (Harding 1960, 6). There are seven notable basins in the Sacramento Valley including Butte, Colusa, Sutter, American, Yolo, Marysville, and Sacramento. There are no exact boundaries for each basin, however, because their extent changes by season and by land use practices.

Differences in soil texture, natural levees and oxbow lakes are evidence of annual flooding, stream side cutting and alluvial deposition over time. The natural depositional levees laced across the Valley bottom are almost imperceptible on the ground today because they have been covered by farming activity and constructed levees. As seen from aerial photographs such as the one shown in Figure 2.2, however, one can detect where the river has moved and left its imprints over the years even after being overlain by urbanization. The natural levees are usually less than ten feet high in this area but that is enough elevation change to allow drainage for Valley Oaks and other trees that would otherwise be deprived of air to their roots.

The Sutter Buttes in the middle and eastern part of the Valley are seen from both the air and ground as a somewhat startling and very visible "island" of peaks emerging out of the surrounding marshes and ranchlands of the Butte Sink. The volcanic mass rises some 2,100 feet from the Valley floor and about nine

Figure 2.2. The Sacramento River.

miles in diameter covering about 75 square miles. When active, the ancient volcano was probably twice this height. The Buttes mark the northern extent of the once vast marshland that stretched as far as Stockton and San Francisco Bay.

As streams flowed out of the surrounding mountains and onto the Valley floor over the years, they created alluvial fans by depositing upstream material collected through erosion. Many of the fans have subsequently been dissected by more recent stream cutting. These ancient features account for many of the hilly lands at the Valley's eastern and western flanks. Other evidences of volcanism in the region exist as well. Between today's cities of Red Bluff and Redding, the eastern side of the Valley also exhibits signs of local volcanic activity. Ash deposits, volcanic flows and a few volcanic cones account for more undulating hills. These dramatic forces that created the study area millions of years ago are still at work but at a rate imperceptible to most of its occupants. The coastal and eastern mountains continue to be uplifted and they continue to bring seasonal water to fill the rivers.

Climate

The climate of the Sacramento Valley can best be described as "two season"—wet and dry. Other contrasting descriptors one might use to define these contrasting seasonal variations are "cool and hot" or "foggy and clear." Spring and fall are transition periods between the two extremes of summer and winter. During the long and hot summer, the relative humidity is low and during the winter it is high, often resulting in blankets of radiation or "tule" fogs. The diurnal range of temperatures is great and is experienced in summer with hot days and cool nights and in winter by warm days and cold nights. Thunderstorms are rare and snow seldom visits the Valley floor. The northern, eastern, and western margins of the Valley are in a thermal belt where cold, stable air can flow unimpeded downwind to the Valley bottom.

The southern portion of the region is greatly influenced by the delta and bay connection to the Pacific Ocean. In late afternoons during most of the year, cool marine air enters the Sacramento Valley from the west and is deflected to the north by the Sierra Nevada barrier. This *delta breeze* greatly moderates heat in Sacramento but grows weaker as it moves north. The areas north of Chico and Orland rarely receive significant benefit from it. For example, the sea breeze pattern dominates the wind flow in spring and summer especially in the afternoon, while in winter more calm conditions dominate the late evening and early morning atmosphere. Figure 2.3 shows typical summer air flow patterns in the Valley.

Summer days in this part of California are hot with a maximum averaging 90° F. or higher in Sacramento and 97° to 99° F. at Redding 150 miles to the north. The average minimum (night time) temperature at Sacramento in summer is 58° and 67° at Redding. Winter low temperatures on the Valley floor average between 13 and 29° F. The mean annual temperature of the Sacramento Valley is 60° at Sacramento and 63° at its northernmost extent at Redding. At Red Bluff, the sun shines an average of 75 percent of the total daylight hours of the year. At Redding the sun shines 88 percent of the time in daylight as compared to Tucson with 85 percent and Chicago, at the same latitude, with 40 percent.

Average Valley precipitation conditions are also quite different seasonally. Overall, Sacramento averages 18.1 inches of rainfall per year, Colusa receives 16.0 inches and Red Bluff receives 23.3 inches. Redding receives less. The majority of the rainfall comes from November to April with January being the wettest month. However, winter flood conditions which are responsible for the Valley's unique physiography and ecology are the product of vast departures from the precipitation norms. Seasonal averages for runoff can vary by as much as 20 inches and rainfall intensities of individual storms can be very high. Rapid snow melt in the surrounding mountains can also cause flooding conditions.

The contrast in summer and winter weather patterns in northern California is accounted for by the sun's relative location over the Pacific ocean. With less solar warming in winter over the North Pacific Ocean (the vertical rays of the sun have shifted south), low pressure storm systems follow the westerly winds onto the coasts of the Pacific Northwest and California. In summer, a relatively warmer high pressure air mass, supplemented by a continental high pressure system, blocks the westerly storm track.

Contrasting microclimates in the Valley were not noted by early explorers, probably because they did not stay long enough to make systematic observations. But, some local differences in temperatures are significant enough for farmers to make decisions based on them. The gradual ascent up the Valley from Sacramento to Redding exhibits an increase in precipitation and decrease in fog in winter and an increase in temperature with a reduction in winds in the summer. Likewise, an increase in elevation up the sides of the Valley brings generally lower temperatures in summer and winter at a rate of about three degrees per thousand feet.

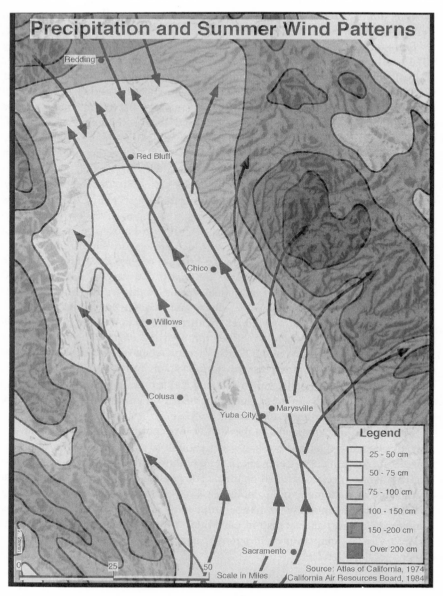

Figure 2.3. Precipitation and Summer Wind Patterns.

Hydrology

The Sacramento Valley is nourished by the flow of the river with the same name producing close to 40 percent of California's annual snowmelt. Its source is on the slopes of Mount Eddy in the Trinity Mountains at about 6,600 foot elevation. In the river's first fifty miles, the gradient is steep and the river rushes through high canyons. From where it is joined by the Pit River at the head of the Valley, the Sacramento River drops another 400 feet in 67 miles until it widens onto the flat Valley floor below the location of Red Bluff. In the remaining 250 miles of its course, the river falls only 240 feet (less than one foot per mile).

The entire drainage basin of the Sacramento River and its tributaries covers about 26,000 square miles. Other major streams flowing into the Valley are the Feather, Yuba, Bear and American Rivers. Lesser streams, but nevertheless important to our understanding of the place, are Antelope, Stony, Cottonwood, Battle, Cache, Indian, Putah, Deer, Mill, Butte and Big and Little Chico creeks. Figure 2.4 shows the Valley's major streams. Nearly all the water that fills these streams comes from the surrounding mountains. The floor of the Valley receives comparatively little rainfall per year and it occurs mostly in the winter season. Without supplemental mountain sources of water, most precipitation in the Valley would percolate into the deep soils below.

The average stream flow of the Sacramento River as it emptied into the delta before historic settlement was probably the same as measured from 1878 to 1985 and compiled by the U.S. Geological Survey. Within this time frame, the lowest annual volume in acre feet was 17.8 million acre feet in 1882-83. This may be compared with our most recent drought year flow of only 7.8 MAF (see Butler 1995). The highest was 32.3 million and it was recorded in 1870-80. This may be compared to today's average flow of 24 million acre feet. This last figure gives us some idea of how the use and overuse of this life-giving resource has been altered in less than 100 years.

The floods for which the Valley has always been noted are caused by the seasonality of precipitation in northern California and the build-up of a tremendous snow pack in the Sierra Nevada/Cascades. The Sacramento River's unimpaired runoff in water year 1995 was 33.9 million acre feet, exceeded only by 37 MAF in 1983 (Butler 1995). The Central Valley once contained 500,000 acres of flooded plains in winter with more than half of that in the Sacramento Valley portion. Herein lies both the cause of the Valley's prehistoric biotic diversity and the motive for it being turned into one of the most altered rural physical environments in the United States.

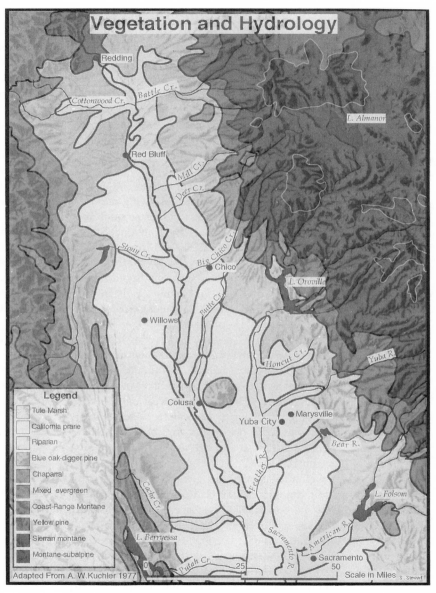

Figure 2.4. Vegetation and Hydrology.

The geologist F. Leslie Ransome described winter in the Sacramento Valley in 1896 as follows (1896, 379):

> The smaller streams flowing from the Coast Ranges on the west seldom reach the Sacramento River directly, but become lost in the intricate plexus of sloughs which meander through the tule-lands bordering the main river. The same is also true of the smaller streams on the east; only the larger tributaries reaching the Sacramento by a definite channel, and that often becoming an exceedingly tortuous one.

The Valley was subject to heavy annual floods. Especially vulnerable were the channels of the Sacramento and Feather Rivers (see Thompson 1960). Lieutenant George H. Derby was caught in a November flood and lost his wagons but saved his mules and records. Part of his description of the Valley notes its flooding potential (Farquhar 1932, 99):

> The whole country between the Creeks is liable to overflow, and is very dangerous to attempt traveling after a heavy rain. The 'tule' swamp upon the western bank of the Sacramento, extending to the vicinity of 'Butte' Creek, and occurring occasionally above is from three to six miles in width, and is impassable for six months out of the year.

Although ground water is in all the younger sediments, only the more permeable sand and gravel aquifers provide enough for pumping. Throughout the Valley, these younger sediments overlie older marine sediments that contain brackish or saline water. The depth to saline water in the Sacramento Valley ranges from less than 500 feet in the north to over 3,000 feet in the south.

Ground water was abundant in the Valley before Euro-American settlement. It occurred under confined (artesian) and unconfined (water table) conditions and was recharged continually by infiltration from streams. It is estimated that before significant extraction of Valley ground water there were over 33 million acre feet available at depths of less than 200 feet.

Soils

Much of the storage of subsurface water is possible because the various layers of alluvial soil allow it. Generally, one may observe rocky or stony soils on the edges of the Valley and a gradation to sandy and loam soils as one travels toward the river lowlands. The soils closest to the rivers are generally clay but may be overlain by the loamy textured soils of natural levees in some places.

Using the U.S. Department of Agriculture's *Seventh Approximation System,* five major orders may be observed in the Sacramento Valley. Alfasols are developed under forest cover where very fine clay particles are leached out and drainage of surface water is good. Vertisols are dominated by clays which expand and contract with changes in water content and make tree root growth very difficult. Vertisols in the Sacramento Valley usually underlayed the prairie lands. Inceptisols represent early stages of soil formation, are generally shallow and are located on the young alluvial deposits at the edges of the Valley. They support grasses, oak woodlands and digger pine associations. Entisols are recent material without developed soil horizons (layers). In the study area, these soils take the form of gravel deposits and outwash plains.

Vegetation and Ecology

Although there were Spanish expeditions into the Sacramento Valley from 1805 to 1821, it was not until the 1830s that the landscape was described in any detail. One of the Hudson's Bay Company's fur trappers, John Work, described the riparian forests near present day Red Bluff in 1832 as (as reprinted in Maloney 1945, 18): "All the way along the river here there is a belt of woods principally oak which is surrounded by a plain with tufts of wood here and there which extend to the foot of the mountain, where the hills are again wooded."

In 1842, Charles Wilkes was overwhelmed with the abundance of large mammals in the Valley. He wrote that "the variety of game in this country almost exceeds belief. The elk may be said to predominate" (Wilkes 1845, 487). The Pacific Railroad Survey in 1857 noted that the large herds of game in the Central Valley rivaled the vast herds of bison that roamed the Great Plains. A later explorer noted that: "At times we saw bands of elk, deer, and antelope in such numbers that they actually darkened the plains for miles, and looked in the distance like great herds of cattle" (Bosqui 1904).

The abundance of grizzly bears was mentioned by Jedediah Smith in 1828 in his journal after an encounter injured one of his trappers. Another early settler in the region, John Bidwell, described his encounter with the great bears in 1843 as follows (Bidwell 1891, 44):

Approaching Butte Creek we camped for the first time since leaving Hock Farm. Here we had an episode with grizzly bears, which will afford some idea of that region of its natural state. In the spring of the year, the bears chiefly lived on clover, which grew luxuriantly on the plains, especially in the little depressions on the plains. We first saw one, which made for the timber two or three miles away; then more, all bounding away to the creek. At one time there were sixteen in the drove. Of course we gave chase, but had no desire to overtake them there being too many of them.

Most of the bears in the Valley were exterminated by 1865 with a few stragglers reported as late as 1860. By 1922, the last California Grizzly had been killed and the state's extermination program hailed a success (Gillis 1995, 15-16).

From the few descriptions that still exist, it is possible to reconstruct in a general way the aboriginal biotic landscape of Northern California. In addition to the original patterns of hydrology in the Valley, Figure 2.4 shows major vegetation patterns as they existed before Euro-American settlement. The Sacramento Valley was a mosaic of lakes, ponds, streams, wetlands, riparian forests, prairie grasslands, and oak savannas. It continually changed with the seasons and its relatively small area housed an extremely large variety of plant and animal species.

Permanent *aquatic ecosystems* included cold, fast running creeks and rivers, shallow and warmer ponds and sloughs, and vast inland marshes. The most remarkable fish in this network of waterways were the Chinook salmon (*Oncorhynchus tshawytscha*) which migrated to and from the Pacific Ocean. There are four varieties of Chinook salmon each migrating through the river system during a different peak run of the year. They are identified by biologists and sports persons as fall-run, late fall-run, winter-run and spring-run. This means that anadromous fishes were in Valley streams and pools throughout the year except during the period of low summer flow and warm water temperatures. It has been estimated that the peak Chinook salmon runs in the Sacramento River system may have been as large as 800,000 to 1 million fish with an average run size of about 600,000 fish (Reynolds 1993). The average salmon runs in modern times range from five percent to 50 percent of historic levels.

Other fish native to Valley waterways are rainbow trout, white and green sturgeon, American shad, Tule perch, Sacramento perch, Sacramento squawfish, and a variety of other suckers and minnows. Striped bass, largemouth bass, catfish and many other fishes present in the Valley today were introduced in the nineteenth century.

Total historic *wetlands* in California are estimated to have been 5 million acres, 4 million of which were in the great Central Valley and the Sacramento/San Joaquin River Delta (Dennis 1984). Most of this wetland was in the form of tidal and freshwater marshes in San Francisco Bay and from the delta confluence of the Sacramento and San Joaquin Rivers stretching all the way to present day

Colusa County (Frayer 1989). These vast, permanently flooded marshes supported tules, bulrushes and other forms of emergent aquatic vegetation, primarily bulrush (*Scirpus spp.*), cattails (*Typha spp.*), spike-rush (*Heleocharis palustris*), and a number of Carex (Dreyer 1984, 27). They teemed with waterfowl and a large number of fish and mammal species, many of which are now extinct or endangered.

The waterfowl in the Colusa area was described by one early resident as follows (Hanson 1953, 2):

> The unoccupied land of the plains, considered as worthless and usually referred to as 'goose land' is where they flocked to roost, unmolested, by the billions. Their flight to the north started at daylight and in the evening they returned south. When a large flock arose they resembled a dark cloud. You could hear their quacks for miles. In the air they scattered, the cloud disappeared, and you could see strings of geese in 'V' formations as far as the eye could see. From daylight until midnight you could hear their continual squawk. Flock after flock arose in the morning and started for the wheat fields.

Today the Valley hosts at least half the Pacific Flyway's Pintail and Wigeon, 80 percent of the Northern Shovelers, 60 percent of the Gadwalls, 82 percent of the Snow Geese, 86 of the Tundra Swans and all of the Cackling Canada, Ross and Aleutian Canada geese. It is a seasonal home to huge numbers of phalaropes, grebes, sandpipers, egrets, herons and rails as well (Steinhart 1987, 23).

The region's permanent waters and wetlands were almost always bordered by dense stands of *riparian woodlands* often dominated by gigantic valley oaks (*Quercus lobata*). Other common trees were Fremont Cottonwood (*Populus fremonti*), willow (*Salix spp.*), and western sycamore (*Plantanus racemosa*). Thick understory shrubs and vines often made the riparian forests difficult to traverse. The riparian zones are usually bounded on one side by aquatic systems from which they obtain needed soil moisture and by dryer upland soils and plants on the upland side. The riparian systems still serve as shelter and a food source for aquatic, wetland and grassland fauna as well as its own populations of animals although more than 90 percent of the original riparian forests have been removed.

Many kinds of insect-producing hardwood trees and berry-producing vines and shrubs provide a diverse and abundant food supply. The density of vegetation afforded by large trees provide cover in areas that are cooler in summer and warmer in winter than the surrounding upland areas. The effects of seasonal flooding, high water tables and lateral water movement through the soil dictates that these zones originally extended no further than about the 100 year flood line or that area that statistically is expected to be flooded one year out of one hundred years. This flood zone was often several miles in extent, however, as indicated by descriptions of explorers and surveyors.

Captain Sir Edward Belcher described his observations of the Valley as follows (1843, 120-123):

> Having entered the Sacramento, we soon found that it increased in width as we advanced, and at our noon station of the second day was about a third of a mile wide. The marshy land now gave way to firm ground, preserving its level in a most remarkable manner, succeeded by banks well wooded with oak, planes, ash, willow, chestnut, walnut, poplar and brushwood. Wild grapes in great abundance overhung the lower trees, clustering to the river, at times completely overpowering the lower trees on which they climbed, and producing beautiful varieties of tint. . . . Our course lay between banks . . . these were, for the most part, belted with willow, ash, oak, or plane, which latter, of immense size, overhung the stream, without apparently a sufficient hold in the soil to support them, so much had the force of the stream denuded their roots.
>
> Within, and at the very verge of the banks, oaks of immense size were plentiful. These appeared to form a band on each side, about three hundred yards in depth, and within (on the immense park-like extent, which we generally explored when landing for positions) they were seen to be disposed in clumps, which served to relieve the eye, wandering over what otherwise be described as one level plain or sea of grass. Several of these oaks were examined, and some of the small felled. The two most remarkable measured respectively twenty-seven feet and nineteen feet in circumference, at three feet above the ground. The latter rose perpendicularly at a [computed] height of sixty feet before expanding its branches, and was truly a noble sight.

In 1841, Lieutenant Charles Wilkes described the forests on the river levees above the Sutter Buttes as follows (Wilkes 1845, 187):

> The river was here only two hundred feet wide, its banks but fifteen feet high. The trees on the shores had now become quite thick, and grew with great luxuriance; so much so, that were the sight confined to the river banks, it might be supposed that the country was one continued forest, instead of an open prairie.

The Derby map and other narrative descriptions indicate that riparian belts were probably two to three miles wide along the river and its major tributaries with large clusters or groves spotted in other environmentally suitable places throughout the Valley. At the time of statehood in 1850, there were an estimated

500,000 acres of riparian vegetation bordering the Sacramento River main stem (Katibah 1984, 23). Today's best estimates are that ten percent of this acreage is currently riparian forest. The largest known historical tree in the Valley was the Hooker Oak near Big Chico Creek. This gigantic Valley oak measured 101 feet in height and 28 feet in circumference.

Each winter, seasonal wetlands were created as grasslands and riparian lands were flooded. The annual process created even more opportunities for food, shelter, and nesting sites in this biological paradise.

Prairie grasses occupied the flat floor of the Sacramento Valley between the riparian forests and the foothills up to about 1,500 feet. They also surrounded the tule marshes of the southern part of the Valley and dominated the upland vegetation patterns of the North Valley as well. In their aboriginal condition, grasslands were dominated by a number of species of bunch grasses, primarily purple needle-grass (*Stipa pulchra*), and nodding needlegrass (*Stipa cernua*) (Broughton, 1988, 52).

Lieutenant George H. Derby conducted a survey and had a map of part of it prepared in 1849. Both the journal and the map note the extent of grasslands on the river levees, in drainage basins and on upland plains. Derby's map, "The Sacramento Valley from the American River to Butte Creek, September and October, 1849," has descriptive notes on it which read: "Plains from 20 to 30 miles wide but with little vegetation or water terminated to the west by Coast Range of Mountains" (Farquhar 1932). His map also showed the Sutter, American and Yolo basins as plains overflowed in winter.

It is generally believed that in pristine times the vast expanses of prairie in the Central Valley, purple needle grasses and nodding needle grass, were supplemented by several other species of perennials and several hundred species of annual grasses. From February through June the Valley formed a continuous bed of grasses, sedges, and flowering plants. Each species usually dominated a particular ecotype or habitat often with some grassland communities occurring in the higher, well drained zones, and others in what were called *hog wallows* in damp swales.

It is interesting to note that these Valley prairies in the presettlement condition were similar in appearance but botanically unlike the grasslands of the Great Plains. California's Central Valley grasslands were made up of annual and perennial bunch grasses with a late winter to mid-spring growing season (in order to take advantage of winter rains). The grasslands of the mid-continent were of different species and utilized a summer growing season. Another difference between these two huge regions is defined by its soil formation process.

California prairie grasses did not form the thick sod soil for which the Great Plains are famous.

By 1855, reports of the Pacific Railroad indicated the presence of an introduced grass they called wild oats. They were described as follows (*Reports of Explorations and Surveys to Ascertain the Most Practicable and Economical Route For a Railroad from the Mississippi River to the Pacific Ocean* 1857, 20):

> The more fertile surface is covered with a growth of wild oat, or grasses, interspersed with a variety of flowering annuals, while the gravelly and more unproductive portions support a thinner growth of coarser plants [Eryngium, Hemizonia, Madaria, &c.]. Of trees, there are none except such as grow in narrow lines along the streams.

These prairie grasslands provided a rich habitat for pronghorn antelope, tule elk, deer, coyote, and grizzly bear. Of these large mammals, only the coyote and deer survive in the Sacramento Valley today.

Spring in the Sacramento Valley provides a dramatic display of hundreds of species of wildflowers. Many are so tiny that they are even overlooked by naturalists. Particularly striking arrangements of flowers may be seen in the *vernal pools* found on the upper edges of the Valley grasslands. Also known as *hog wallows,* these depressions in shallow, hardpan soils retain spring runoff long enough for flowers to bloom in concentric circles around the deepest part of the pool as water evaporates from March to May. They hold water long enough to allow some purely aquatic organisms to grow and to reproduce, but not long enough to permit development of a typical pond or marsh ecosystem. The pools are sometimes separated by small hillocks called *mima mounds* but which there is no agreed upon explanation as to their cause. Many of the plants and some of the invertebrate creatures that inhabit the pools are very rare and, in fact, are found nowhere else but in the Sacramento Valley. Over half of these pools have lost their unique ecological value having been graded for development or farming or heavily overgrazed.

The *Oak Savanna* community is one of the driest tree associations in the state and is restricted in the Valley to its margins except in the far north where it becomes the dominant vegetation. This biome receives from 15 to 40 inches of annual rainfall but loses most of it through spring runoff and summer heat and evaporation. Oak Savanna is identified by the predominance of blue oak, foothill or digger pine, interior live oak (*Quarqus wislizenii*), and some Valley Oaks scattered, park-like amidst annual grasslands. At its upward boundaries, chaparral plants such as manzanita and chamise are mixed in with the trees.

Of the nineteen species of oak trees found in California, three are common in the Sacramento Valley. The Valley Oak (*Quercus lobata*) is found throughout the Valley and generally serves as a good indicator of where riparian or savanna forests may have been before human impact. Bidwell Park in Chico is one of the largest remaining areas of Valley Oaks in both foothill and riparian settings. The Valley Oak is the most impressive local tree of the oak group for sheer size and patriarchal demeanor. It is most easily identified by its height and trunk girth, its lobed-edged leaves, and by its characteristic long acorns. In contrast, the blue oak (*Quercus douglasii*) is primarily a foothill tree. Blue oak is very drought tolerant and fire resistant enabling survival on the edges of the Valley where both conditions are common if not frequent. This tree is best identified by its bluish leaves and light gray bark. Oaks have evolved different solutions to survive in the hot dry climate of the Valley. Seedlings produce a deep tap root, leaves are small so as not to lose too much moisture through transportation, and when drought-stressed, most oaks will drop their leaves in late summer to prevent moisture loss.

Foothill pines, also named digger pines after the derogatory description given to the local aboriginal people who depended on their seeds for a seasonal food supply, are usually found in association with the blue oaks and drought-tolerant shrubs around the edges of the Valley. Oak savannas seem not to have suffered as much removal as the riparian forests or wetlands and, therefore, may still be seen on cattle ranches on both the Coast Range and Sierra sides of the Sacramento Valley. Seasonal deer herds and their natural predators, the mountain lions, are at home in this community as are literally hundreds of other vertebrates. Oak woodlands, in fact, provide food, and shelter for over 300 different species of vertebrates (amphibians, reptiles, birds, and mammals) on a seasonal as well as a full time basis.

Detailed local examinations of various parts of the Valley display a mosaic of different biotic communities based on characteristics of drainage, topography, and microclimate. For example, much of the river bottom land in Shasta County harbors wetland and upland plants mixed together.

Environmental factors in the Sacramento Valley that would affect future settlement included its warm and sunny climate, its surrounding timber, mineral, and water resources, its rivers and streams, and its rich soil with excellent farming potential. Before settlement, the natural conditions of the Sacramento Valley were similar to the Willamette Valley in Oregon but somewhat different than the rest of California and vastly different from the Great Basin to the east and the arid Southwest. Here was a land that was described by its first foreign visitors as rich with pastureland, an ample fresh water supply, and fertile soils. Here also were beaver and other animals for the taking by trappers. Gold was not known to be here but the potential for good drainage and/or irrigation of the land for farming were obvious to most who came. Here was a place where, with a sense of vision and a little hard work, dreams might be fulfilled.

Chapter 3

Earliest Visions

In the late eighteenth century, the aboriginal population of the state of California formed the densest population of Native Americans in the entire United States (Meriam 1905, 595). Although absolute numbers are still uncertain, most scholars agree that the population in California was at least six times the national average of all Native American groups (Bean 1968, 6).

But by 1846, starvation, epidemics, relocation, warfare, and forced labor had all but decimated the number of these original Valley residents to only about 100,000 remaining in the entire state (Hendrix 1980, 1). By the turn of the century, the *United States Census of Population* listed less than 16,000.[1] The story of what happened to these earliest Valley residents is not only a story of longterm adaptation to the natural environment of the Sacramento Valley, but is also a story of greed and betrayal—a tale filled with the geography of despair.

Traditionally, California Native peoples have been portrayed as docile, unambitious people, who openly accepted the invading Euro-Americans and were easily subdued and conquered. In reality, this simplistic explanation grew out of an attitude of racial and cultural superiority of incoming groups which emphasized the "strength" of new arrivals and the perceived "weakness" of aboriginal people (Heizer 1978, 99). The eventual extermination of most of these earliest residents of California was accomplished by miners, cattlemen, farmers, soldiers, barbed wire, dogs, and guns. Some of these newcomers were willing conspirators in the race to eliminate Native Americans. Others were relatively unaware of their complicity in this process. Along with the activities of newcomers to the region went the complete uprooting of ancient cultural and social units and the elimination of the original inhabitants of their former means of subsistence. Although faunal reserves had been depleted by Native Americans over the course of many centuries (see Broughton 1994a, 1988), human impact on game animals, fish, and plant communities intensified after the arrival of outsiders in the region in the 1840s. Big game was driven out of the region, fish were depleted, and the life sustaining acorn reserve reduced by farming and grazing.

Box 3.A details some of the all too common newspaper accounts of events involving Native people in the Sacramento Valley after the arrival of settlers from Europe and the United States.

Box 3.A
Early Newspaper Accounts:
Native American Experiences in the Valley

Newspaper Article, Red Bluff, 1862
Outrages in Tehama County

Editor Beacon:—It is well known that there is, or has been, a body of soldiers in this country for several weeks past, for the avowed object of defending and protecting the citizens of the county against Indian depredations. It is equally well known that the depredatory Indians were on the east side of the river. By the neglect, carelessness, mismanagement or something worse, of the present Superintendent of Indian Affairs for the Northern District of California, it is known that there has been nothing raised either on Nome Lackee or Nome Cult for the subsistence of the Indians. Under the belief, and with the facts to substantiate it, that the Indians at Nome Cult were either to starve to death, or kill off, or be killed off, by the settlers, both Indians and settlers came to the conclusion that it was best for the Indians to leave the valley; and in this they were advised, counseled or favored by the Government employees at Nome Cult. Pursuant to this open, or at least tacit understanding between the Indians and the Government authorities, two tribes, the Hat Creeks and Con-Cows, left Nome Cult undisturbed, and without resistance or remonstrance, to make their way to their old haunts, in the hope of escaping death by starvation, With the morality or the policy of this, the writer has nothing to do. But to the sequel.

It is after these Indians had left Nome Cult—in starving condition—and made their way into the Sacramento valley, an effort was made by the Agent's employees to stop them. To do this they summoned to their aid Company E, 2nd California Cavalry, or a portion of it. The command promptly obeyed, and on the 1st day of October, they left the town of Red Bluff, on their mission. The command, or a portion of it, arrived in the neighborhood of Nome Lackee, to arrest and re-capture the Hat Creeks on Thursday or Friday. So far was their duty.

It is but proper, after consulting with those who are acquainted with the outrages, to say the Lieut. (or pretended Lieut, if such he was,) did not arrive at the scene of action until after the larger portion of his men were on the ground—But it is absolutely certain that he was there—that he put his horse in the stable to hay, and then prowled around and through the Indian rancherias in quest of some squaw. Whether he found a fit subject upon which to practice his virtuous and civilizing purposes, the writer is not informed. He, however, saddled up and left the scene or moral exploit about daylight.

Box 3.A cont'd

In justice to decency, humanity and civilization, these brutes should be punished. It is due to the honor, the reputation, the chivalry of the army of the United States, that the insignia of rank and position should be torn from the person of the Lieutenant (if it was he who was there,) as an officer unworthy of its trust and confidence.

Oct. 6, 1862 Foot Hills

Newspaper Article, Marysville, 1862
Fight with The Indians

From private information, we learn that Capt. Good's company of volunteers overtook a party of Indians near the site of the late massacre in Butte county, near Chico, and gave them battle. Seventeen of the Indians were killed and scalped by the volunteers, who, being from the immediate vicinity of the former massacre, are highly exasperated at the red-skins. None were killed on the side of the whites. They are determined to drive off or exterminate the Indians, it is said.

Newspaper Article, Sacramento, 1852
Indian Difficulties

The Yreka correspondent of the Shasta Courier states that a fight took place a short time since at Wright's Camps with 21 Indians. Two citizens were severely wounded. On the arrival of the party at Yreka, they paraded through the streets—the wounded being borne in litters—each of the party, consisting of 16 whites, 2 Indians, and a negro, having a bow and arrows, and the muzzle of his gun decorated with a scalp taken from the enemy.

Newspaper Article, Marysville, 1859

A new plan has been adopted by our neighbors opposite this place to chastise the Indians for their many depredations during the past winter. Some men are hired to hunt them, who are recompensed by receiving so much for each scalp, or some other satisfactory evidence that they have been killed. The money has been made up by subscription.

Location Patterns

A population distribution map of the Sacramento Valley drawn in the year 1800 would reveal a place populated by tens of thousands of Native American people. Most of the dots shown on this cartographic depiction of the original inhabitants of the region would show people clustered along the Sacramento River and along both sides of other smaller streams flowing out of the Sierra Nevada/Cascade foothills on the east or the rolling Coast Ranges on the west.

Local village locations were linked to food supplies (e.g., acorns, fish) and the availability of fresh water (see Dreyer 1984 for a complete discussion of the subsistence patterns of selected Valley groups such as the Mechoopda).

It was a fertile land then, filled with a diversity of people and a lush cover of wild plants and animals that provided sustenance for its human inhabitants. Vast areas of grassland, quantities of variable woodland and chaparral, combined with rivers provided one of the richest habitats on Earth. The woodland/chaparral provided deer, vegetables, and the staple acorns; the grasslands provided antelope; the river provided salmon and other fish; and the dense forests along the riparian corridors provided more acorns (State Lands Commission 1994, 6-7). The Maidu story of a Sacramento River flood summarized in Box 3.B provides a dramatic illustration of the close relationship between the all important river and its people.

The availability of native plant and animal foods and the complete reliance on them by Native Americans in the Sacramento Valley largely dictated settlement patterns. Ethnographic data collected during the late nineteenth and early twentieth centuries provides evidence of Native groups in the region that Dreyer defines as "storage hunter-gatherers" (Dreyer 1984, 2). This level of economic development is characterized as consisting of sedimentary dwellers with relatively dense populations and well developed exchange networks.

Villages were located on sites that provided plenty of fresh water, a dependable food supply, security from flood waters, exposure to sunlight, and shelter from winds (Hill 1978, 7). Limited in density by local food supplies, most people lived in settled villages of kindred families of between 100 and 500 inhabitants. In the Valley, villages were apparently inhabited year round, although small purposeful groups may have periodically left their village to exploit resources in nearby areas (Dreyer 1984, 45).

Although many of these earliest Valley residents traveled from one village to another to trade goods and attend festivals, most knew that the place where they had been born was also the place they would die. Land "ownership" was shared by village residents, but most had a strong attachment to their community and maintained a vital connection to home space throughout their lifetimes.

Although the earliest available ethnographies of Native American life are incomplete and filled with biases common in the mid-nineteenth century, a partial listing of the diverse groups inhabiting the Valley is instructive. As shown on the map in Figure 3.1, many different groups of Native Americans resided in the Sacramento Valley before the arrival of Euro-American settlers.

Box 3.B
A Native American View of Natural Hazards:
Maidu Legend of a Sacramento Valley Flood

In the not so distant past, Native Americans lived happily in the Sacramento Valley. But one day Big Water came in and covered the land so deep that none could measure. Many fled and many were drowned. Frogs and salmon chased the Indians beneath the water and ate them. Only two Indians escaped to the foothills.

The Great Man blessed these two with much fertility so that from them many tribes resulted. A mighty nation was formed with one Chief known everywhere.

This Chief went out on a hill and viewed the rich valley, once the home of his ancestors. He lay for nine sleeps on the knoll, thinking of his people, the flood, and how it had come so suddenly on the land. For these nine sleeps, the Chief lay without food, "feeding on his mind," and wondering about the deep water that covered the earth.

After his nine sleeps, the chief was much changed. No arrow could harm him. Even if a thousand Indians shot at him, they could not harm him. Like the Great Man in Heaven, the Chief could not be slain.

The Chief spoke to the Great Man, asking that the water flow off the plains of his ancestors. So it happened thus. The Great Man opened the side of the mountain, and all the flood water flowed away into the Big Water.
Source: Adapted from Hendrix, 1989, p. 31.

These groups included:

- The Maidu, divided into the Mountain Maidu in the Sierra Nevadas, the Konkow in the central region, and the Nisenan in the southernmost extent of the Valley. Together, they formed one of the largest linguistic groups in the region. Maidu villages were located east of the Sacramento River;
- The Winton who lived west of the Sacramento River from Suisun Bay north to Mt. Shasta;
- The Chimariko, Karok, Shastan, and Yana who inhabited the northern end of the Valley.

Large linguistic and socioeconomic groups were divided into smaller tribelets. These relatively small sociopolitical groups were first described by early explorers in the region who were unable to distinguish between the languages andcustoms of various sub-groups. Their descriptions, in fact, did a great deal to encourage the belief among outsiders that "all Indians are the same" —a stereotype that lingers among outsiders all too frequently in modern times. The Indian sub-agent for the United States government, Adam Johnson, for example, who

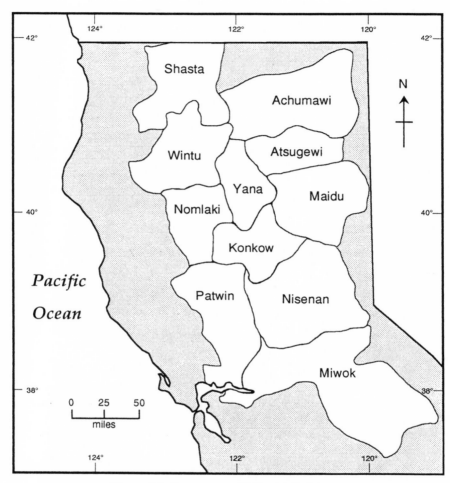

Figure 3.1. Sacramento Valley Tribal Areas.
Source: Adapted from Burrill 1988, 12.

traveled at least 800 miles throughout the Sacramento Valley in 1850, noted no great differences among the customs and habits of life among the people (despite the great diversity of native groups and cultures in the area). Johnson listed the following groups and their estimated populations living in the region: (*Sacramento Daily Transcript,* August 17, 1850, 1):

• The Hocks who lived near the Hock Farm near Sutter's home south of Yuba City (70-100);
• The Yubas, located near the mouth of the Yuba River (180);
• The Olippas who lived about 32 miles above the mouth of the Feather River (70);
• The Bogars, located near the Olippas on the opposite side of the Feather River (70);
• The Erskines, located near Lawson's Rancho on Butte Creek (60);
• The Cushnas, who resided on the South Yuba River near Bidwell's and Potter's ranches, near the foothills (600);
• The Machucks, located near Potter's Rancho on the south branch of the Yuba river (70-90).

Johnson's naive observation of groups listed here forms only a partial representation of what ethnographers now believe defined the political and economic organization of Native Americans in the Valley. Individuals lived in distinct villages based on familial associations and spoke a dialect related to dialects spoken in neighboring villages but who were thoroughly unique as well (Heizer 1966, 5). A certain tribelet was often concentrated in one village, but, in some cases, members of the same group lived in a number of different villages located near one another. This type of socioeconomic and political system was described by Kroeber as follows (1932, 257-259):

It has gradually become clear that in the region west and northwest of the Patwin there prevailed a type of political organization which has been veiled by the shrinkage, removal, and amalgamation of the native in recent generations, by the fact that the units were small and often nameless, and they frequently lived in several settlements, and that each settlement has a recognized headman who, as well as the group head, was called chief. . . . Each group acted as a homogeneous unit in matters of land ownership, trespass, war, major ceremonies, and the entertainment entailed by them.

Figure 3.2 locates Patwin and Maidu villages along the Sacramento River. Data shown on this map were gathered from personal interviews with Sacramento Valley Native Americans by C. Hart Merriam between 1902 and 1935.

Adding to our knowledge of these demographic patterns and the locations of their villages is a tabulation compiled by John Bidwell in 1846 and 1847 recorded in a letter to his employer, John Sutter. Bidwell's estimates are shown in Table 3.1. Bidwell's list is of interest for several reasons. First, it records the diversity and size of various tribelets scattered throughout the entire region. Second, it provides evidence of the lingering importance of the names of several

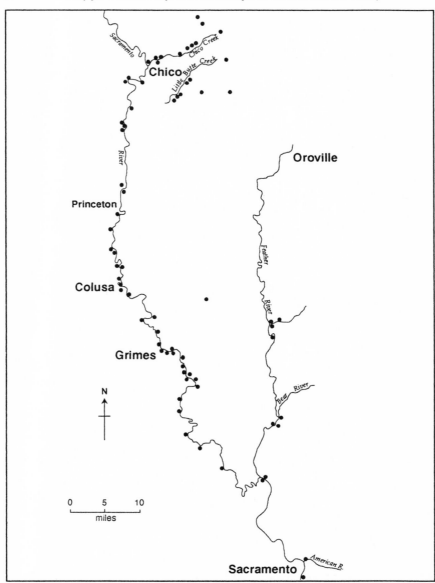

Figure 3.2. Maidu and Patwin Villages along the Sacramento River.
Source: Heizer and Hester 1970, n.p.

Table 3.1. Native Americans in the Sacramento Valley, 1846

	Male	Female	Total
Lakisimne	28	16	44
Shonomnes	11	6	17
Tawalemnes	25	21	46
Seywamenes	21	24	45
Mukelemnes	45	36	81
Cosumne	34	25	59
Sagayacumne	27	20	47
Louklumnes	43	45	88
Olonutchamne	31	23	54
Newatchamne	31	30	61
Yumagatock	21	15	36
Shalachmushumne	32	18	50
Omutschamne	18	9	27
Yusumne	35	49	84
Yule eyumne	124	113	237
Yamlock-lock	40	27	67
Lapototot	45	29	74
Yalesumne	228	257	485
Wapoomne	75	67	142
Kiskey	48	45	93
Secumne	23	26	49
Pushune	43	40	83
Oioksecumne	16	19	35
Nemshau	29	21	50

Table 3.1. Native Americans in the Sacramento Valley, 1846

	Male	Female	Total
Palanshau	17	18	35
Ustu	25	14	29
Olash	30	22	52
Yukulme	12	11	23
Hock	39	40	79
Sishu	54	49	103
Mimal	22	16	38
Yubu	56	65	121
Bubu	19	16	35
Honcut	41	45	86
Total	1,224	1,149	2,373

Source: John Bidwell, November, 1846 (list included in a letter to John Sutter).

of these Native American groups still recorded on contemporary maps of the Sacramento Valley. Place names such as Honcut and Yuba (and many others not recorded by Bidwell such as Colusi) remain as evidence of the importance of these earliest Valley residents in shaping today's visible geography of the region.

A Closer Look: The Maidu of Chico

Chico ethnographers William Dreyer (1984) and Dorothy Hill (1978) located specific village sites of the Maidu of the Chico Rancheria as shown on Figure 3.3. Their original village, located near the Fourth Street entrance to Bidwell Park was relocated nearer the Bidwell residence in 1869. According to Hill, there were several reasons for this relocation of the settlement (1978, 52):

In March, 1869 the Indian village was relocated approximately one mile from the Bidwell's residence on Sacramento Avenue, where the Chico Ran-

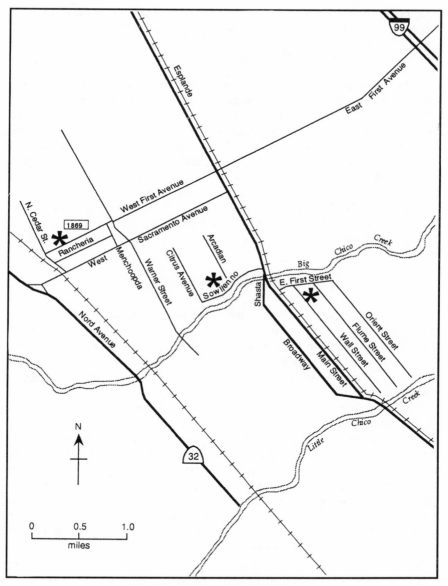

Figure 3.3. Native American Villages in Chico.
Source: Adapted from Hill 1978, 53.

cheria was established and where it has remained since. The reason for this move was stated by Mrs. Bidwell as the necessity for the Indians to have more ground. . . . However, the noise of the ceremonial wailing which reportedly disturbed the Bidwell household was probably another reason.

Despite heavy dependence on a diet of fish, small game, and acorns among early Chico residents, recent work suggests that three slightly different economic strategies were followed by the Mechoopda of Chico (see Dreyer 1984). These include: (1) a general economic system characterized by exploitation of acorns, fish, and game; (2) a more specific economy based on the exploitation of acorns and fish, and a secondary reliance on game; and (3) a specialized economy based on the exploitation of acorns and game. As in many other parts of the Sacramento Valley, the availability of acorns, however, most influenced the settlement patterns of Chico area Native Americans. A dramatic reminder of the lingering importance of Maidu people in the Chico area is the cemetery located on West Sacramento Avenue in the heart of the town's university district.

Human-Environment Interaction

Despite their adjustment to similar physical environments in the Sacramento Valley, a significant diversity of Native American languages, cultures, and lifestyles existed in the region Over 135 native languages were spoken in California, each spoken by about 1,000 people (Caughey 1970, 7). A dwindling number of people in the state remain fluent in only a few of these languages at the present time.

Resident peoples in scattered villages north of Sacramento were quite diverse in their lifeways particularly in how they adapted to local environments. Although anthropologists and archaeologists have maintained for decades that early California Indians were all hunters and gatherers who lived *off* the land rather than managing the land, recent research has begun to unravel facts that illustrate a much more complex human-environmental relationship. In a recent book co-edited by ethnobiologist Kat Anderson, evidence is presented that argues that tribes living in the Sacramento Valley tightly controlled and managed their environment through a variety of methods, most notably through the use of fire (Anderson 1994, 6C). Through the study of archival materials, interviews with local Native people, and an analysis of baskets and tools used by early people, Anderson's research reveals that Native Americans used fire regularly to both encourage and control plant species. Using several branches of redbud as an example, Anderson reported at a recent conference in Willows that (Brown 1994, 6C):

> Shoots come up after an area is burned. They are used to make the baskets. To get a supply necessary year after year, it would take 1,000,000 shoots to make all the baskets produced—the Native Americans burned the fields, a concrete example of managing, not just living off the land.

Despite lingering images to the contrary in numerous academic and popular publications, videos, and movies, it has become more clear in recent years that Native people not only understood, but also controlled their environment to meet specific needs of their community. Fish catches were maintained through careful use of resources in rivers and streams and plant species needed for food, medicines, baskets, and tools were "cultivated" to assure continued availability. Recent work has documented that, over a long period of time, these original Californians actually had quite a major impact on their local environment. Using vertebrate data from archaeological evidence (rather than ethnographic records), for example, Broughton established that Native people had a major impact on the elimination of large game animals and drastically reduced fish populations in the Valley (Broughton 1994a, 1994b, 1988). His work differs widely from more traditional studies of Sacramento Valley pre-Euro-American environmental impacts which emphasized aboriginal subsistence as based on an unlimited supply of high quality natural resources and an almost total lack of environmental degradation (see, for example, Kroeber 1925; Baumhoff, 1963).

Despite this rather surprising evidence of early impacts on physical systems in the study area, it is evident that Native Americans maintained a close, caring, and quite well informed relationship with their local environment, especially when compared to later arrivals. Box 3.C details an example of the close relationship that existed between one group of Native Americans in the North State, the Koncow Maidu, and the physical environment. It is based on research done on a group of early residents who lived along the eastern edge of the Valley and in the foothills.

Conflict

The region's original settlement patterns and human impacts on the environment were severely and rapidly disrupted when Euro-American settlers arrived. The relationship between food supply and population density was the first disruption caused by the arrival of these new Valley residents. In addition, mining

Box 3.C
Sacred Sites of the Konkow Maidu
Environmental Perception Among Native Americans
By Kari Forbes-Boyte, Geographer-Ethnographer

North American Indians generally have an extremely close relationship with the environment. Take, for example, the Konkow Maidu who reside in the Sierra Nevada foothills of north central California. Although these people are acculturated for the most part, they still gather their traditional food sources and worship nature in much the same way as their ancestors.

The Konkow feel that food was given to them by Worldmaker, whom they call Wonomi. In the beginning of time, Wonomi made the Earth and all its inhabitants. For humans he provided an endless supply of food sources, including fish and acorns, the traditional dietary staples. These foods are still gathered by the Konkow. As food was given to the people by Wonomi, it is considered sacred, and therefore the act of gathering is a religious observation.

Before gathering traditional foods, one must be pure in heart and leave an offering of acorn meal, scraps of material, or pennies as a sign of thanks to the Worldmaker for providing for his people. When gathering food sources, a respect toward the gathering area is always observed. Therefore, the Konkow gather only what actually will be utilized, and the area itself is never decimated with trash or any other signs of human intervention. The gathering places are considered sacred, as well as the act of gathering itself. It is important that these areas be left in the natural state. However, the traditional gathering areas are becoming scarce through land development, and thus the Konkow feel it is important to protect the remaining areas from further encroachment.

The Konkow could be considered nature worshipers. Their religion is based on an interrelationship between themselves and their homeland. They are animistic, which means they believe the world is filled with spirits, so there are places that they consider to be sacred. These places included prominent landform features, mountain tops, groves of trees, waterfalls, and mountain lakes. Many of these places are mentioned in their mythology, which is considered to be truth and not mere stories. Other places are considered sacred because they are the homes of the ku kini, or guardian spirits who help the Konkow in life. The ku kini are the manifestation of power, which is the "cosmic breath of the world"; it is what makes the world alive, and is considered part force and part object.

These sacred places are scattered throughout their territory. Some places are considered important for showing respect to the gods. They are used in the vision quests or ritual acts, such as the spring and fall feasts held there. Other places are discussed in mythology. for example, there is a place in the Konkow territory where Bat, one of the first people,was said to live. Another mythological area is a lake which is considered poisonous due to the presence of a large snake that is believed to reside there. It is a place to stay away from in the Konkow perception.

Box 3.C cont'd

The perception of these traditional sacred sites influences the psychological makeup and lives of the foothill Konkow individuals. it is an aspect of their environmental perception to note these sacred areas and to incorporate these values in their daily lives. The Konkow feel an adherence to their homeland, stabilized by this perception of sacred sites. This sense of sacredness in regard to the landscape leads to a powerful sense of communion between the society and the environment. To the Konkow Maidu nature is not just natural, it is given religious value because it is created from the hands of Wonomi.

Source: Reprinted with permission from Patterns on Our Planet: Concepts and Themes in Geography, Susan W. Hardwick and Donald G. Holtgrieve, New York: Macmillan, 1990, pp. 280-281.

---

operations affected salmon fishing and destroyed fish dams (Heizer 1978, 108). As large ranchos were divided into smaller and smaller land holdings after the arrival of new settlers, more intense grazing and a better developed system of planting of field crops resulted in increased destruction of the natural food supply for native people.

Overall, the national context for the government's "management" of Native Americans centered on a unique set of circumstances in the state of California. As mentioned earlier in this chapter, the population density of California aboriginal people was higher than in other parts of the country. A second issue was that whites arrived and settled in large numbers in California more quickly than in other areas. Finally, Indians could not be removed to the West as they had been in earlier decades of our nation's history. There was simply no place else for them to go.

Although California state law, as summarized in Box 3.D, had established clear legal responsibilities for Native American-Anglo relations in the state, national law soon superseded the state's jurisdiction. One of the first and most damaging of the "California solutions" was an attempt to remove Indians entirely from their homelands within the state. The commonly accepted philosophy that "the only good Indian is a dead Indian" reappears in many works of fiction written about the era as well as in numerous nineteenth century diaries and historical accounts (see, for example, Sim Moak's *Last of the Mill Creeks* published in 1972). Other negative and hostile attitudes about these earliest residents of the state were expressed by the general public. Many believed that all Indians should be slaughtered or even moved to a remote island in a faraway sea. The vast majority of newly arriving settlers had extremely negative feelings

---

Box 3.D
An Attempt to Control the Valley's Earliest Residents

The act provided for the following:

1. The Justice of the Peace would have jurisdiction over all complaints between Indians and Whites; "but in no case shall a white man be convicted of any offence upon the testimony of an Indian or Indians."
2. Landowners would permit Indians who were peaceably residing on their land to continue to do so.
3. Whites would be able to obtain control of Indian children. (This section would eventually be used to justify and provide for Indian slavery.)
4. If any Indian was convicted of a crime, any White person could come before the court and contract for the Indian's services, and in return would pay the Indian's fine.
5. It would be illegal to sell or administer alcohol to Indians.
6. Indians convicted of stealing a horse, mule, cow, or any other valuable could receive any number of lashes not to exceed 25, and fines not to exceed $200. (It should be noted that the law provided that abusing an Indian child by Whites was to be punished by no more than a $10 fine. It is hard to compare the penalty with the crime.)
7. Finally, an Indian found strolling, loitering where alcohol was sold, begging, or leading a profligate course of life would be liable for arrest. The justice, mayor, or recorder would make out a warrant. Within 24 hours, the services of the Indian in question could be sold to the highest bidder. The term of service would not exceed four months.

This law was widely abused with regard to the use of Indians as laborers, though it did allow Indians to reside on private land.

Source: *Act for the Government and Protection of Indians,* by the first session of the California State Legislature in 1850.

---

about Native peoples. Many pitied them, others hated them, and just about everyone wanted them entirely out of the way. In contrast, the earlier Latino population had hoped to Europeanize the Native Americans. Later North American hostility toward Native Americans is even more disturbing in light of Kroeber's and other early observers' descriptions of local people as fundamentally peaceful and harmless.

These negative attitudes exerted pressure on the United States government and ultimately resulted in the passage of the Indian Appropriation Act of 1852. This law authorized the President to make:

> Five military reservations from the public domain in the state of California, or the territories of Utah and New Mexico bordering on said state, for Indian purposes. Provided that such reservations shall not contain more than

twenty-five thousand acres in each; and provided further, that said reservations shall not be made upon any lands inhabited by citizens of California.

The first reservation to be established under this new system was located at Fort Tejon near Bakersfield in 1852. The second was located in Tehama County in the heart of the Sacramento Valley, a few miles north of the town of Flournoy. Early government agents searching for an appropriate site in Northern California, described their travels through the area as passing through well watered valleys endowed with plentiful oaks and grasslands. In a letter sent by H.L. Ford to Thomas Henley on September 4, 1854, it was stated that they:

> Moved camp south about two miles and a half to a small valley containing about six hundred acres of as good and fine land as the Northern portion of the state affords.

This second Indian reservation in the United States was eventually named Nome Lackee after a group of Tehama County Native Americans who lived between Thomas and Elder Creeks. The initial number of the region's earliest inhabitants brought to the reservation in October, 1854, was about 200. The number increased to more than 1,000 by August of the following year (Hislop 1978, 16, 21). In addition to the original Nome Lackee families, Pit River, Trinity, and Nevada Indians were added over the course of the following year. Tight military control was maintained to control this diverse group of residents.

Despite overly optimistic and repeated accounts by local newspapers of "the good life" provided inside the reservation, by 1859, the reputation of the Nome Lackee reservation had fallen into an abyss. When the truth finally came out in local papers, it told a sad story indeed. The much bragged about successes in agriculture among residents of the reservation had lagged by then due to a failure of the local water supply. Most of the residents of the reservation had escaped, leaving far less than 1,000 people still inside. In an argument to close down Nome Lackee, government agent Vincent Geiger reported that "the only way to provide for the safekeeping of these Indians is, in my opinion, to put them on the reserve either at Round Valley or Mendocino" (Hislop 1978, 50).

In February, 1859, a pro-Indian petition unique to its time and place was sent to Washington asking for the closure of the reservation. The petition filed in the town of Tehama on February 24, 1859, offered the following arguments for the total elimination of Nome Lackee:

1. The few Indians on the reserve were peaceful.
2. Good land was being wasted.
3. The Indians, were, by that time, capable of earning good wages.

4. The evil influence of the people on the reservation should be ended.
5. The agent would not let the settlers live within one mile of the reservation.
6. The mismanagement of the whole project was a disgrace to Tehama County.
7. The personal conduct of Vincent Geiger and his employees was objectionable.

After several more years of complaints reported in local newspapers and numerous local attempts to eliminate the reservation at Nome Lackee, in 1863, everyone remaining on the reservation was forced to walk overland to Round Valley in Mendocino County. The route of this forced march is shown on the map in Figure 3.4.

According to the final report of Captain Augustus Starr of the Second Cavalry, California Volunteers, who led the difficult journey across the rugged Coast Ranges, he left Chico for Round Valley on September 3, 1863 with 461 Native Americans. Although his report fails to mention Nome Lackee, Starr no doubt picked up the remaining Indians in Tehama County on his way through the area. By far, the most disturbing aspect of Starr's report were his comments on disease and other hardships along the trail. Only 277 of the original 431 Indians arrived safely at the Round Valley reservation. There they found insufficient food and accommodations (Goldschmidt 1951, 212).

Numerous other Native Americans died of disease in the Sacramento Valley during these early years of European and American settlement. Ample evidence exists that there were devastating epidemics of smallpox and malaria that swept through the region even before 1840 (Wollenberg 1970, 30).

One of the most severe and devastating epidemics swept through the Central Valley and Coast Ranges in 1833. The following on site descriptions vividly tell the tale:

• F.T. Gilbert in his *History of San Joaquin County, California* (1879) reported:

On our return in the summer of 1833, we found the valleys depopulated. From the head of the Sacramento to the great bend and slough of the San Joaquin, we did not see more than six or eight Indians while large numbers of their skulls and dead bodies were to be seen under almost every shade tree near water, where uninhabited and deserted villages had been converted to graveyards.

• A.S. Cook (1955) hypothesized that the disaster which spread from the north end of the Great Valley was malaria. He wrote:

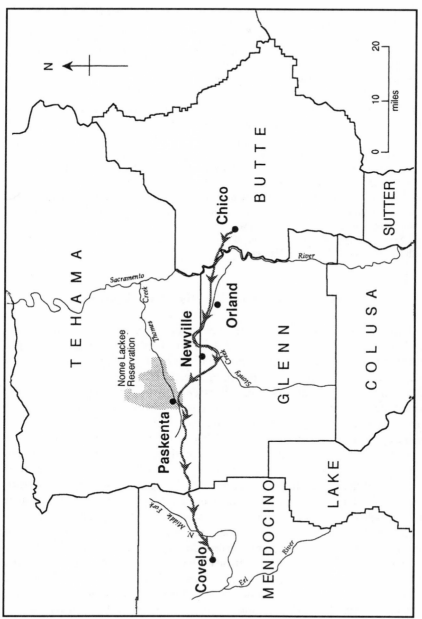

Figure 3.4. Route of Forced Drive to Round Valley.

This is a startling and disturbing result. It means that fully 20,000 natives of the Great Central valley died in 1833. It means that 3/4 of the Indians who had resisted 70 years of Spanish and Mexican domination were wiped out in one summer. It means that the red race in the heart of California was so crippled that it could offer but the shadow of opposition to the gold mining flood which swept over it in 1840.

Later, accounts of the toll of disease became even more vivid. According to a newspaper article in the *Sacramento Union* in 1851:

Dr. Harkness informs us that a brother of his, who has just come down from the upper Sacramento, brings intelligence that sickness prevails to a considerable extent among the tribes of Indians in the vicinity of the river. He noticed on the road a number of unburied bodies, and in the huts and woods many who were lying prostrate with disease. The ranks of the aborigines are rapidly wasting away before the onward march of the pale face; and very soon, the last son of the forest will have been summoned to the presence of the 'great Father.'

Native American Landscapes Today

Accounts of disease and the total destruction of Native American villages and their inhabitants contribute sordid details to the evolving and deeply disturbing geography of aboriginal people living (and dying) in the Sacramento Valley after 1850. A lethal combination of disease, social and economic change, military intervention, and eventual displacement to reservations drastically affected these earliest Valley residents. The story of Ishi, last of his tribe in the foothills rimming the eastern side of the mid-Sacramento Valley (Box 3.E), serves as a final case study of this tragic tale of conflict and despair in the region.

In the late twentieth century, Native American groups in the Sacramento Valley are involved in a continuing effort to regain tribal status and associated recognition of their rights to land and resources. The Chico Mechoopda described earlier in this chapter have already received notification of the approval of their official tribal status. In addition, as this book was going to press, the federal legislature finally agreed to restore national recognition to the Paskenta band of Nomlaki Indians of Tehama County. Tribal Chairman Everett Freeman, a Bureau of Indian Affairs maintenance worker in Williams, reported on October 5, 1994, that tribal status will assist the Nomlaki to secure better housing and improved educational and employment opportunities. One wonders what the outcome might have been if the United States government would have provided recognition of tribal status in its earliest years of initial contact with Native Americans rather than following violent and restrictive policies of internment and attempted eradication.

Table 3.2 summarizes the total number of Native Americans counted in Sacramento Valley counties in the *U.S. Census of Population* between 1860 and 1990. Dramatically increasingly numbers in recent decades is no doubt due to an increased awareness of the importance and value of claiming Native American heritage for personal and economic reasons. Perhaps nowhere is this increase more evident in the local landscape than in recent efforts to open profitable "Indian Bingo" establishments. These operations have become highly successful economic ventures for local groups and have increased an awareness of the Native American presence among other Valley residents. Three of these gambling establishments are currently in operation in the region at Redding, Colusa, and Brooks.

The next chapter continues the story of Valley settlement, economic development, environment, and landscape evolution. These impacts, inspired by developments in the world beyond the Valley, brought about the continuing decline of Native American life and landscape in the region, dramatically changing both its physical and human geography.

Table 3.2. Native Americans in the Sacramento Valley, 1860-1990

County	1860	1880	1910	1930	1950	1970	1990
Butte	121	522	298	377	207	890	3,212
Colusa	75	353	169	107	172	132	305
Glenn	*	*	32	31	39	188	505
Sacramento	251	14	62	186	325	2,670	11,786
Shasta	8	1,037	756	687	525	1,321	3,885
Solano	21	21	1	18	84	1,048	3,070
Sutter	10	13	18	12	39	209	914
Tehama	656	167	94	125	130	306	956
Yolo	*	47	32	54	78	476	1,692
Yuba	72	67	16	86	81	210	1,671

Source: United States Census of Population, 1960-1990.
* Census data not available.

Box 3.E
Ishi: Symbol of a Forgotten Time and Place

The story of Ishi, perhaps the most famous Native American in Northern California has been told and retold many times in many places. It is indeed a fascinating tale, full of discovery, adjustment to new experiences and new cultures, and ultimately of sadness. As such, Ishi symbolizes the end of a way of life in the North State. Indeed, Ishi's life (and death) in many ways represents the end of an era that had dominated life and landscape in the region for tens of thousands of years.

Ishi grew to adulthood in the wild Sierra-Cascade hill country east of the mid-Sacramento Valley. His tribe had survived easily on the numerous wild plants and animals of the Deer Creek drainage area for many generations before the arrival of Euro-American miners, railroad workers, and farmers. Then their life suddenly began to change.

Left only with his elderly uncle, his mother, and his sister, Ishi's small family unit, the last of the tribe, tried to avoid these new Californians. After the death of everyone in his family, Ishi stumbled into a cattle yard outside Oroville in 1911. Afraid and uncertain of his identity, local townspeople quickly locked him in the local jail. Alerted by a newspaper story about their "capture of California's last wild Indian," a well known anthropologist from the University of California, Kroeber, came to Oroville and eventually took Ishi back to live at the university in bustling San Francisco.

But it wasn't Kroeber who became Ishi's closest confidant. It was Kroeber's friend and colleague, T.T. Waterman, who remembers Ishi as follows:

> He convinced me that there is such a thing as a gentlemanlyness which lies outside of all training, and is an expression purely of an inward spirit. It has nothing to do with artificially acquired tricks of behavior. Ishi was slow to acquire the tricks of social contact. He never learned to shake hands but he had an innate regard for other fellow's existence, and an inborn considerateness that surpassed in fineness most of the civilized breeding with which I am familiar. His life came to a close as a result of an over susceptibility to tuberculosis, to which he was at some time or other exposed, and to which he never developed the slightest immunity. He contributed to us the best account he could give of the life of his people, as it was before the whites came in. To know him was a rare personal privilege, not merely an ethnographic privilege. I feel myself that in many ways he was perhaps the most remarkable personality of this century.

Source: "Ishi, The Last Yahi," by T.T. Waterman (in) R.F. Heizer and M.A. Whipple, eds. *The California Indians: A Source Book.* Berkeley: University of California Press, 1973, and *Ishi in Two Worlds* by Theodora Kroeber, Berkeley: University of California Press, 1961.

Endnote

1. Many widely varying estimates have been given by scholars regarding the actual number of Native Americans living in California over the years. The earliest estimate, provided by C. Hart Merriam, was based on mission records. He suggested an approximate total of 260,000 ("Indian Population in California," *American Anthropologist*, V. 7, 1905, 594-606). The well-known Berkeley anthropologist, A.L. Kroeber, cut this number back to 133,000 in his *Handbook* published in 1925. Later work published by Kroeber suggested that the number was probably much larger. Census calculations for counties and cities in the Sacramento Valley for the years 1850 through 1990 should be used in research with caution since census takers often missed local residents in their count or overlooked entire villages for the sake of convenience.

Chapter 4

New Arrivals

The displacement of Native Americans in northern California by the Spanish, Mexicans, North Americans and others was described in the last chapter. Exploration and early Euro-American settlement of the Sacramento Valley are described here because the two processes were really simultaneous and were often played out by the same actors. As with most North American frontier areas, the *first effective settlement* of a place (excluding aboriginal settlement) had the greatest potential for leaving a lasting imprint on the land. Such was the case in the Sacramento Valley where a vast expanse of what they perceived as "virgin" land was occupied by a few determined families of ranchers and town builders. The results of their decisions and actions are still visible on the landscape today.

People

Spanish Exploration

The motives for Spanish incursion into Northern California were based on a global strategy for control of what we now call the Pacific Basin. Settlement of Mexico in the sixteenth century and most of South America in the seventeenth allowed trade and religious conversion to reach the Philippines and east Asia. Transport to Asia by ship was made possible by using the trade winds to sail west along a line roughly following the 20° parallel. The return voyage required use of the global westerly winds that flowed along the 40° parallel. To reach these westerly winds, ships had to follow the Japanese Current northward for 2,500 miles. Since landing on the Japanese islands was forbidden and dangerous, the voyage from Manila was 5,000 nonstop miles to the coast of North America, a long trip by anyone's standards. To add to the difficulty of a return voyage to Mexico, the westerlies carried Spanish ships to land at approximately 39° north latitude (near today's town of Mendocino), still 1,500 miles from their home port of Mazatlan.

Sea exploration of the California coast by Cabrillo in 1542 and Viscanino in 1602 confirmed the feasibility of a northwest coast port for the Spanish. The 1769 expedition by Portola and Serra made it a reality. The Spanish claim to Alta California was reinforced with the construction of Presidios at San Francisco, Monterey, Santa Barbara, and San Diego as well as a chain of missions along the coastal mountains and valleys from San Diego to Sonoma. By the 1820s, coastal California was occupied and settled by outsiders along with total subjugation or removal of most of the Native American population.

During these early years, the Central Valley remained unexplored because it was not considered important. The region was viewed as insignificant because it not only did not possess perceived resources but it also harbored the more "difficult" natives who refused to be subjugated to the mission system. Eventually, a need to secure the northern frontier of "New Spain" and significant horse stealing by local Native Americans necessitated exploration and military activity in the Valley. The Spanish government also gave some thought to constructing a second string of missions in the interior portions of California.

The first Spanish incursions into the Valley were tentative and reached only as far as the area near Mount Diablo (1772) and the delta of the Sacramento and San Joaquin Rivers (1776). The 1776 expedition named today's Sacramento River the Rio Rogue. In 1793, Francisco Eliza sailed into the Sacramento River portion of the delta. The first recorded expedition to the Sacramento River Valley consisted of eleven men led by Lieutenant Gabriel Moraga in 1808 (see Cutter 1950). On his search for possible mission sites, he named the present Feather River, calling it the Sacramento, and the Sacramento River, which he named Jesus Maria. The American River was named Las Llagas. His Sacramento (Feather) River was described in his journal as "a wide overflowing plain." The Moraga expedition went as far north as Stony Creek, passing the Sutter Buttes which he referred to as the "mountain range in the middle of the valley" (Cutter 1950, n.p.). Upon completion of the trip, Moraga reported that he had found no suitable mission site because the plains were subject to flooding, the river banks were too high to build a water delivery system, the tules were an obstacle, and there was no available stone for building foundations.

Larger vessels began exploration in 1511 when priests by the names of Abolla and Fortini took a short trip up the "northern river of San Francisco." Land expeditions by the Spanish priests and soldiers through 1520 wandered through Montezuma Slough and up the Sacramento River as far as today's city of Redding (State Lands Commission 1994, 7).

Lt. Luis Antonio Arguello and a priest who recorded the adventure, Father Narciso Duran, also traveled to the Sacramento Valley, arriving in 1817 by boat. They camped on Brown's Island in the delta then rowed upriver with a party of twenty men in two boats. Their trip to the regionrecorded that there was significant flooding. Herds of deer and elk and bands of grizzly bears were seen frequently. Duran observed and noted the Sutter Buttes and Arguello named El Rio de las Plumas (or Feather River) from the many feathers of the waterfowl seen there (McGowan 1961, 20).

This expedition probably turned around at the junction of the Sacramento and Feather Rivers later to become a town known as Verona. They also noted that they hoped a pass through the great barrier of the Sierra Nevada would be discovered. It is interesting to note that there is also record of an 1817 expedition in the Valley led by a priest, Narciso Duran. His purpose was the selection of mission sites but no record of his route or accomplishments exists today.

Later, in 1821, Arguello again headed an expedition up the Valley toward Oregon. This group was in search of reported "white men" who may have been Russians from Fort Ross or Hudson's Bay Company fur trappers. In spite of encounters with hostile Native residents in the area that were provoked by the Spanish, and various other mishaps, Arguello sketched a crude map of the Sacramento Valley, naming several mountains and creeks. His party of explorers traveled as far north as the site of present day Redding, noting twin peaks which were probably Mt. Shasta and Shastina. The group also described a volcanic peak now known to be Mt. Lassen. The expedition was prematurely aborted, however, and they then returned to San Francisco by following the Coast Ranges south. Unfortunately, their original map was lost.

Early Russian Explorers

It is important to note that despite these early travelers in the region, Northern California was not exclusively Spanish in the early years of the nineteenth century. The Russians established a modest settlement at Fort Ross on the Sonoma Coast and were able to explore the Sacramento River Valley, with reluctant Spanish permission, in 1823-24 (Bancroft 1886, II, 523). Their leader, Captain Otto von Kotzebue, described the landscape as a sweep of beauty and luxuriance. While very critical of the Californians the river was described in glowing terms as (Bancroft 1880, V. 2, 523):

Broad, beautiful streams, sometimes winding between high, steep banks, sometimes gliding through smiling meadows where great herds for deer were grazing. White and gray pelicans, twice the size of our geese, were here in great numbers. We saw many great fish leap beyond the surface of the water.

Early cartographic evidence of the Russian presence in the Sacramento Valley appeared on a map drafted by a Spanish cartographer in 1833 (Hardwick 1986, 284). On this early map, the Sacramento River (near today's Discovery Park) bore the Russian/Spanish name Rio Ojetska, in Russian meaning "land (or *place*) of the hunter." This Slavic place name continued to appear on other early maps, including John Cooper's grant application map for land near the American River.

The British also made brief contact with the Sacramento River in 1837. The crews of the British navy ship, the *Sulphur,* produced the oldest surviving chart of the lower Sacramento River during and after their expedition (State Lands Commission 1994, 7).

Visitors from North America

The first known explorer from the United States to visit the Sacramento Valley was Jedediah Smith who trapped beaver there in early 1828. Smith followed the Sacramento River upstream from its junction with the American River thinking that it was the mighty Buenaventura River, believed to flow from the Rocky mountains to the Pacific Ocean. He then crossed the Bear River, naming it Brush Creek, describing it as being twenty yards wide. Smith followed the Yuba and Feather rivers, crossing Honcut Creek, eventually reaching Butte Creek, then traveled west to the Sacramento River again. Following the winding Sacramento River, Smith eventually reached Deer and Mill creeks. Here, in the vicinity of today's town of Red Bluff, he noted in his diary that he intended to continue to follow the Sacramento River but "rocky hills coming in so close to the river . . . make it impossible to travel" (McGowan 1961, 21-22). Smith finally made his way west to the coast and north to Fort Vancouver. Figure 4.1 shows the approximate route of the earliest explorers of the Sacramento Valley.

Brigades of the Hudson's Bay Company trapped beaver in the Valley every year between 1830 to 1844 (see Leader 1928; Maloney 1945). They are credited with introducing the toponym *Butte* which translates in French to "small hill." Chief traders Alexander McLeod, John Work, and Michel La Framboise of the Hudson's Bay Company were there. Work's expedition is credited with bringing malaria into the Valley to the Indian population in 1832 and killing 75% of the

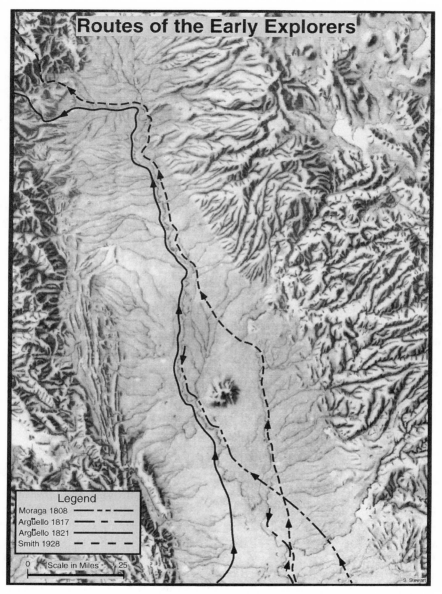

Figure 4.1. Routes of the Early Explorers.

native people in four years as described in the previous chapter (State Lands Commission 1994, 8).

Other North American frontier travelers of note who were also in the region include Ewing Young, Peter Skeen Ogden, Joseph Walker, and others who worked the Valley's fur resources in the 1830s. They probably numbered at least 200 in all. By the end of the fur trade era in 1841, the Sacramento Valley had been traversed, mapped, claimed, and partially settled. The rest of the settlement process would continue into the 1850s and is described in detail in the following chapter.

Mexican Ranchos

Although many had passed through the Sacramento Valley prior to 1839, none except the aboriginal people had attempted to settle it on a permanent basis. Mexican authority had replaced the Spanish policy of excluding foreigners and it was now possible for Mexican citizens (including foreign born who were granted citizenship) to receive land grants of not less than 4,400 acres and not more than 48,712 acres. By 1840, the rancho had become the predominant settlement institution in California and the most common way to acquire land (Hornbeck 1983, 58). Since much of the prime coastal land was already granted and it became more important to settle northern areas so as to keep out possible incursions by the British, Americans or Russians, official government policy encouraged newcomers.

German entrepreneur John Sutter was the first to take advantage of this optunity. He was authorized to claim any land east of the Sacramento River and made his way to an area near its junction with the American River in August, 1839. In 1841, Sutter submitted a map of his claim to New Helvetia which included a selection of several areas near the Sacramento and American rivers as far north as present day Marysville. Box 4.A describes Sutter's view of his own life in the American West.

In 1841, construction of a fort was begun on a hill three miles from the junction of the American and Sacramento Rivers in a place now called Discovery Park. Livestock and military equipment were purchased from the Russians who were about to abandon Fort Ross. At the same time, overland immigrants from the United States were beginning to arrive. With Native American labor and help from the newcomers, Sutter planted crops and expanded facilities. In 1842, he established his mid-Sacramento Valley Hock Farm, located on the north bank of

---

Box 4.A
Sutter's Biographical Statement of 1850

He arrived in Monterey in the month of July 1839. He then and there made his declaration of his intention to become a citizen of the Mexican Republic. At the same time he wished to procure a grant of land, and the Governor told him that he could not procure a grant at that time, but must wait one year and then he could become a citizen and receive a grant. At the same time, he (the Governor) gave him a passport and permission to select and settle upon any lands in the Sacramento Valley; he then proceeded to San Francisco and thence he set out in search of the Sacramento, which search continued eight days before he was able to discover the entrance to the Sacramento River. He had engaged fourteen men exclusive of himself and capt. Davis and his crew, said Davis being the commander of the schooner, "Isabella" which he, John A. Sutter Senior had chartered for the trip the launch of the boat were his property and the men employed thereon were engaged in the service of himself. J.A. Sutter Senior—after discovering the mouth of the Sacramento River, he extended his explorations as far as the mouth of the Feather River, and then on account of a mutiny he was compelled to abandon his researches and return to the American River and land at the old Tannery, near the North east corner of Sacramento City, on the 15th day of August, 1839.

---

the Feather River between present day Nicolaus and Yuba City. There, Sutter sub-granted 640 acres to Nicolaus Allgier who founded the town with his given name. A second grant that year to Theodore Cordua resulted in the birth of Marysville, which was first named New Mecklenburg.

While Sutter was making his imperial dream a reality along the banks of the Sacramento River, he played host to an official visit from Commander Charles Wilkes and his *Around the World United States Scientific Expedition*. The expedition's goal was to construct the first maps of the Valley from its source to the Pacific Ocean. The log of this journey included detailed descriptions of places visited. At the same time, an overland segment of the Wilkes expedition walked from the Willamette Valley in Oregon to the upper Sacramento, following it downstream to Sutter's Fort.

While this development of Sutter's holdings east of the Sacramento River was taking place, several large tracts of land were granted by the Mexican governor in the Valley and settled on the west side and to the north. Of the more than 800 ranchos granted during Mexico's 25-year reign over California, 40 were in the Sacramento Valley. Table 4.1 lists these Mexican era grants by present day county, recipient, date of patent and acreage. Figure 4.2 shows their locations and boundaries as they were confirmed by American courts and the

State Lands Commission established in 1851 (Robinson 1948, 91-110). The large cattle ranches of this Mexican period of settlement had first begun under a new and more liberal colonization policy adopted by the Mexican government in 1824. In all of California about 26,000,000 acres or about one fourth of the land in the state, was made by Mexican authorities under this legislation (Hutchison 1946, 25). Of this total, 1,328,913 acres were in the Sacramento Valley. The average rancho size in the Valley was 33,222 acres. Land was provided to citizens or naturalized citizens of Mexico without payment, although Mexicans were given preference. The land unit specified by law was a square league, about 4,438 acres; no more than a maximum of eleven square leagues could be awarded to one person. Including earlier Spanish and Mexican land grants, the United States government later confirmed titles to 563 of these large properties.

Reference to the map of ranchos in the Sacramento Valley in Figure 4.2 allows several observations. First, most of the owners had Anglo names and were recent immigrants from the United States. Second, some of the ranchos were located in what were to become two or more counties under United States rule. Third, even after the land commission downsized many of the original rancho claims, only about half of the Valley was owned privately after 1851, the rest becoming part of the public domain to be disposed of by the federal government or the state. Much of this public domain was awarded to the railroads via land grants which were in-turn sold to newcomers to the Valley. Most of the rancho lands were also immediately broken up and sold to speculators or new settlers.

One of the first to take advantage of this bounty of free or very cheap land was John Bidwell who had entered the Valley in 1841. By 1843, land north of the Sutter Buttes was explored for settlement. In that year Bidwell, who worked for Sutter, drew a map of the north Valley, identifying and naming features on the land as he went. Literally "falling in love" with the area, Bidwell also selected a location for a Mexican grant of his own. He enthusiastically described the area near Big Chico Creek as follows (Bidwell 1891, 44):

> Hastening up the Valley, we at last struck the trail of the Oregon Company, on what is now known as the Rancho Chico. The plains were dotted with scattered groves of spreading oak, while clover and wild grasses three and four feet high, were most luxuriant. The fertility of the soil was beyond question. The water of Chico Creek was cold, clear and sparkling; the mountains flower covered and lovely. In my chase for stolen horses I had come across a country that was to me a revelation.

Table 4.1. Sacramento Valley Mexican Ranchos

Grant	Patentee	Patent Date	Area in Acres
Butte County:			
Aguas Frias	Todd	07-19-1860	26,761.40
Arroyo Chico	Bidwell	04-04-1860	22,214.47
Boga	Larkin	10-05-1865	22,184.66
Esquon	Neal	04-04-1860	22,193.78
Farwell	Williams	07-01-1863	22,193.78
Fernandez	Fernandez	10-14-1857	17,805.81
Llano Seco	Brenham	06-18-1860	17,767.17
Honcut	Covillaud	03-09-1863	31,079.96
Colusa County:			
Colus	Semple	07-23-1869	8,876.02
Jimeno	Larkin & Missroon	07-18-1862	48,854.26
Larkin's Children	Larkin	12-18-1857	44,364.22
Glenn County:			
Capay	Soto	08-18-1859	44,388.17
Jacinto	McKee	09-19-1859	35,487.52
Larkin's Children	Larkin	12-18-1857	44,364.22
Placer County:			
San Juan	Grimes	07-09-1860	19,982.70
Sacramento County:			
Arroyo Seco	Pico	08-29-1863	48,857.52
Cosumnes	Hartnell	04-29-1869	26,605.37
New Helvetia	Sutter	06-20-1866	48,839.30

Table 4.1. Sacramento Valley Mexican Ranchos

Grant	Patentee	Patent Date	Area in Acres
Omochumnes	Sheldon	07-01-1870	18,661.86
Del Paso	Norris	05-04-1858	44,371.42
Rio Americanos	Folsom	10-28-1864	35,521.36
San Juan	Grimes	07-09-1870	19,982.70
Moquelumnos	Chabolla	05-13-1865	35,508.14
Shasta County:			
San Buenaventura	Reading	01-17-1857	26,632.09
Solano County:			
Los Putos	Vaca & Pena	06-04-1858	44,383.78
Rio de los Putos	Wolfskill	12-18-1858	17,754.73
Suisun	Richie	01-17-1857	17,754.73
Suisun (part of)	Fine	12-16-1882	482.19
Los Tolenas	Armijo	10-12-1868	13,315.43
Los Ulpinos	Bidwell	08-09-1886	17,726.43
Sutter County:			
Boga	Larkin	10-05-1865	22,184.66
New Helvetia	Sutter	06-20-1866	48,839.30
Tehama County:			
Barranca Colorada	Ide	07-03-1860	17,707.49
Bosquejo	Lassen	01-21-1861	22,206.27
Capay	Soto	08-18-1859	44,388.17
Las Flores	Chard	09-19-1859	13,315.58
Primer Canon	Dye	02-28-1871	26,637.11

Table 4.1. Sacramento Valley Mexican Ranchos

Grant	Patentee	Patent Date	Area in Acres
Los Molinos	Toomes	12-03-1858	22,172.46
Saucos	Yhomas	10-14-1857	22,212.21
Yolo County:			
Canada de Capay	O'Farrell	02-16-1865	40,078.58
Jimeno	Larkin & Missroon	07-18-1862	48,854.26
Quesesosi	Gordon	02-04-1860	8,894.49
Rio de los Putos	Wolfskill	12-18-1858	17,754.73
Rio Jesus Maria	Harbin	07-03-1858	26,637.42
Yuba County:			
Honcut	Covillaud	03-09-1863	31,079.96
Johnson Rancho	Johnson	08-03-1857	22,197.31
New Helvetia	Sutter	06-20-1866	48,839.30

While John Bidwell's map of the region was not the first map of the Valley, it was the most utilized with copies going to John Fremont, Landsford Hastings and other land claimants as a reference for their land grants. More information about Bidwell is provided in Box 4.B below.

Former fur trapper and another Sutter employee, Peter Lassen, accompanied Bidwell on this trip and likewise obtained a grant in the northern part of the Valley near Deer Creek. In 1848 he brought a group of settlers over the mountains by way of Deer Creek to the ranch. Box 4.C details Lassen's experience and lingering impact in the region.

The most northerly Mexican land grant in the Sacramento Valley, almost entirely within today's Shasta County, was San Buenaventura, awarded to rancheros working as Sutter's clerk and head of trappers. The cities of Redding (named for railroad land agent P.B. Redding, not ranchero Pierson Reading!) and Anderson are located within the boundaries of the now historic San Buenaventura Rancho.

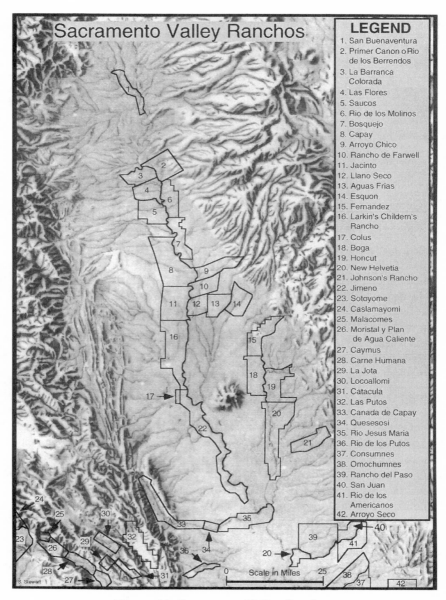

Figure 4.2. Sacramento Valley Ranchos.

Box 4.B
John Bidwell's Memories of His First View of the Valley

It was early March, 1843 when we struck the trail of the Oregon Company on what is now known as Chico Creek. Rancho Chico—to me one of the loveliest of places. The plains were covered with groves of spreading oaks; there were wild grasses and clover, two, three, and four feet high, and most luxuriant. The fertility of the soils was beyond question, and the waters of Chico Creek were clean, cold, and sparkling; the mountains were lovely and flower-covered, a beautiful scene. In a word, this was the means of locating me for life. . . . I never was permanently located till I afterward located here.

Source: John Bidwell, *Echoes of the Past*, (Chico, CA: Chico Advertiser, n.d.), p. 77 and reprinted in *A Precious Sense of Place*, W.H. Hutchinson and Clarence F. McIntosh (Chico, CA: Friends of the Meriam Library, 1991), p. 2.

In 1847, after California had come into possession of the United States, John Bidwell counted 82 Euro-Americans north of the Sutter Buttes, two-thirds of whom were men. Many of those who had missed the initial settlement period under Mexican rule or had given up gold mining became squatters on land confirmed by land claims. Such trespassers brought about suits, ejections and sometimes outright warfare between owners and land seekers. Land historian Paul Wallace Gates reports that (1967):

> In the Sacramento Valley were half a dozen or more [squatter] claims. Together they contained over 300,000 acres. However, because of the slowness of the judicial process and because they were not clearly located by the terms of the alleged grants, these claims actually kept out of the public domain a far larger amount of land.

Eventually all of these fraudulent claims were rejected.

A Closer Look: Native Americans and Hawaiians in the Sacramento Valley

Not included in Bidwell's informal census is any record of an ethnic group who lived closely among Native American residents of the region. A fascinating and little known aspect of life in the multicultural Sacramento Valley in its earliest years of settlement was the presence of a small group of people from the Sandwich Islands (Hawaiian Islands). Although most married local Native Amer-

---

Box 4.C
The Lassen Trail: Traveling into the Valley—The Hard Way

There is no better example of (Lassen's) confidence than the fact that he induced twelve emigrant wagons to follow him over this cutoff to California before he ever traveled it himself. There are no better examples of the paradoxes in the character of Peter Lassen than stem from this first journey over the Lassen Trail.

The emigrants threatened to hang Lassen after he led them into some of the damndest country in California. The party almost starved in Big Meadows (Lake Almanor) and reached the valley only by the timely aid of a party of gold seekers coming down from Oregon. Yet, when they did reach the valley at Benton City, after the crowning horror of the Narrows on Deer Creek ridge, Lassen killed the beeves for them. And, after this firsthand acquaintance with the Lassen Trail, Peter Lassen could recommend it two years later as a suitable railroad route across the Sierra.

Source: Tales From "Old Hutch," 1990, pp. 53-54.

---

ican women (and thus lived in Native villages and were often labeled "Indians" by outsiders), some were recorded as Kanakas in early census records.

The earliest arrival in California of this ethnic group is a complex and adventurous story. Originally, the hardy Sandwich islanders had signed on as deck hands on whaling ships and trading vessels which had visited their islands in the early nineteenth century. Treated brutally by ship captains and others on board ship, many braved icy waters and "jumped ship," swimming frantically for the California coast. Almost without exception they were reported lost at sea, since no one could believe that even these capable swimmers could survive exposure to the cold water and pounding surf of the Pacific, or ever be able to reach the mainland (Calhoon 1986, 33). But many did survive. Some scholars say, in fact, that these early adventurers formed half the population of San Francisco (Yerba Buena) in 1847.

The earliest arrival of Hawaiians in the Sacramento Valley began with Sutter's connection with a man known as "Kanaka Jack," owner and operator of the ferry that transported Sutter and his crew up the Sacramento River from the San Francisco Bay to Sacramento. Impressed with his first encounter with a Hawaiian, Sutter later recruited ten people from the Sandwich Islands to work for his increasingly large and economically successful operation in the Sacramento Valley.

One of the members of this earliest group of Sandwich Islanders in the Sacramento Valley in 1839 was a man the Americans called "John Kelly." John's real name was Ioane Keaala o Kaaina. His marriage to a Konkow Maidu woman,

Su-mai-neh, near Oroville is romantically recounted by Anne H. Currie in *A Maidu Story* (1963). Kaaina and his family were later forced to travel to the reservation at Round Valley with most of the other Native Americans of the area. Because of his Hawaiian heritage, however, Keaala (Kelly) was eventually allowed to leave the reservation (Hill 1978, 97). Keaala's son, Hiram, married an American woman and settled in Washington state. His daughter, Mele Kainua Keaala, married John B. Asbill of San Francisco. After Asbill's family disowned him because of his marriage, the couple settled in Chico on land given to them by John Bidwell (Hendrix 1980, 44) (see Figure 4.3).

Many of the original Valley Hawaiians and their families found their way to what came to be known as the "Kanaka Colonies" located on the Feather River at the settlements of Vernon and Fremont. There they supplied the residents of Marysville with sturgeon and salmon from the Feather and Yuba rivers and fresh vegetables from their gardens for many years. This ambitious colony of workers was eventually forced out of business by the declining fish supply due to hydraulic mining and the arrival of Chinese, and by Japanese farmers after 1870 (Calhoon 1986, 45-46). An important part of the increasing ethnic diversity of Gold Rush-era Northern California and the resultant changes in the economy and culture of the North State, these early people from the Hawaiian Islands ultimately became an almost invisible piece of the increasingly complex demographic flavor of the Sacramento Valley in the later part of the nineteenth century.

Economy

According to Bancroft's estimates, the number of foreign residents in California had grown to about 380 by 1840. Although many of these newcomers from Europe and the United States believed California would eventually become independent from Mexico and were aggressive in developing local trade and business networks, they were a conservative lot politically (Caughey 1970, 207). Despite their successes in economic development in the region, therefore, these early residents did not pose any threat to the Mexican government. This gave them ample opportunities to develop their new environment in any way they saw fit.

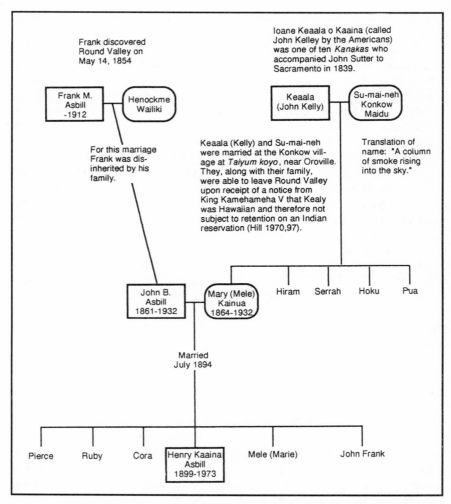

Figure 4.3. Hawaiian and Native American Family Genealogy:
The Asbill Family.

Reprinted with permission of The Anthro Company, Sacramento, California, as reprinted from Appendix I of Richard Burrill's *River of Sorrows: Life History of the Maidu-Nisenan Indians,* 1988.

Agricultural Development Before 1850

Typical of these pre-Gold Rush Sacramento Valley farmers was German-born Theodore Cordua, originally an associate of Sutter's. This enterprising settler raised wheat, beef, hogs, sheep, and dairy cattle on land located between the Feather and Uba (aka Yuba) rivers. When Fremont visited Cordua's ranch, he recorded yields of about twenty-five bushels of wheat per acre (Hutchison 1946, 30). According to Scheuring (1987, 17):

Cordua sold ham, bacon, butter, and flour to the San Francisco trade. Like Sutter, he was just staring to make money ranching when the Gold Rush destroyed his monopoly in the area and ruined his plans. Eventually he became partners with a Frenchman in early Marysville.

As the area's population increased over the years, especially after the Gold Rush-induced stampede began in earnest after 1848, food production took on an increasingly important function in the region. Dependent on wagon trains with supplies from Oregon and the East and shiploads of goods arriving at coastal ports, these earliest residents of the North State soon grew tired depending on outsiders for their survival. According to one historical account of this dependence on the outside world in the 1840s (Caughey 1965, 260):

The wagon trains brought household goods, tools, and implements that in the aggregate were important. These trains and more formal drives brought horses, cattle. and sheep. Ships from Puget Sound and the Columbia delivered lumber while the agricultural settlements of the Willamette Valley sent eggs, garden produce, and grain. Dried beef—charqui of jerky—came from Chile and diversified cargoes were sent from Hawaii and the Orient.

It clearly was time for the residents of California to begin producing their own agricultural products and developing their own economic potential. A major transition in culture, economic development, political systems, and environmental issues was set in motion by the great demographic upheaval sparked by the discovery of gold just east of Sacramento. This major global event quickened the tempo of agricultural production and potential in the North State as many of the newcomers came to realize that the longterm wealth of California was to found in the soil rather than in the mines.

Following a pattern well established during the Mission period, livestock ranching formed the most logical beginning for this agricultural development. Northern California's climate, soils, and ample level land fostered the success of early ranchers who devoted their attention primarily to cattle and sheep much as the Spanish padres had done in prior decades. Richard Henry Dana's dramatic account of the hide and tallow trade in *Two Years Before the Mast* made the importance of California's early cattle ranches familiar to several generations of readers. It has been estimated that between 1,250,000 hides and 62,500,000 pounds of tallow were shipped from California between 1826 and 1848 (Gates 1967, 4).

According to geographer Terry Jordan, a unique Anglo-California system of cattle ranching evolved began in the early 1840s when the Mexican government awarded land to forty-six people with Anglo surnames (1993, 208). Most of these ranchers were located in the Sacramento Valley. This ranching core remained geographically and culturally distinct from the older Hispanic core in southern California, described by Jordan as (1993, 212):

> By contrast, northern and interior California, including the great Central Valley, became considerably anglicized, serving both as the focus of the cattle boom and the center where the Anglo-California ranching systems evolved in ways very different from the south. Anglos developed many new ranches in the remaining Mediterranean prairies where excellent bunch grasses could still be found. By 1860, fully forty percent of all California cattle grazed ranges in the Anglo-dominated Central Valley.

But dried beef jerky and other products from animal ranching in this pre-refrigeration era did not provide enough diversity or quantity of food to meet the needs of the region's residents. Local markets created by hungry gold seekers and other newcomers soon created a "back to the farm" movement in the lower Sacramento Valley. The population surge after 1848 created severe shortages and very high prices for goods and services, and, along with the Valley's proximity to gold districts in the nearby Sierra Nevada foothills, and a benevolent climate and fertile soils, intensive domestic farming was encouraged. The emphasis in these dry farming years was on grain farming and experimental efforts with a variety of vegetables and fruits. Indeed, "after a fling at digging gold, many settled down to the more reliable, and usually more profitable business of feeding other pioneers" (Rice, Bullough, Orsi 1988, 262). A discussion of the importance of the "Wheat Era" in the evolving geography of the Sacramento Valley is presented in the following chapter.

Agricultural Location Patterns in the Valley

According to research on early agriculture in the North State conducted by historical geographer Margaret Trussell, the attractions of the region for early agricultural development and settlement were described in a letter to the *Marysville Herald* on October 22, 1850 as (Trussell 1969, 221-222):

- Good timber;
- Abundant grass;
- Nearness to the mines; and
- Towns well supplied with provisions and luxuries by boats from the river.

Using newspaper accounts such as this one and other archival evidence, Trussell summarized three factors that influenced the settlement patterns of early farmers in the Sacramento Valley (1969, 224). These include (1) the desire for good soil; (2) the need for ready water and wood supply; and (3) the belief that a treeless plain was not good agricultural land. These factors encouraged farmers to choose land along rivers and streams rather than developing farms on vast expanses of available land located on the Valley's immense expanses of "treeless plains." Two nineteenth-century scholars described the perceived relationship between soil fertility and lack of trees as follows (Nordhoff 1875, 119):

In 1847, when I spent eleven months on the California coast, it was universally believed that but a small part of the soil would produce crops. 'There are no trees on these great plains,' said everybody, 'and if not a tree will grow, of course the soil must be sterile.' But many of these treeless plains have since yielded from fifty to eighty bushels of wheat per acre.

Despite its limitations of overlooking a great deal of fertile and available land, this riparian settlement pattern did have the distinct advantage of access to markets provided by connections via the Sacramento River. These early farmers, many disillusioned miners recently "down from the hills," laid the foundation for more extensive and intensive agricultural development after 1850. This and other important issues involving life and landscape in the Sacramento Valley are discussed in the following chapter.

Chapter 5

Early Impacts

By comparison, the impacts left on the landscape by Euro-Americans before 1850 were minimal when compared to those left after the initial wave of the Gold Rush. Farmers, city folk, and miners created numerous new settlements in the Sacramento Valley after 1850. Others built roads and developed river transport systems to connect these new settlements. The map in Figure 5.1 shows these new towns and routes as well as the first railroad into the Valley that linked Sacramento with Folsom. A comparison of Figure 5.1 with Figure 6.1 (1880 settlements) in the next chapter shows how roads, railroads, and towns expanded between 1860 and 1880.

People

Early European Settlement

California has often been called the "America of the Americas." Whatever our country was and is becoming is represented within the state's borders. The American dream of owning land in a free and open countryside of well watered and well drained soil, good weather, and unlimited economic opportunities has long been symbolized by the "Golden State." Nowhere in the state does this "Jeffersonian Ideal" come together quite as strongly as in the fertile Sacramento Valley.

And the people came. Indeed, in both numbers and diversity, the surge of people into the state of California during and after the Gold Rush represents one of the most phenomenal population movements in all of human history. More than two centuries were required to settle the United States as far west as the Mississippi River while only a few decades were required to settle the western

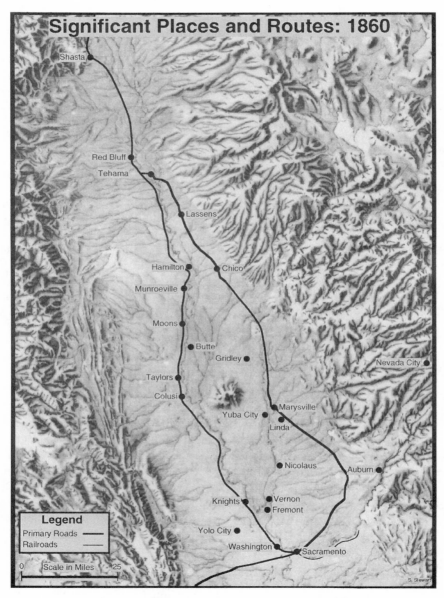

Figure 5.1. Significant Places and Routes, 1860.

coast of this vast continent. It was the powerful magnet of golden California that most encouraged this rapid westward expansion.

It is significant to note here that despite recent concerns about uncontrolled population growth impacting negatively on the state's natural environment and its cultural and social fabric, a former governor of California, Pat Brown, set aside a four day celebration in 1963 to honor the fact that California already had become the most populous state in the union. This event recognized the importance of this mass migration to the west and celebrated the diversity of cultures and lifestyles in evidence here. Because of its proximity to the gold country and its promising agriculture land, the Sacramento Valley has long played a key role in this major expansion of population in the west.

One of the Valley's most remarkable and relatively unknown characteristics is its multicultural settlement patterns and varied ethnic landscapes. Densely populated groups of Native Americans who settled the region first, have been replaced by successive "layers" of equally diverse settlers seeking their own version of the promised land. Both rural and urban communities in the North State are an ethnic mosaic of people from many European, Latin American and Asian nations, along with African-Americans from many parts of the United States. This regional polyglot has formed a fascinating blend of colorful landscapes and lifestyles very visible in the Sacramento Valley today. In Butte County alone, for example, there was a convergence of immigrants from thirty-eight nations and thirty-five states in the United States between 1848 and 1880 (Monaco 1986, 7). In Shasta County, in the frontier town of Redding, as in other counties in the Valley, thousands of new arrivals came not only from foreign countries, but also from many parts of the eastern and southern United States (see Figures 5.2 and 5.3).

As examined in the preceding chapter, the complex story of the peopling of the Valley began with Native American settlement. Then, beginning in the eighteenth century, Spanish Franciscan priests were the first Europeans to arrive in California, settling here in the hopes of saving souls for Christ. From 1769 through the 1830s, their combined mission/military system not only altered Native life forever, but also established an agricultural tradition and put into place a strong undercurrent of Latino culture that lingers today. Although no missions were ever built in the isolated and far distant Sacramento Valley, this early connection with Spanish (and later Mexican) culture spilled over into the Valley, leaving an indelible mark on local landscapes and subcultures.

It wasn't only the Spanish that influenced early demographic patterns and culture of the Valley. Other Europeans were also early inhabitants of the region. By 1847, the European population of the Valley north of the Sutter Buttes

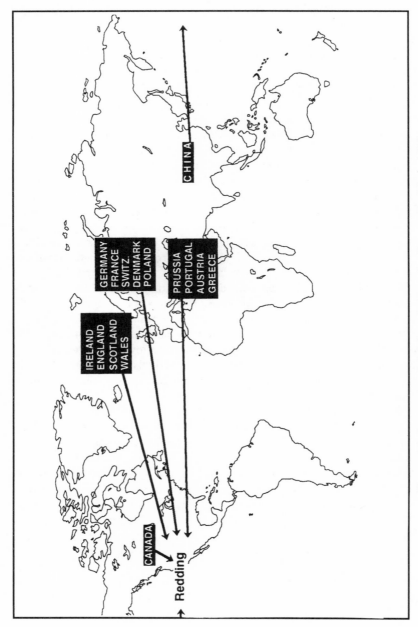

Figure 5.2. International Origins of a Frontier Town—Redding, 1880.
Source: United States Census of Population, Shasta County, 1880.

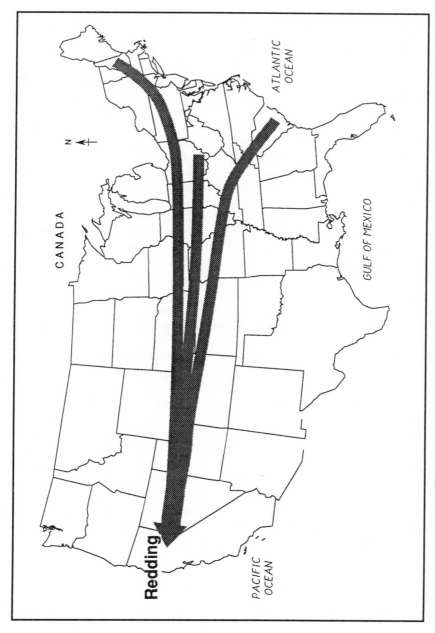

Figure 5.3. United States Dominant Population Flows to Redding.

was estimated at 82 (Bidwell Census, December 21, 1847, in McKinstry 1872).

Although not as plentiful as the Anglo-Americans or Irish in regional census counts, German financial clout dominated economic development in the Valley in the years following the Gold Rush. The language barrier posed less of a problem for Germans than for many other groups because most had lived in the United States or Canada before coming to the West. Germans, Dutch, Danes, and perhaps Swedes were indiscriminately referred to as "Dutchmen" (Borthwick 1917, 233). According to a recent study of ethnic contributions to California agriculture, some of the most powerful capitalists in later nineteenth century California history were of German origin (Scheuring 1987, 17). Many German entrepreneurs established businesses to serve the needs of growing communities in the Sacramento Valley like Matthew Schwein of Chico.

Since large land holdings made it difficult for newcomers to buy land individually, many of these earliest European immigrants came to the Valley in large groups, or "colonies." German, Slovenian, and Russian Mennonite groups were encouraged to settle in Shasta County, for example, by large scale promoters and land speculators (Scheuring 1987, 35). A more detailed discussion of land colonies in Corning, Los Molinos, Durham, and several other locations in the Valley is presented in Chapter 7.

Census records for late nineteenth century Sacramento Valley towns and counties document other ethnic settlement nodes in the area. A dramatic example was the population of the town of Shasta. As shown on the map in Table 5.1, the census of 1880 lists residents from the following countries (in numerical order) for this small, but diverse community: Germany, China, Ireland, African-American, England, Canada, Native American, France, Poland, Prussia, Scotland, Austria, Denmark, Switzerland, Bohemia, Chile, Greece, Portugal, Wales, and Mexico.

Newcomers brought their languages, religions, and value systems with them to this new land. They built churches, held festivals and social events, and established traditional farming practices in the region. Despite the optimism of boosters and speculators, however, some of these ethnic colonies never got off the ground such as the Danish colony just west of the town of Chico and the Italian colony at Tudor. The Danish Tract was developed in 1868 with the intent of putting small farmers on the land (Trussell 1969, 277). After plans were made for this new ethnic colony, the local newspaper reported excitedly that:

> The Danes! The Danes! Some months since we announced that the Mandeville and Soloman tract of five thousand acres of the choicest farming land in the State, a little east (sic) of town, had been purchased by the Danish Consul of San Francisco, to be parceled out among five hundred Danish immigrants now

on their way to this coast. . . . An addition to our population of five hundred wealth producers at one dash is no small item (*Butte County Press*, Nov. 2, 1867).

Table 5.1. Non-Anglo-American Residents in the
Town of Shasta in 1880[a]

Nationality	Number of Residents
German	41
Chinese	31
Irish	26
African-American	16
English	10
Canadian	5
Native American	3

[a]Also: France, Poland, Prussia, Scotland, Austria, Denmark, Switzerland, Bohemia, Chile, Greece, Portugal, Wales, and Mexico.

Source: United States Census of Population, 1880.

The Danish Colony's progress was mentioned in subsequent issues of the newspaper which reported that it was surveyed, mapped, fenced, and a contract let for clearing. For unknown reasons the tract never attracted people from Denmark to settle in Butte County, and by 1872, a final sale had been made of the entire Taafe Farm and adjacent lots to James Morehead (Trussell 1969, 285).

Despite the similar failure of early Italian settlement in Tudor, Italians did successfully settle in other parts of the region between 1880 and 1900. Northern Italians settled on fertile farmland along the Sacramento River, forming partnerships in garden and truck farms. An Italian farmer is even credited with beginning the tomato industry in the Central Valley after he taught Merced farmers to grow them on stakes as was the custom in Italy.

Basques from the Pyrenees Mountains also settled in the Sacramento Valley in the decades following the Gold Rush. Many herded sheep, an animal well suited to pastures of the rolling Coast Ranges that formed the western border of the region. Most Basques chose these pastoral slopes in Tehama County just east of Corning and Red Bluff for settlement. Others opened restaurants and hotels in small towns in the region. They supplied local residents and visitors with much appreciated urban amenities in these outlying communities which were distant from more sophisticated California cities. The historic Hotel Español in Colusa is still a popular restaurant and bar. It was built to cater to the Basque population who primarily engaged in sheepherding in the early 1880s.

The Basque presence is also expressed in the region's religious and social traditions. Annual Basque potluck dinners draw Basque families from all over the North State. Organized by a Basque from Yuba City and catered by a Basque restauranteur from Chico, this regular event provides ethnic and cultural solidarity to an otherwise far flung group of Valley residents. In addition to social events, the Basque identity is also enhanced by the work of visiting priests who are affiliated with the Catholic church from the Basque homeland, the Pyrenees Mountains. The springtime celebration begins with a traditional Basque Mass led by visiting priests, followed by a picnic with traditional Basque foods. Live ethnic entertainment has been provided year after year by local and Bay Area Basque dancers and musicians.

Portuguese immigrants also came to the Sacramento Valley. Most were farming people who first came as sheepherders. They then turned to cattle and crops when the wool industry declined and irrigation was made available, permitting cultivation of alfalfa for feeding dairy cows. Most settled along the Sacramento River in 40-50 acre strips of land best suited for dairying and vegetables such as the small town of Princeton in the heart of the Valley.

Other Portuguese settlers had lived in nearby mining communities such as Portuguese Flat in Shasta County before relocating to the Valley. By the census of 1880, the rich farm land in South Sacramento along the Sacramento River had the densest population of Portuguese in the entire United States (Mayne 1992, 4). This "Lisbon District," as it came to be known, also thrived on fruit and truck farming and dairying. Towns such as Princeton still celebrate Portuguese festivals regularly to commemorate their ethnic heritage. According to Jerry Williams, chronicler of the Portuguese experience in California (1982, 90):

Summer was a great time to be Portuguese in California. A fiesta, or celebration was held almost every weekend in some community in the Central Valley or along the coast and everyone looked forward to the occasion; it was a time for dancing, eating, and socializing. Traditionally, every Portuguese community of any size would hold an annual celebration. Most of these began with a candlelight procession on Saturday night. The procession transported the queen's crown from the house of the sponsoring family to a chapel near the church. Afterwards a dance was held in the local Portuguese Hall where the *chamarita,* a traditional fold dance, shared the floor with less traditional dances. The following day a parade, complete with suitably gowned outgoing and incoming queens, participants from fraternal organizations in all nearby towns, and statues of saints from the church, would transport the queen's crown from the chapel, through town, and end up at church where participants attended mass. At the conclusion of the mass, the crown would be blessed, the new queen crowned and the procession would march back to the chapel. Afterwards a traditional meal of meat and bread was served free to the public.

The town of Biggs provided a focus of Portuguese settlement at the turn of the century. According to Osborn (1953), the Portuguese were by far the largest group of immigrants in the Biggs region although they are now well assimilated into the community. The earliest Portuguese settler came to Biggs about 1908, settling on Larkin Road on Ord Ranch east of town. Like most of the other Portuguese in this part of the Valley, these first arrivals came from the Azores Islands not from mainland Portugal. They initially worked in Biggs in the dairy industry, but later expanded into grain farming. Many still own productive dairy farms in the Biggs and Gridley area, although many members of the more upwardly mobile second, third, and fourth generations have entered non-agricultural employment and moved out of the area.

Despite the importance of these diverse groups of people from Europe, no ancestry group so dominated the census records of the Sacramento Valley as the Irish. In almost every community and county listing, people from Ireland outnumbered all other European groups throughout the later decades of the nineteenth century. Most came by way of east coast cities in a sometimes desperate search for the rural lifestyle they had left behind in Ireland. Driven from their homeland by famine and political oppression after the Potato Famine of the 1840s, these hardy immigrants had arrived in the United States in time to acculturate to American life before the Gold Rush in 1848. Despite a certain amount of hostility and discrimination from Anglo residents of the region, most of the Irish soon settled comfortably into their new life in the Valley (Caughey 1948, 192; Buck 1930, 144).

The French were also an important ethnic group in the nineteenth century Sacramento Valley. Most of the French who came to California before the Gold Rush were from Canada or were Creoles who came by way of New Orleans. Others came as a part of Fremont's party (whose mother was a French Creole).

Gold fever was highly contagious in Paris in the 1850s and many came to seek their fortune, ending up in other occupations when the gold ran out. The

French government apparently considered emigration to be a partial remedy for survival of the chaotic situation in France after the Revolution of 1848. Riots, disorder, and famine made life difficult for the people of this nation after the Revolution and, as a result of these challenges (along with the attraction of the discovery of gold), several societies were formed in Paris for the transportation of emigres to the United States in 1850 (Martin 1981, 24).

Moreover, the French government was attempting to make connections with California as a new field of merchandising for French products. It was viewed as a vast, unexplored place with a great deal of potential for the establishment of trading linkages. The French government, therefore, strongly supported the emigration to California as a way to relieve the economic depression, to expand its power overseas, and to get rid of trouble makers at home. Thus, when official companies were founded to promote and organize trips to California from France, they had the full backing and support of the government.

Companies of all types were started in France. They were created for various purposes—colonization, mining, agricultural development, and business. These companies bore very alluring names such as La Toison d'Or ("The Golden Fleece"), La Ruche d'Or ("The Goldhive"), and La Moisson d'Or ("The Gold Harvest"). They used various schemes to entice the public, many of which were outright fraudulent and so most enjoyed an extremely ephemeral existence.

There were three large settlements of this ethnic group in the state in the nineteenth century—Marysville, Mokelumne Hill, and San Francisco. Another smaller node of French settlement developed in Vina. In the early 1880s, railroad magnate and investor Leland Stanford and his family traveled to Europe and hired about fifty French families to come to Vina to help plant and raise grapes and teach the locals how to make fine wines. Cuttings from select vines were brought from France by these employees and planted in Vina vineyards.

Although other ethnic groups such as the Germans and the Irish were more numerous in the Sacramento Valley at this time, the French apparently kept their identity and were more visible than most other European groups. They were not violently discriminated against as were the Chinese or the Native Americans —or even persecuted as much as the Irish or the Mexicans—but the French were often referred to as "clannish" by local residents. Their idiosyncrasies and personal attire were often considered humorous by others in the area. The attitude of the locals toward the French seemed to range from amusement at what was considered their outlandish practices, to indifference, condescension, discrimination, and even cruelty (Caughey 1948, 192). Anglo-Americans were apt to refer to them irritably as "Keskydees" because whenever an English-speaking person tried to communicate with them through an interpreter, the French keep interrupting and asking: "Qu'est-ce qu'il dit?" (Borthwick 1975, 241-242).

As a fitting summary of the multicultural character of Sacramento Valley communities in the late nineteenth century, the children with various ancestries and backgrounds looking out from the photo shown in Figure 5.4 were enrolled in an elementary school in Colusa County in 1890. We wonder what their impressions of life and landscape in the Sacramento Valley would be if they were here today?

The Arrival of the Chinese

Tens of thousands of Chinese also played a major role in the development of Sacramento Valley communities in mining, in agricultural development and land reclamation, in the building of railroads that linked the region with the outside world, and in urban commercial development. Although the history of this ethnic groups is truly a "living history" (since many thousands of fourth, fifth, and sixth generation descendants of the first settlers still reside in California), this narrative concentrates on the settlement of Chinese in the Sacramento Valley during their earliest decades of settlement in the state, between 1850 and 1900. This is a story not only of migration and settlement, but also of racial violence, discriminatory legislation, restrictive covenants, and limited opportunities for the economic survival of ethnic groups other than Anglo-American.

In the early 1850s, most Chinese immigrants entered California through the port of San Francisco. By 1860, the 50,000 Chinese in California made up one-tenth of the state's total population (Scheuring 1987, 35). The United States Constitution in the 1850s, however, only permitted the naturalization of white immigrants to this country; in fact, the law recognized only two racial groups—black and white. Since these early Asians were neither, some were allowed to become citizens but most were not. Without citizenship, the Chinese could not vote or hold government office so most had little voice in determining their future lives in this country. They were designated "aliens ineligible for citizenship" and so were unable to own land or file mining claims (*Five Views* 1988, 107).

The first large influx of Chinese into northern California was triggered by the discovery of gold in 1848. News of this event spread fast, reaching as far as the Kuangtung Province near the port of Canton. The attraction of gold encouraged many Chinese to leave their homeland. In addition, extremely difficult conditions of war, famine, political oppression, rebellions, civil disorder, and drought had

Figure 5.4. School Portrait in Colusa County, 1890.
Reprinted with permission from Meriam Library Special Collections, California State University, Chico and Sacramento Valley Museum, Colusa, California.

disrupted China for many decades and made earning a livelihood difficult in their native land (See Book 1974, 1976).

Most of the earliest Chinese to arrive on the West Coast traveled from San Francisco to the Sierra Nevada foothills, settling first in emerging Mother Lode communities. As gold became depleted, many moved into the Sacramento Valley finding employment in domestic work and truck gardening. Others opened small businesses in towns like Marysville, Oroville, Chico, Tehama, and Red Bluff. More than 10,000 Chinese laborers were recruited by the Central Pacific railroad to help lay tracks across the Sierra Nevada from Sacramento to Utah. Whatever the economic motivation for these early Chinese, the vast majority were forced to leave their families at home (because of the prohibitive high cost of the trip and difficulties of life in the mining camps).

It is important to mention here that the Chinese living in the Sacramento Delta, although beyond the scope of this book, were instrumental in draining valuable wetlands for early agriculture. Chinese crews were contracted to work in the tule and bottomland marshes and build hundreds of miles of levees, cut drainage ditches, and construct floodgates. These Chinese work crews reclaimed at least 88,000 acres of rich Delta land between 1860 and 1880 (Scheuring 1987, 35). Their rich ethnic landscape is visible today not only in the thousands of acres of fertile farmland now used by Delta farmers, but also in the intense and memorable Chinese landscape in the town of Locke.

Butte County also had several well developed Chinatowns by the mid-1860s. Because of its location on the Feather River, one of the primary arteries connecting the gold country with the Valley, Oroville long contained the largest and most well known of all Valley Chinatowns. Many thousands of Chinese lived and worked in this community, reworking the white miners claims near Baghdad just south of the city and at Lava Beds, due west of Oroville. By 1880, Oroville had the largest population of Chinese in the United States living outside of San Francisco (Book 1974, 27).

As in other towns in the Valley, the Chinese neighborhood in this Butte County community consisted of a few brick and wooden buildings, but was actually a "town within a town." Oroville also had a Chinese theater, several stores, and a Joss House or Chinese Temple which is still standing in the 1990s. The temple is now a museum and historical landmark now maintained by the city. It is still used as a place of worship by several Chinese families who still live in the area (*Sacramento Bee,* Oct. 13, 1993, 6).

The Chinese also settled in many other parts of the Sacramento Valley. In Chico, the number of Chinese increased steadily throughout the decades of the late nineteenth century. Most of the earliest Chinese to come to this rapidly growing Valley town came first to work for the Southern Pacific Railroad. When the rail line was completed, many stayed on, finding employment as gardeners, laundry owners, and domestic laborers.

Chico had two Chinatowns, one west of the downtown and one to its east (See Figure 5.5). "Old Town" was founded about 1865 and consisted of wooden, two-story buildings with porches extending along the front of the whole row (Kelly 1950, 286). As was the custom in villages in their homeland, shops and restaurants were on the first floor of these buildings with living quarters directly above. After a major fire in 1880, brick buildings replaced damaged wooden ones which resembled the older frame buildings in style. All had extensive basements underneath. Because of their closeness, most basements were connected by doorways and small hallways. These so called "Chinese Tunnels" so well known to most Chico residents were actually just doors and walkways connecting the old buildings (Tochterman interview, Chico, 1973). These interconnected cellars were the inspiration for popular stories about a mysterious network of Chinese tunnels under the city.

Chico's second Chinatown was built west of the downtown and was known to locals as "New Town." This new Chinese neighborhood was built mostly of one-story brick houses with comfortable wooden porches along the front. Most had ample room for vegetable gardens in the front yard, adding color and charm to Chico's westside residential district. The best known feature of New Town was its Joss House located on the corner of Cherry and West Eighth Streets.

Smaller Chinese settlements were established elsewhere in Butte County during this period. The census count at the original county seat at the town of Hamilton on the Feather River, for example, listed 55 Chinese residents in the year 1860. By 1880, there were at least 210 Chinese men living in this community with occupations listed as cooks, railroad workers, merchants, farmers fishermen, washmen, huckster, barber, printer, and gardener (*U.S. Census of Population* 1880).

Other Chinese settled in the towns of Biggs and Gridley in the heartland of the Valley. By 1873, there were 47 inhabitants of Biggs and 23 of these early residents were Chinese (Osborn 1953). The Chinese in these small communities were very much a part of the local landscape. In 1877, the Oroville newspaper reported that during their Chinese New Year's holiday, for example, "so many whites joined in the festivities that the Chinese took a back seat and watched them" (*Oroville Mercury,* Feb. 16, 1877, 1). Gridley's Chinatown was even larger than the one in Biggs because of employment opportunities on the Southern Pacific Railroad and in the town's rapidly developing agricultural sector. The Chinese in Gridley raised vegetables on fertile and well watered flood

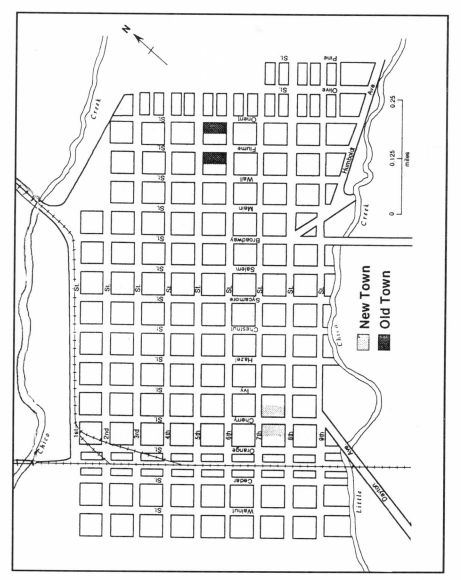

Figure 5.5. Chinese Neighborhoods in Chico, 1870-1910.

lands along the Feather River and picked and sold blackberries to local residents (Boulware interview, Sacramento, 1974). Other small nodes of Chinese settlement in Butte County had developed in Dayton, Durham, Nord, and at the site of Richardson Springs by the early 1870s. A photograph of Sing Gah, the nineteen year old cook of a Durham family, is shown in Figure 5.6.

Significant numbers of Chinese also lived in Yuba and Sutter Counties especially in the well developed Chinatown just below the levee on the Yuba River in downtown Marysville. Chan's seminal work on the Chinese in California documented that Marysville and Sacramento had the largest number of Chinese businesses establishments in the Valley in 1870 (Chan 1986, 66). Marysville also had a large number of Chinese truck gardeners working in its hinterland. In cities such as Yuba City, Marysville, Chico, and Sacramento, Chinese-grown fresh produce supplied the consumption needs of most of the local population (Chan 1986, 88). There were thirty-four Chinese truck gardeners in Yuba County in 1860 located all around the city and also inside the city limits. Chan found that early on Marysville became particularly famous for its Chinese-grown bitter melons and string beans. Because of its warm climate and strategic location on the Yuba River connecting the mining country with Sacramento and the Bay Area, Chinese-grown produce from Marysville supplied the consumption needs of residents in not only the local area but also in San Francisco and in the mining camps (Chan 1986, 98). By the early 1880s, at least 75 percent of all California farm workers were Chinese (Scheuring 1987, 35).

In the late 1860s, Chinese farmers began to lease larger plots of land and expand from vegetables to field crops. An early example of this patterns occurred in Colusa County where Ah Chow and Company leased 35 acres in 1869 to grown wheat on fertile land along the Sacramento River. Soon after, land was also leased on the other side of the river in Colusa County by another Chinese agriculturalist (Chan 1986, 158; and Colusa County, *Leases* Book B, 162). These Chinese wheat farms became very profitable ventures within a relatively short period of time contributing to Colusa County's ranking as California's top wheat producing county in the year 1880 (McGowan 1961, V. 1, 244).

In Tehama County, several very significant settlement nodes of Chinese developed in the Valley towns of Red Bluff, Tehama, and Vina. Lyonsville, in the foothills also had Chinese residents working in its lumber camps. The 1860 census listed 104 Chinese in Tehama County out of a total county population of 4,044 (*U.S. Census of Population* 1860). It is interesting to note that none of these Chinese residents of Tehama County in 1860 were listed as miners. All were a part of community life in the emerging towns of this developing county and, as such, had occupations such as cooks, doctors, laborers, merchants, wash-

Figure 5.6. Sing Gah, 1880.
Source: Meriam Library Special Collections, California State University, Chico.

men, or homemakers (Reed 1977, 14-15). Surprisingly, as compared to other Chinese communities in the state at this time which had a total of only 5 percent females in its total population, Tehama County had 28 percent female Chinese residents listed in the census. Overall, the Chinese comprised nearly 72 percent of the non-white population of Tehama County in 1880 (Reed 1977, 46).

Red Bluff had the largest Chinese settlement anywhere in Tehama County. As in other counties in the Valley, many well established white families in the area employed Chinese cooks and domestic helpers. Chinatown was located near downtown Red Bluff on High Street between Walnut and Hickory (see Figure 5.7). Most of the original buildings were frame and had cloth-lined ceilings. There were also several cabins in this small Chinatown located on the bluffs high above the Sacramento River (Insurance map for Fireman's Fund Insurance Company 1886).

Perhaps the most exciting rumors about the perceived glamour and intrigue of Red Bluff's Chinatown was in regards to its tunnels. As in Chico and other Valley towns, Chinatown was reputed to contain mysterious secret tunnels far beneath its buildings. Early newspaper accounts such as the one quoted here after a fire in Chinatown in Red Bluff amplified these rumors (*People's Cause,* August 1, 1886):

> It was observed during a fire that nearly all the cellars were connected by gratings a little below the level of the street, which indicates at least a neighborly disposition towards each other among the heathen.

And, according to another story in the *Cause* on April 2, 1887:

> The tribunals meet in a subterranean recesses beneath some of the largest buildings of Chinatown. The entrances to these "courts" are through many a winding and darkened passage, in the labyrinth of which a stranger would surely lose himself. Sheet-iron doors bar the passages at regular intervals, and owing to their narrowness, which will permit but one man to work at a time, the police have been unable to devise a means of entrance to the dens of torture.

Despite stories that persist into the 1990s about the existence of Chinese tunnels beneath the cities' downtowns, according to Dr. Calhoone Yuen of Red Bluff, the real explanation of the tunnels is much less dramatic. To escape the extreme heat of Valley towns in the summer, the Chinese built enlarged cellars and hung burlap on the walls. They then soaked the burlap in water to keep the cellar cool (Yuen interview, Red Bluff, 1977 as cited in Reed 1977, 51). Some of the cellars may also have been used as drains to remove the water from springs that seeped to the surface beneath the downtown area of these communities (Osborn interview, Red Bluff, 1977 as cited in Reed 1977, 52). These cellars resembled tunnels when the old buildings burned down or were torn down for urban renewal in later decades.

The Chinese in Red Bluff used a portion of the local town cemetery to bury their dead, although, according to religious requirements, most of the deceased were eventually shipped back to China to be buried alongside their relatives (see Book 1974b for a more detailed description of Chinese burial practices in early Sacramento Valley communities).

Another smaller but equally significant Chinese settlement node developed in the town of Tehama. Many of the Chinese residents of this small town raised peanuts in fertile floodplain soils along the Sacramento River (Hisken 1948, 2). Their large vegetable and peanut gardens extended along the east side of the river as far as Mill Creek. Chinese here also raised broom corn, radishes, onions, squash, and other vegetables which were transported to San Francisco by the Southern Pacific overnight train (*Wagon Wheels,* V. 22, 12-15).

Unlike the Chinese in most other towns in the Valley, according to county deed books, the Chinese in Tehama owned a great deal of property in the town. As recently as 1947, some of the lots in Chinatown were still in the names of former Chinese residents who had long since returned to China (Reed 1977, 57).

The third largest settlement of Chinese in Tehama County in 1880 was located in Vina. This Chinese settlement node had a Joss House, a Chinese general store and pharmacy, and a cemetery. Most local Asian residents in this agriculturally-based community were gardeners, although some were listed as cooks and woodchoppers. Chinese-owned gardens were farmed by Hop Sing and Lui Hing and others along Deer Creek. Others worked for white farmers in the area including Leland Stanford who hired more than 140 Chinese to pick and pack grapes and 35 more to work in his winery in 1886 (*People's Cause,* Aug. 28, 1886, 1).

Shasta County was another important destination for Chinese leaving the mining camps in the 1860s and 1870s. As early as December, 1853, there were at least two or three thousand Chinese miners in Shasta County (Reed 1977,14). As gold supplies became depleted in the hills, as in other places in the region, many of these miners moved into towns in Shasta County, soon becoming an important part of the evolving economy and multicultural ambience of these towns.

In Shasta City, for example, a Chinese settlement developed at the lower end

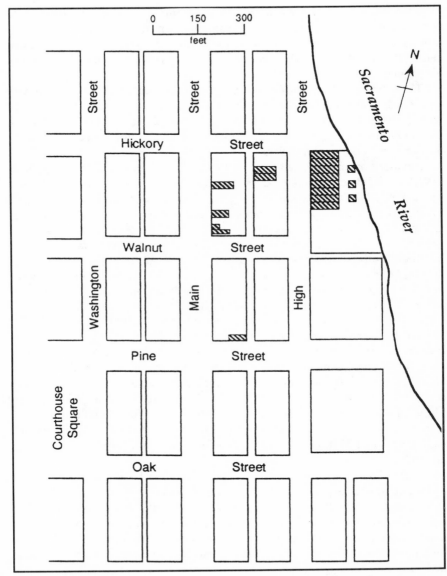

Figure 5.7. The Chinese Neighborhood in Red Bluff, 1870-1910.
Source: Adapted from Reed, 1892, 117.

of town, named "Hong Kong" by local residents. It was estimated that there were at least 500 residents of this small Chinatown in the mid-1850s. The early Chinese of the community raised vegetables for local needs, opened laundries, and worked as cooks. A significantly large Chinese settlement also existed at Igo during its boom period. Most of the homes were clustered around Piety Hill where, according to Reid (1969, 106):

> The families raised vegetables for consumption and to sell to the white miners. Most of them had pens of ducks in their back yard. They built large brick ovens which they used for cooking meat and rice. In their spare time, they could be seen reclining on reed mats with a block of wood for a pillow.

Despite their contribution to economic development in Shasta County, many of the local residents remained stubbornly opposed to the presence of the Chinese in the area. There were numerous floggings of Chinese workers by whites in the community. Another common practice was to catch two Chinese men and tie their queues together. Everyone would be invited to join in the laughter and ridicule as they attempted to free themselves. The most severe punishment inflicted on the Chinese of the area was the cutting off of their queues. This meant not only a loss of honor, but, in addition, because queues were required by the Mandarin rulers in their homeland, loss of this important hair piece meant they could not return to China (Southern, *Chinese in the Mines,* Scrapbook, V. 3 as cited in Reid, p. 104).

These hostile attitudes towards local Chinese residents of Shasta county were spelled out by attendees at a convention called to seek solutions to the "problem" of the Chinese. Held in Shasta City in 1855, the following items were spelled out at this meeting (*Courier*, Jan. 20, 1855, 1):

- A large number of Chinamen has become too large an evil to let it go. We must take measures to stop this evil which threatens to overcome us;
- Prohibition and total expulsion seems the only practical solution;
- Senator Sprague and Representative Bates will be given the grievance to consider so they may ask the legislature for immediate relief;
- Miners in California should forbid the Chinamen from working the mines after February 25, 1855;
- Miners should ask the cooperation of the rest of the miners in the state;
- All persons with Chinamen in their employ should notify them and discharge them by the date mentioned;
- All papers should print these resolutions.

This early hostility against the Chinese in the Sacramento Valley was a premonition of even more serious things to come. As Chinese workers began to take over more and more jobs in the region, white workers began to protest by discriminating against them in many often violent ways. The early 1870s witnessed a deepening of California's economic depression, the growth of the Workingman's Party, and the rise of anti-Chinese politics. As in other times of economic hardship (including the early 1990s in the state), a scapegoat to blame for economic hardships was needed. Because they were easy to identify due to their non-Anglo appearance and because of their willingness to work for lower wages than white laborers, the Chinese easily fell, although unwillingly, into this role.

In 1872, the completion of construction of the California and Oregon Railroad in Redding released several hundred Chinese into the labor market. They were in direct competition with other workers in the area and soon were blamed for its economic problems. The Panic of 1873, followed by the San Francisco banking collapse in 1875, further stimulated the seething anti-Chinese sentiment in the state (Reed 1977, 31). Local ordinances against the Chinese were thereafter passed throughout the Valley. Acts of violence against the Chinese increased. In Chico in 1877, six Chinese tenant farmers were attacked on the Lemm Ranch in Chico. Five were killed and their bodies burned.

Efforts to force this ethnic group out of the Valley took many forms, perhaps none as ugly as the establishment of the Order of the Caucasians. Organized in Chico in 1872, this secret anti-Chinese society flaunted to the community that they intended to annihilate all persons who did not join their group and listed the following as public nuisances (Mansfield 1918, 276):

- Anyone who removes a white man or woman or black man or woman (native born) and instates an Asiatic in his place;
- He who retains in his family an Asiatic nurse;
- He who gives bail or bond to an Asiatic;
- He who defends an Asiatic against a white in a court of law;
- All public officials who, having the opportunity, fail to work in the interests of the white man against the Asiatic;
- All proprietors of saloons, coffee houses, cigar stores, restaurants, etc. who employ Asiatics;
- He who teaches Asiatics any of the trades or arts of the Caucasian civilization;
- He who rents property to an Asiatic.
- Newspapers advocating the presence of Mongolians in America.

Continuous agitation by anti-Chinese organizations finally forced the passage of the national Chinese Exclusion Act in 1882 by the congress of the

United States. This law specified that both skilled and unskilled Chinese laborers were excluded from entering the United States for ten years. Only merchants, tourists, diplomats, students, and professional people were allowed to enter the country. Chinese workers were forced to decide whether they should stay in the United States and perhaps never see their families again or return to China (*Five Views* 1988, 117).

Following the passage of this act, numerous acts of violence were committed against the Chinese residents of the Sacramento Valley and elsewhere. Suspicious fires burned many Chinatowns in the region including parts of those in Chico, Red Bluff, Marysville, and Wheatland. In 1886, a group of thirty masked men from Wheatland in Yuba County, raided Chinese workers on H. Roddan's ranch, beat eleven hop pickers, then burned down the Chinese bunkhouse on C.D. Wood's ranch (*Five Views* 1988, 118). In 1888, the Scott Act was passed by Congress which barred Chinese laborers from returning to the United States if they left the country (even if it was temporarily). As a result of this law, along with the Chinese Exclusion Act, and violence and discrimination against the Chinese throughout the United States, immigration of the this ethnic group began to decline after 1880 decreasing to an insignificant number entering the country after 1890.

Economy

Early Agricultural Patterns

After 1852, as the supply of gold decreased in the Sierra Nevada, miners were displaced to other parts of the region. As discussed in the previous chapter, a new boom in the economic development of the region occurred. It focused on agricultural production, built upon the foundation established during the Mexican Rancho Era when large operations based primarily on cattle raising had dominated the Valley's agricultural activity.

Large scale American farming in the region emerged after 1855, the year the State Lands Commission put government land on sale for the first time (McGowan 1961, 157). The opening up of vast stretches of open, level land by the United States government encouraged immigrant farmers to settle in the region. Some continued the cattle operations already in place; others turned to raising grains such as wheat and barley which were extremely well suited to the Valley's natural environment.

Natural forces also encouraged the transition from cattle to other operations.

A series of natural disasters occurred in the mid-1850s that severely affected the cattle industry, starting with a number of invasions by hungry grasshoppers in the summers of 1855, 1857, and 1858. Damage caused by these invaders was compounded by years of drought between 1856 and 1864 which seriously dried up rangeland. Numerous cattle died of starvation because of these calamities. As if these decimating dry periods and insect invasions were not bad enough, they were exacerbated by other equally devastating natural disasters in the early 1860s in the form of floods and heavy snow storms. According to historian Joseph McGowan, hundreds of cattle were drowned in the great flood of 1862 and "numerous carcasses were strewn about the plains" (1961, 158). The cattle industry in the Sacramento Valley, in fact, never fully recovered from this damaging combination of environmental disasters.

Grazing

Following these challenges, an expansion of sheep raising was the second major event in the transition in Sacramento Valley agriculture. Despite poor climatic conditions, sheep raising continued unabated in the Valley in the decades after the Gold Rush since sheep were more able to adjust to fluctuations in water and pasture supplies. In the 1850s, tens of thousands of sheep were imported overland from southern California and from the midwestern states. In 1857 sheep arrived from Australia; in 1859, four Merino sheep bred in Vermont reached California (McGowan 1961, 159). The surprising story of other Merino sheep brought to the Red Bluff area by abolitionist John Brown's son is told in more detail in Chapter 8. The largest producers of sheep were Solano County (in 1857), Colusa County (in 1866), and Tehama County (in 1872). In Colusa County alone, sheep outnumbered cattle by a ratio of 45.1 by 1878 and yielded some 340 tons of wool (Hutchinson 1988, 10).

Meanwhile, in the wake of the disastrous drought that dealt the livestock business of Northern California a devastating blow in 1863-64, a bonanza era of grain farming emerged. It is important to note that the period of agricultural development that followed the decline of cattle did not eliminate the importance of livestock altogether. Instead, the addition of wheat and barley to the local agricultural scene became one of many successive layers of new crop introductions to occur in the Sacramento Valley from 1850 to the present day. It has been said that one of the unique aspects of Valley agriculture over the years has been the addition of new crops along with the continuation of the old. Livestock ranching continued on the periphery of the Valley, even after grain farming and sheep production emerged and intensified.

Dry Farming

In these post-Gold Rush years, the Sacramento Valley was especially well suited to grain farming over other crops. First, before the advent of irrigation, wheat and barley were two of just a few domesticated plants that could withstand the region's summer drought. In addition, wheat was the only crop durable enough to export before the invention of refrigerated railroad cars in the 1880s. The long hot summers of the Sacramento Valley produced a hard, dry wheat that could withstand without damage months of sea transport to Europe and elsewhere (Bauer 1970, 8).

Other advantages of the area were the rich, flat land which required little work to prepare for planting. Wheat was extremely easy to plant and required almost no care during the growing season. Even inexperienced farmers could find success in this type of farming. According to Pisani (1984, 6):

> He could get by without a house, barn, of even quarters for hired hands. Farm laborers were seldom needed for more than three or four weeks a year, and the mild California climate permitted them to sleep under the stars. Setting up and operating a farm required little capital, and wheat usually returned a good profit from the first year . . . little wonder, then, that wheat had the reputation as the 'poor man's crop,' even though the industry was dominated by huge farms after the 1860s.

Connections with the outside world via the Sacramento River also encouraged early wheat production. Wheat was transported from docks (as far upstream as Red Bluff) to Port Costa in the Carquinez Strait to foreign markets in China, Australia, and Europe (Lantis, Steiner, and Karinen 1963, 356). By the early 1850s, downriver traffic was as important as upriver traffic as far upstream as the town of Red Bluff because of wheat exports from the Valley.

Between 1891 and 1896, the wagons, steamboats, and barges of the Sacramento Transportation Company hauled an average of over 100,000 tons of wheat to market each year (Magliari 1989, 459). This represented roughly a quarter of the entire traffic carried on the Sacramento River!

Later, railroad connections enhanced opportunities for the shipment of wheat to distant places. These transportation linkages, along with an ideal natural environment and vast expanses of level land increased acreage planted in wheat in the Sacramento Valley from 200,000 acres in 1866 to over 1 million by 1884 (Lantis, Steiner, Karinen 1963, 356). There was no wheat country in the world like the Sacramento Valley at this time in history. Its almost perfect environmental, economic, and locational advantages were indeed perfect for the emergence of the region's "wheat kings."

One of the most successful and best known of these early land barons was Hugh J. Glenn who enthusiastically acquired land until he had 55,000 acres extending 20 miles along the west bank of the Sacramento River, mainly in Colusa County (see White 1995 for more information on Glenn's impact on regional economic development) After his death in 1891, Glenn's important contribution to Sacramento Valley agricultural development was memorialized in the naming of the newly formed Glenn County (see White 1995). Glenn's dream was for his "bonanza grain farm" to produce 1,000,000 bushels of wheat in one year. Later, historian William Hutchison described the labor crews at work on his immense expanses of land as (1980, 137):

> The great reapers were drawn by thirty mules, moving like an army through the square miles of waving wheat. Threshing crews worked from sunup to dark, their cooks even longer; and the mountains of chaff rose high enough, it seemed, to tower above the Sutter Buttes.

John Spencer Cone was another early settler who took advantage of the opportunities available in wheat production. One of the "Wheat Kings" of Tehama County, Cone had tried stock raising in the 1850s and had shifted his attention to growing wheat after the 1863-64 drought. It seemed that his desire for land was unstoppable. Beginning with his purchase of 100,000 acres of Job Dye's Antelope Ranch, part of one of Tehama's early land grants, in 1868 and extending through all land lying north of Mill Creek (part of the Toomes grant) in 1882, Cone added piece after piece of new property to his estate. By 1884, this rich land, along with other sections of public land adjacent to his property, made Cone one of the largest wheat growers in the North Valley.

Cone, like so many other wheat growers of his generation, was called by Julian Dana, "the most colossal splendors of resources in our history" (1939, 179). Unfortunately, these owners of huge properties planted the same crop year after year with little regard for the land. And they expanded their operations every year. Another drought in 1889 drove many small farmers out of the Valley so that by February, 1890, most of the property had been snatched up by these wheat barons (Pisani 1982, 262). By 1892, fewer than one hundred people owned 1,600,000 acres in the Sacramento Valley (Bauer 1970, 15).

The rapid expansion of wheat growing no doubt could not have happened at this immense scale without the plows, threshers, and other machinery that made such large scale operations possible. During the 1870s and 1880s, these labor saving devices boosted wheat growing in the state to become one of the most mechanized and structured forms of agriculture in the world. On John Bidwell's ranch in Butte County, his fifty "trained Indians" who had enabled him to culti-vate 300 acres of wheat and oats in 1857 and 435 acres in 1858 soon gave way to work crews backed by powerful farm equipment. As early as 1860, on his 39,000 acre ranch, it was recorded that Bidwell used 20 plows, 4 harrows, 2 mowers, 200 reapers, and 100 threshers (Gates 1967, 44-45).

The Sacramento Valley's flat land and dry summers made it possible for land owners to use the largest steam powered tractors and harvesters in the world. Without these labor saving devices, the state of California could not have boosted its wheat production from 17,000 bushels in 1850 to 5,900,000 in 1860, to 16,000,000 in 1870, to 40,000,000 by 1890. Barley was a close second with 4,500,000 bushels in 1860, 8,700,000 in 1870, 17,500,000 in 1880, and 25,000,000 in 1900, a year in which wheat production fell to 36,000,000 (Caughey 1970, 262).

As these yields illustrate, barley was also an important grain crop in the Valley in the second half of the nineteenth century. Especially well known was the barley grown in Yolo County between 1870 and 1900. The main buyers of this coveted grain crop were beer makers in the United States and in Europe; indeed, in English pubs during these years, ale made from "Yolo Barley" was in great demand (Larkey and Walters 1987, 39).

After 1890, wheat, and later barley, became less significant in California largely because new grain farms had begun producing on the Great Plains and in Europe, Asia, and Australia, where they used machines and techniques imported from Sacramento Valley operations. Other factors, such as the effects of severe erosion of the Central Valley, improved irrigation facilities, and rail connections with the East encouraged subdivision of wheat lands for more profitable crops. The "Bonanza Wheat Era" ended suddenly in 1893 due to a major financial panic from rapidly dropping prices of wheat. The panic was caused by overplanting in the United States and in Europe.

Early Irrigated Crops

Specialty crops such as fruits and vegetables emerged after 1870 and replaced wheat as the Valley's most profitable crops. Although certain fruits and vege-tables had been grown on earlier Mexican Rancho land, these crops were more difficult to grow and market than hardier grain crops. The first Constitution of California specified that "The legislature shall encourage by all suitable means, the promotion of intellectual, scientific, moral, and agricultural improvements." Accordingly, specialty crops received special attention from state and local agencies and were ultimately nurtured into importance by innovative, locally developed water control systems. Although much smaller in scale in terms of acreages and labor involved, the early efforts to encourage specialty crops in the 1850s had a much larger influence on the longterm future of the region's agriculture than did wheat farming or livestock. As irrigation systems developed in selected parts of the Valley, it became possible for a wide variety of vine, row, and orchard crops to flourish.

Grapes were one of the first fruits to be grown in the Sacramento Valley because wine was easier to market and transport than more perishable fresh fruits. One important immigrant who influenced the development of vineyards in the Valley was a native of Germany, Henry Gerke, who settled near today's town of Vina in Tehama County. With funding supported by earnings from the gold fields, this emigre became one of the largest landholders in Northern California in the 1850s (*Memorial and Biographical History of Northern California,* 1891, 149). After purchasing a large plot of land for his vineyard in 1852, Gerke became the first to cultivate and export wines from the Vina area. He later set aside the land for the town of Vina, deeding the site to the Southern Pacific Railroad Company in 1871. The following account of Gerke's successes was provided by a chronicler of the time (in *History of Tehama County* 1880, 35-36):

> Henry Gerke demonstrated successful growing of grapes started in the 1850s and manufacture of wines in the upper Sacramento Valley. He has the finest wine cellar in this portion of the state. It is capable of taking care of 100,000 gallons of wine. The grape grows so freely that it does not pay to adulterate the juice. The winemaker assures us that his red or white wine is the pure juice of the grape. The sweet Angelica, Sherry, or Muscatel make it keep. . . . The main brands of wine now being made are Claret, Angelica, Sherry, Riesling, and others.

Vineyards were also planted by other European immigrant vintners and investors in other parts of the Sacramento Valley. In Yolo County near Woodland, the largest holding devoted to grapes was the Orleans Hill Vineyard located on 450 acres six miles west of Madison (Larkey and Walters 1987, 45). This vineyard was established in 1861 by German born Jacob Knauth and was later purchased and expanded into a champaign-producing establishment by Arpad Haraszthy. Haraszthy, sometimes called the father of California viticulture. His successes in the Valley as well as in San Mateo and Sonoma counties after emigrating here in the 1840s attracted many other Europeans into the wine industry of the state, including such well known names as Charles Krug, Pierre Mirassou, Paul Masson, Carl Wente, and the Korbel brothers (Scheuring 1987, 18).

Compared to grapes, the growing of orchard fruits involved a much longer wait for profitable return, greater difficulties in marketing, and was a more expensive operation. Although numerous local farmers, such as John Wolfskill in Yolo County and John Bidwell, experimented with various fruits, it was not until the railroad was completed in the 1870s, enhancing marketing possibilities, that orchard crops became a truly profitable venture.

Improved irrigation networks discussed in the following section of this chapter made it possible for new specialty crops to be planted on fertile Sacramento Valley soils. In Yolo County along the Sacramento River north of Washington (now West Sacramento), Reuben Merkley planted his first hop vines in 1875. By 1878, Yolo was producing almost half of the state's total production of this crop (Larkey and Walters 1987, 43). Sugar beets were also planted in several parts of the Valley, most notably near Woodland and Hamilton City, with refineries constructed nearby in the early twentieth century.

With expanding crop production in the Valley, agricultural patterns became increasingly complex. Along with this complexity, new conflicts among cattle ranchers and orchardists and wheat farmers emerged. One was the challenge of keeping animals sufficiently away from orchards and fields to prevent them from damaging (or eating!) crops. In 1872, farmers were required by law to construct fences to prevent their livestock from destroying neighboring field crops.

The passage of this and other laws designed to solve conflicts between the region's farmers and its cattle and sheep ranchers as is so vividly depicted in the song from the musical *Oklahoma!* —"The Cowboys and the Farmers Can't be Friends"—did not ease all conflicts among various interest groups in the region. In an effort to protect their interests and enhance marketing opportunities for their products, the California Fruit Union was organized in Woodland in 1887. This action was followed by the creation of other similar organizations such as the Davisville Almond Grower's Association in 1897 and the Winters Dried Fruit Company in 1897.

These cooperatives enhanced opportunities for fruit production in the Valley. The formation of land "colonies" also intensified settlement for purposes of agriculture. Several of these colonies, including the citrus colonies of Oroville, peach colonies of Gridley, and other land colonies in Corning and Los Molinos are discussed in Chapter 7 as examples of the importance of these tightly controlled real estate ventures in the economic development and settlement of agricultural land in the Sacramento Valley.

Environment

Some environmental impacts of settlement and development of the Sacramento Valley were immediate and obvious such as cutting of the riparian forests, killing of wildlife, and denuding grassland vegetation with overgrazing. For example, the *Marysville Appeal* reported how the railroad removed thousands of cords of oak wood from newly cleared land to supply the fuel demands of city homes and industries. Five or six carloads of wood were shipped daily from the Live Oak, Gridley, and Biggs areas in 1872-73 when the land was being cleared for farming (McGowan 1961, 224). After the Gold Rush had begun, the numbers of livestock throughout California increased over ten-fold (California Division of Forestry 1988). By the late 1880s, almost all of the Valley and surrounding foothills were very heavily grazed with devastating results including soil erosion and the conversion of native grasses into a range dominated by poor quality, weedy species. Although some government control over public lands was begun in the 1930s, overgrazing impacts to watersheds and streams continued unabated until the environmental movement of the 1970s and 1980s (State Lands Commission 1994, 36). Other impacts were more subtle in their effects and the causes were disputed. Such was the case with flooding.

Floods

One of the major environmental impediments to more intensive economic development of the Sacramento Valley in the nineteenth century was the "problem" of flooding. Although alternating cycles of floods and droughts were acknowledged natural processes in the region, these vagaries of climate nevertheless were seen as one of many aspects of nature to be conquered and eliminated if possible.

Early farmers who developed land in the Sacramento Valley, therefore, had two serious issues to deal with regarding water—droughts and floods. Unlike the situation in their homeland in the humid East, Northern California's alternating patterns of too little water or too much water, tarnished dreams of easy prosperity in the region's Mediterranean climate. Water, rather than cold temperatures, ultimately became the limiting factor for crop survival.

Native American traditions indicated that a flood in 1805 had inundated the entire Valley floor and taken many lives. Devastating floods have occurred in the Sacramento Valley regularly between this first recorded one in 1805 and, most recently, in the winter of 1995. Extreme high water also occurred in 1833, when employee-hunters of the Hudson's Bay Company, experienced a huge flood in the Valley while en route from New Helvetia (Sacramento) to their home base in Vancouver, Washington. Trapped for weeks in the high ground of the Sutter Buttes, these early observers of this common occurrence in the region (perhaps more than 150 men, women and children and assorted pack animals and riding horses), lived comfortably off local game that "used the Buttes as their ever present ark when floods came" (Hutchison 1988, 12).

During this same flood, Captain Belcher reported in 1837 that (1843, 123-124):

> The annual rains do out of necessity inundate these low lands, but in severe seasons, after heavy falls of snow, they produce one immense sea, leaving only a few scattered eminences which art or nature have produced, as so many islets or spots of refuge.

And the 1841 Wilkes expedition reported that (1845, 189):

> At the place where the survey ended, the river was 200 feet wide, its banks being twenty feet above the river; but it was evident that its perpendicular rise exceeded this, a s there is every appearance of it overflowing them; and according to testimony of the Indians, the whole country is annually inundated.

Winter flooding was a natural part of the Valley's climatic cycle. Its Mediterranean climate balanced water losses during summer months with water excesses during the winter in a continuing annual cycle of wet and dry. As such, winter flooding was a natural part of the seasonal cycle of the region.

In another "disastrous" flood in 1850, however, the normal cycle saw new extremes. No levees or water control systems had yet been constructed, making damage from the flood even more serious (Kelly 1989, 10). The journal of Riley Root helps us visualize the extent of this flood, which devastated the entire Sacramento River drainage basin, and made rowboats the only acceptable means of transportation throughout most of the Valley. According to this account (1955, 119):

> During the winter of 1849 and 50, one of the greatest floods occurred which had ever been known in the valley of the Sacramento. From the top of a high hill on the left bank of the Feather River, not far from Table Mountain (near Oroville), where I could command an extensive view of the valley, I estimated that one-third of the land was overflowed. Hundreds of cattle, horses, and mules were drowned, being carried away by the rapidity of the

current in their attempt to reach higher ground; and the Sacramento City, then being without its levee, was almost entirely submerged. A small steamboat actually run up its principle streets, and discharged its freight on the steps of the principle stores.

Even with the Valley's newly constructed levees, another major flood in 1862 caused even more destruction. One eyewitness account described the high water as extending from the site of Sutter's Fort on a hill in Sacramento to the city of Davis ten miles to the west with water three feet over the tops of the riverbanks (Harding 1960, 148.). This flood devastated the lower twelve miles of the Yuba River drainage. It also caused water to rise ten feet in one night at Colusa during the storm. During this event, Colusa newspaperman, Will Green, calmly stated that it was now possible to travel from Colusa to Yuba City by boat (Hutchison 1988, 13). In the winter of 1995, this same area was under water during a flood that inundated Route 20 between Williams and Colusa and Colusa and Yuba City. Hamilton City residents were likewise briefly flooded out of their homes during this flood. It is obvious from this recent natural disaster that flooding remains a serious environmental concern for Sacramento Valley towns, cities, and farmland even in modern times.

The Valley's flood control system is linked with its major water delivery systems, the Central Valley Project and the California Water Project. Major flood waters flow in natural stream channels until capacity is reached. Overflow water then flows through the Sutter and Yolo bypasses. Water delivery projects in the Sacramento Valley are discussed in more detail in Chapters 8 and 9.

Reclamation and Early Irrigation

Reclaiming swamplands was an issue that received a great deal of public and legislative attention between 1850 and 1870. Congress had first granted swamp and overland lands to the states in 1850 providing that proceeds from their sale be applied to their reclamation. In 1866, responsibility for these valuable lands was shifted to the county level whereupon any sort of cohesive statewide plan was abandoned in favor of local development decisions.

The cycles of floods and droughts encouraged early immigrants unaccustomed to the uncertainties of the Valley's climate, to conceive of numerous projects and schemes to add to the flow of water on their newly developed land when necessary. Irrigation was first practiced on a small scale by orchardists, vineyardists, and truck farmers who grew vegetables for local markets. In the Valley, the usual method for obtaining water was let it flow naturally out of wells or streams into small canals. In 1856 and 1859, a number of canals were built to irrigate wheat near Woodland and Cacheville in Yolo County. These were apparently the earliest irrigation enterprises in the state. Public interest in the creation of larger and more extensive irrigation systems first came together in 1866 when the state legislature authorized a survey for a canal to be built from the Sacramento River extending through Colusa, Solano, and Yolo counties (Hutchison 1946, 45). Later, in 1874, in a premonition of the future comprehensive Central Valley Project, a national commission authorized by Congress, submitted a report that laid out a proposed irrigation plan for the entire Central Valley.

In 1850, a statute was passed by the legislature providing that *The Common Law of England* be applied to water ownership in the state. A conflict over riparian (streamside) rights then was battled in court when Lax vs. Haggin precipitated arguments over the riparian doctrine and its effect on the development of riparian issues (Harding 1960, 37-40). The court ruled that each riparian owner along a stream had the right to "reasonable" use of water, but could not unnecessarily diminish the quantity of water in its natural flow. The volume of a stream could be reduced if the water was necessary to meet domestic needs and to water cattle, no matter how much the diversion reduced the supply of water to downstream riparian owners. The upstream riparian owner, however, had no right to obstruct the channel of the stream itself (Pisani 1984, 36-37). Arguments over whether water is owned and controlled by riparian rights, groundwater appropriation (those who own the land own the water beneath it), or through "prior appropriation" (earliest users of the water continue to have rights to it) still rage on in California courts in the 1990s.

Valley Impacts from Hydraulic Mining

The conflict between miners and farmers extended well beyond water use, however, and fostered another set of issues resolved in the state's courts. When California became a state in 1851, all lands except those in Mexican or Spanish land grants were owned by the federal government. Technically, miners were trespassers on these federal lands. As the mining industry expanded, so did mining technology. As such, water was used in virtually all mining practices and water demands in the foothills increased year by year. Eventually, it became necessary to devise a system of appropriate water rights for mining and this required the construction of works to divert and store water that would ultimately have a serious and lasting impact on the natural environment of the Sacramento Valley.

Since mining was largely unchecked by law, debris ran into canyons and then into the flatlands below. It was reported by ship captains in the lower Sacramento River as early as 1854 that the river was becoming more and more muddy as a direct result of this debris (Kelley 1959, 25-27). As this intensity of mining and mining technology increased in the foothills, a number of problems were created in the Valley below. Hydraulic mining (the use of water under high pressure to wash away huge amounts of dirt to expose placer deposits), had become the mainstay for extracting gold in many mining districts especially in the Feather, Yuba, and American River drainage districts. Hydraulic mining was so powerful that it could wash away entire hillsides, meadows, and stands of timber. The destruction was extraordinary but profits from gold extraction soared.

Deposition of excess sediment from hydraulic mining operations and the subsequent diversion of streams was the first major change to occur in the Valley. This influx of hydraulic debris increased the sediment load of the river beyond their transport capacity and resulted in extensive deposits of tailings in the Sacramento Valley. The "debris plain" of the Yuba River was particularly noticeable and noteworthy. It covered over 40 square miles (State Lands Commission 1994, 10). The streambed of the Yuba River at Marysville was raised by seventy feet according to local county histories. Stabilization of the bed of the Yuba River continued for decades, influenced in large part by channelization and the construction of Englebright Dam upstream of the debris plain in 1940 (State Lands Commission 1994, 10).

Another impact caused by this invasion of debris from the foothills was an increase in river flooding. In addition, smooth navigation of rivers and streams became impeded as sediment buildup clogged formerly navigable channels. Thousands of acres of farmland and orchards were regularly buried under layers of mining debris, decreasing land values and ruining crops (Hundley 1990, 76). Since mining was an unregulated industry at this time, Sacramento Valley landowners could do nothing to stop the damage. Some of the richest farmlands in the state became barren wastelands as orchards, grain fields, and houses were buried out of sight (Kelley, 1956, 332). Hundreds of acres of fruit orchards along the rivers were dying out as the debris spread into the Valley (Kelley 1959, 58).

The situation became desperate for Valley communities and farmers. After the flood of 1862, which deposited a broad sheet of mining debris over farmlands, people began a desperate fight to keep rivers in their beds. When the water finally receded in the Marysville region, a large part of the hydraulic tailings which had been accumulating since 1853 were removed from canyons in the foothills and redeposited in Valley streambeds. The land south of the Yuba River was reported to be a "desolate waste . . . a thick sediment of sand destroying all hopes of vegetation for some time to come" (Kelley 1959, 72). By the 1870s, the drainage system of the entire Valley was so overloaded with mining debris that it was unable to carry off even normal rainfall. Many people had begun to move out, especially from the Yuba and Bear river drainage areas. Clearly something had to be done.

As early as 1824, the US Supreme Court had ruled that it was the federal government's responsibility to control the country's navigable streams and rivers. However, little effort was made by the government to clear out mining debris from the Sacramento River and other natural waterways in the Valley. The first federal appropriation for the improvement of navigation on the Sacramento River came in 1875 when snag removal was officially authorized. Then, in 1883, the Caminetti Act created the California Debris Commission. This Commission was authorized to oversee and license hydraulic mining to those who promised not to damage the rivers. Contributing to this effort at the state level, California courts ruled in 1884 to place an injunction on any hydraulic mining operation that would deposit debris into navigable channels on the Sacramento River and its tributaries.

But conflicts between foothill miners and Valley landowners intensified despite these rulings in the courts. Reform efforts to create a drainage system that would protect the farmland and allow hydraulic mining to continue went on for many years. The debate created animosity between farmers and miners because each group felt it was struggling for its own economic survival.

After the cessation of hydraulic mining, there remained a similar but not as extensive mining activity that also caused downstream siltation and flooding. Large floating barges worked the alluvial deposits of Butte Creek and the Feather, Yuba, and American Rivers until the 1950s. The resulting pattern of parallel ridges and swales were made up of coarse sediments overlain on top of finer materials. They formed a huge rock pile on which vegetation was unable to become established. Impacts of the dredgers are still easy to see in the Oroville and Marysville areas along and within river drainage channels.

Eventually farmers in the Valley were to prevail. In order for this to happen, however, modification of the natural flow of the Sacramento, Feather, Yuba, and American Rivers; swampland reclamation in the natural basins; and irrigation systems would have to be approved. This massive and complex set of variables ultimately were to come together and find expression on the landscape of the Sacramento Valley through the federally funded Central Valley Project discussed in Chapter 8.

Chapter 6

Urbanization

As long as the economy of Northern California was based on extractive industries such as farming, ranching, lumbering and mining, its population was dispersed in rural areas and in small towns. As linkages with the outside world expanded, transportation systems improved, the importance of trade increased, local manufacturing expanded, and larger settlements evolved. With this urban expansion came the development of new services. Both education and government became more important in the later years of the nineteenth century. New migration increased urban populations and the increased contact with the rest of the country and the world supported them. Figure 6.1 maps early settlements and routes in the Sacramento Valley in the year 1880 and provides a fitting introduction for this chapter. Clearly things were changing rapidly.

Economy

The Evolution of Transportation Systems

From the beginning of Euro-American interest in California, it was apparent that settlement and economic development could only succeed with adequate transportation linking the vast region to other parts of the Pacific Coast and the nation. As transportation to California by ship became more commonplace in the early 1840s, San Francisco and other coastal areas received significant numbers of new migrants. For overland travelers during the same period, New Helvetia, later to be named Sacramento, developed as the earliest growth node. As the Valley filled with new inhabitants, Sacramento was the beginning and end of most northerly movements of goods and people.

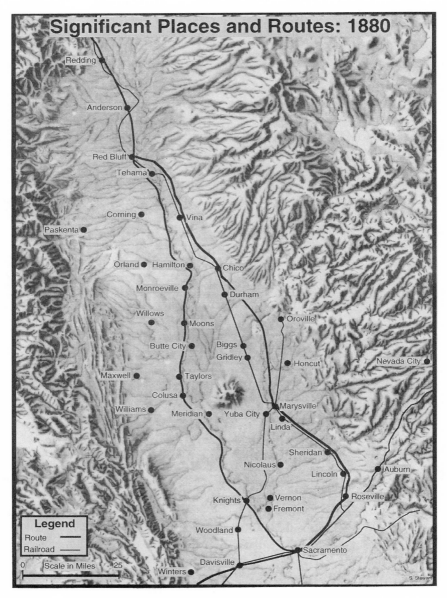

Figure 6.1. Significant Places and Routes, 1880.

Early Roads and Trails

As with most unplanned trail systems, the routes used by pack animals and wagons in the Valley formed a network of links between destinations. The destinations were places of settlement, many of which would evolve into towns and cities. Likewise, overland trails leading to the mines in the foothill region and to Valley farms and ranches that supported them were created out of a need for commerce and communication both internally within the region and externally to the outside world.

Major trails leading to the Valley, to the northern mines, and to the central Mother Lode were, for the most part, blazed by the fur trappers and improved by those who followed. James Beckworth, for example, one of the early trapper-adventurers, is credited with the route of the Beckworth trail which entered the Valley by way of Berry Creek to Oroville via the Feather River from Truckee and Quincy. Hudson's Bay Company trappers are credited with locating a trail used by immigrants in the 1840s from Donner and Truckee Passes down to the Bear River east of today's town of Wheatland. This road became the most popular of the trans-Sierra routes for the gold seekers in the 1840s and 1850s and is acknowledged as the "California Trail" (Gilbert 1966, 173-174).

Another route across the Sierra to the Valley included the Pit River route to Red Bluff known most commonly as the Lassen Trail. The Sonora and Walker Passes, discovered by John Bidwell in 1841 and Joseph Walker in 1833, were dangerous and fell into disuse until paved roads were built in the twentieth century. In addition to these major routes, many parallel trails, cutoffs, and unnamed roads also existed.

Various wagon roads were surveyed and promoted in an effort to attract state or federal financing for grading and other improvements. Routes over the Sierra Nevada were advocated from Marysville, Placerville, Downieville, Georgetown, and Calaveras Big Trees but none materialized as a reliable route that would support government mail contracts or private stage line activity. Eventually, in 1858, the Johnson Pass route was adopted by the State Wagon Road Commissioner and subscribed to by several financial backers. This early road followed the general route of today's Interstate Highway 50 except that Johnson Pass was located a few miles south of today's Echo Summit. In the 1860s, this became the main wagon road for shipping supplies from Sacramento to the Comstock mines.

A more northerly entrance to the Valley was conceived in 1857. It became the National Wagon Road from Ft. Kearney, Nebraska to Honey Lake, now Susanville (Jackson 1952, 193-200). From there this road continued to Mountain Meadows (now Lake Almanor) where it met the Chico-Humboldt

Wagon Road and the Tehama County Wagon Road from Red Bluff (McIntosh 1962, 12-14).

Roads from Jelly's Ferry, known locally as the Old Oregon Road, joined the easterly road from Redding to cross the Cascades and then proceeded on to eastern Oregon and Idaho. Most roads in the Sacramento Valley were not federally funded nor were they connected to transcontinental routes. They were simply tracks delimiting the shortest routes from farm to river landing, ferries, or small settlements. Eventually, most of these individually initiated roads would become owned and maintained by city and county governments. Later, some of these roads would be designated as state highways.

The major staging area for the northern Sierra mines was Marysville which was the head of reliable navigation on the Feather River and was located at the junction of the Yuba River. This settlement was founded by Theodore Cordua who selected the site because it offered alternate routes into the foothills and mountains and was often used as a camping spot on the "California-Oregon Trail." He called his town New Mecklenburg; others called it Nye Ranch. The Marysville name won out, however. The town quickly out-competed its neighbor, Yuba City, because it had the advantage of location on the foothill (mining) side of the river. Both "cities" claimed to be the head of navigation but Marysville residents were more aggressive in attracting steamboats. The February 15th, 1850 issue of *The Golden Gazette* described Marysville as follows:

> This town at the junction of the Feather River and Yuba River is prospering. It has now 500 inhabitants, with a floating population of perhaps 1,000 and lots are selling fast. It is expected that soon there will be regular communication with Sacramento by steamer and other boats.

From Marysville, a number of roads radiated out to other towns in the Valley as well as to foothill mining communities. The major road was on the east side of the Sacramento River from Marysville through Chico to a ferry at Tehama where it continued on to Red Bluff. The Shasta mines were supplied with pack trains and a wagon road on the west side of the river from Washington, across the Sacramento River from Sacramento, to Colusa to Red Bluff and on to Latona (Redding) and Shasta City (Boggs, 1942). Shasta, located eight miles west of the site that would become Redding, was the northernmost head of wagon navigation in the early 1850s. From this point, as many as 100 pack trains per day would fan out to the Klamath Mountain region. By 1851, mail contracts made it profitable to run two stagecoach lines on the east and west side routes throughout the region. By 1852, the Hall and Crandall Company claimed to make the trip from Marysville to Shasta in 24 hours (Boggs 1942, 137).

This quotation from the Red Bluff *Beacon* illustrates the importance of the roads to the mines (as cited in Ostrander 1968, 63):

> With the road already made by the Pitt River, and another in prospect, we are now commanding all the trade of Siskiyou and with the road now in progress from Shasta to Weaver, and the South Trinity road, to command the Trinity River trade, we have the whole in our hands.

In 1854, a merger of small stage coach companies created the California Stage Company which dominated overland transport in the North State in much the same way that the California Steam Navigation Company did on the rivers.

The role of ferries in determining the locations of road systems is fairly obvious. Red Bluff, Tehama, Colusa, Princeton, Butte City and other major river towns owe part of their success to ferry service. However, ferry service alone was rarely the factor that created a new community. One of the first ferries in Tehama County was begun by William Moon in 1845 near Woodson Bridge.

River Navigation

When Sutter bought out the Russians at Fort Ross in 1841, the purchase included a Russian sailing vessel renamed the *Sacramento*. This little ship was the first to carry on regular service between New Helvetia and Yerba Buena (now called Sacramento and San Francisco). The trip usually took a week each way (State Lands Commission 1994, 8).

The first steamboat to navigate on the Sacramento River was the Russian-American Company's thirty-seven foot *Sitka* which took seven days to reach Sacramento in 1847 (Shaw 1963, 6). Two more years passed before regular service would be established but by 1853 service to "Calvertsburg" (Red Bluff) was advertised in San Francisco newspapers.

The era of the dominance of steamboat transportation in the Sacramento Valley lasted from 1849 to 1871 although there was a revival of river traffic in the 1890s. Even after railroads became established in the Valley, however, river traffic continued to hold a place of importance. In 1873, there were twenty-two steamboats on the river ranging in size from 60 to 864 tons (McGowan 1961, 303). That same year, over five hundred steamboats arrived in California's capital city.

The most important steamboat company was the California Steam Navigation Company which began operations in 1854. After 1871, boats owned by the railroad carried more goods and passengers. In addition, much of the middle and upper Valley was serviced by smaller independent operators. In 1850, twenty-eight steamboats were operating on the Sacramento and Feather Rivers (Ostrander 1968, 11).

Beginning with just one barge and a steamboat, the Sacramento Wood Company began cutting oak along the river near Colusa and transporting it to Sacramento. While in the process of totally defoliating riparian forests, the operators were able to take on other cargoes, especially wheat. Historian Michael Magliari has compiled extensive data establishing that approximately half of the state's entire 1890 wheat crop either travelled by water (on the Sacramento or San Joaquin Rivers) or benefitted from rail rates lowered by water-borne competition (Magliari 1989, 453). By 1913, the name of the Sacramento Wood Company had been changed to Sacramento Transportation Company and was operating seven steamers and twenty-three barges between Chico landing and San Francisco Bay (McGowan 1961, 305). Upon reaching Sacramento, most of the smaller steamboats transferred their cargoes to larger deep-water draft steamboats capable of towing up to four fully loaded barges to Port Costa, the wheat shipping center of the Pacific Coast (Harney 1908, 7).

A variety of smaller, single operator, endeavors competed with the larger companies stopping at over two hundred landings as well as the thriving towns of Knights Landing, Verona, Colusa, Butte City, Tehama, and Red Bluff. Red Bluff was the acknowledged head of navigation until 1881 when mining debris made the water too shallow and hazardous. However, as Magliari points out, navigation did not cease completely on the Sacramento and Feather Rivers (1989, 455). The revival of steamboat traffic in the 1890s was due to the introduction of light-draft stern wheel vessels and the efforts of the U.S. Army Corps of Engineers to clear obstructions in the river. For awhile, weekly steamboat service to Red Bluff resumed and at least eight grain warehouses were constructed on the riverbank at Tehama (Magliari 1989, 456-457). During the 1890s, at least fifteen steamboats and thirty barges operated in the Sacramento River. Thereafter, steamboat visits were infrequent although some trips were recorded as late as 1911, 1918, and 1936.

Steamboating was as important on the Feather River as it was on the Sacramento River until 1869. By that year, mining debris in the river and competition from the railroads decreased river traffic on the Feather although there was a regular schedule in effect until about 1900. The last steamboat to reach Marysville did so in 1914 (McGowan 1961, 309).

In the early 1850s, most freight carried by the river boats was hauled upriver. In 1860, the downriver cargo of mostly agricultural products, hides, and lumber equaled the upriver supplies for the mines. Downriver freight dominated the industry by 1870 and on into the 1890s. During this period, however, rail lines connected Sacramento with Marysville, Red Bluff and Oakland and steamboat traffic faced the competition of time and cost for movement of goods. The last commercial Sacramento River freight traffic ceased regular operations in the 1940s.

Railroads

Grandiose ideas and plans for railroads in the Far West were not uncommon but few actually materialized before passage of the Pacific Railway Act in 1862. One exception was California's first rail line, the Sacramento Valley Railroad. It was constructed in 1856 and extended from Sacramento to the Sierra foothill mines. It was so successful that an entirely new town, Folsom, was built at the end of the line. This early success and the visionary efforts of Theodore Judah, encouraged the development and ultimate construction of the now well known transcontinental line, which opened in 1869, which also focused on Sacramento.

The planning and building of the first transcontinental railroad from Omaha is an exciting but lengthy story told elsewhere. But the partners of the Central Pacific and others would not stop with one railroad line to its west coast hub. Connections to Oregon and to Mexico and beyond were also envisioned by these early "dreamers."

Within the Sacramento Valley, it was plain to see that those communities with access to the rail center at Sacramento had an advantage in marketing their farm products. For upriver communities, grain had to be hauled by wagon to river landings then on to ports for ocean shipping. Paying a minimum cost for transport meant the competitive difference between success and failure for Valley farmers. Marysville and Sacramento supplied food to over two-thirds of the population of California in 1854 over muddy roads and shallow spots on the Feather River. A more reliable and cost effective mode of transport was certainly in great demand (McGowan 1961, 170).

The California Pacific Railroad was incorporated in 1857 to extend tracks from Folsom to the Yuba River. By 1861, tracks were laid to Roseville and to the new town of Lincoln named for one of the promoters of the ambitious railway. Under the new name of the Yuba Railroad Company, this line extended connections to Wheatland in 1868. Later it became part of the California and Oregon Railroad which, in turn became part of the Central Pacific.

The California and Oregon Railroad was organized in 1865. Congressman John Bidwell had introduced a bill which provided for a public land grant to run the line from the Central Pacific yard at Roseville to the Columbia River in Oregon. At the same time, the Oregon and California Railroad was chartered to be constructed from Portland south toward Sacramento. The California and Oregon railroad was completed from Sacramento, through Marysville, to Chico in 1870 and later, on to Red Bluff. It crossed the Sacramento River at the Sesma-Tehama bridge which was opened in 1871. Redding was reached in 1872. Besides providing connections with the outside world, another primary benefit of this effort was the granting of land to railroad companies. They each received ten square miles of land on each side of the right-of-way for every mile of track completed. The *San Francisco Chronicle* on May 22, 1889 estimated that the railroads had received 1,800,000 acres between Roseville and Redding from the government and that they were worth six million dollars (McGowan 1961, 224). Most of this land was sold to farmer-investors who would be attracted to the Valley by promotion efforts sponsored by the railroads.

By this time, however, the Central Pacific was in the process of acquiring small railroad companies throughout the West. The first to fall was the Sacramento Valley Railroad whose owners sold out in 1865. In 1868, the Central Pacific purchased the Southern Pacific Railroad and consolidated all its lines under one name. The Southern Pacific Railroad bought the California and Oregon Railroad in 1875 while purchasing most other smaller railroads in California. In 1887, this huge company acquired and completed the Oregon and California Railroad thereby connecting Portland and Sacramento by rail. By the end of the 1880s, the Southern Pacific monopolized transportation in California and most of the other western states.

It is interesting to note that the application to the State of California for the chartering and construction of the California and Oregon Railroad was objected to by the Butte County Board of Supervisors. The county had raised $200,000 to finance the Northern Railroad from Marysville to Oroville. The railroad company, in an effort to defray the debt, had issued its own bonds and as it became apparent that the California and Oregon Railroad would become a reality, the bonds declined in value. Supervisors' loud protests, however, failed to persuade the state to deny the application (McGie 1982, 178).

A sample of the optimism the railroad brought to Valley residents is reflected in this excerpt from an article from a local newspaper (*Gridley Herald* 1882, 7):

Rapid Transit. The new timetable went into effect for the C & O lines together with connections for westbound overland trains. Letters from New York are received here on the sixth day. From St. Louis, five days. Less than twenty years ago the trip across the plains occupied six months. Now it can be made inside of five days. In less than 20 years hence we think the trip to Omaha will be shortened by three days.

While the Southern Pacific system dominated the region in the latter part of the nineteenth century, a few modest independent railroads were built to augment it. Such was the case of the Colusa and Lake Railroad constructed in 1885 as a narrow gauge line running from Colusa to the quarries at Sites on the west side of the Valley twenty-two miles distant. The word *Lake* in the name of the company referred to the stockholders' intention to build the line to the town of Lower Lake in Lake County. This extension was never built. The main reason for construction of this short line, though, was to address community agitation to move the county seat from Colusa to Williams which had Southern Pacific service. This strategy seems to have worked. The city of Colusa remains the county's seat of government and administration today. The line carried passengers, agricultural products and sandstone until its abandonment in 1915 due to competition from the Northern Electric line connecting to Marysville.

Other smaller lines remained important during these years of growth. The California Northern Railroad was created in 1876 and laid track up the west side of the Valley to be joined to the California and Oregon Railroad in 1882 at Gerber (McGowan 1961, 231). The Butte County Railroad Company was franchised in 1902 by the Diamond Match Company and ran from Sterling City to Barber just south of Chico. It was used for transporting logs to the Diamond Match factory. The line was eventually purchased by the Southern Pacific Company in 1903 who operated it until 1975 when the plant was closed.

While anyone was free to promote business growth along the lines, the railroad had an interest in controlling growth encouraged by outside investors by limiting the number of stations. They were usually located at seven to ten mile intervals. The location of rail lines that existed in the Sacramento Valley in 1930, as shown in Figure 6.1 illustrate the success of this strategy in that most such stops evolved or were promoted into towns. Lincoln, Wheatland, Sheridan, Gridley, Biggs, and many others provide evidence of this successful development scheme. Southern Pacific passenger service was eliminated in 1966 which resulted in the closure and demolition of several railroad stations along the lines.

Transportation and Agricultural Development

The development and expansion of transportation linkages in the Sacramento Valley provided a tremendous boost to its potential for agricultural production. According to historian Joseph McGowan (1961, 379):

> Prior to 1869 and completion of the Central Pacific, the only agricultural exports from California were non-perishable products such as wheat, flour,

wool, wine, cattle hides, dried fruit or an experimental shipment such as grapes packed in sawdust.

The sale and shipment of fresh fruit to the east was only possible after transcontinental rail connections were established. Even then, problems of spoilage had to be worked out with faster schedules and the introduction of the refrigerator car. By 1895, it was common practice to cool the rail cars with ice and by 1906 it was even more economical when an ice plant was established at Roseville. Thereafter, Sacramento became the fruit shipping center of the west, forwarding about ninety percent of California's deciduous fruit (McGowan 1961, 383).

Historian Richard Orsi has listed and documented several ways that the Southern Pacific Railroad promoted agricultural development in California (1975). His work includes a discussion of the Sacramento Valley from 1865 to 1915. The railroad encouraged crop specialization based on local climates and soils and demonstrated that horticulture, rather than grain farming, would result in higher profits, more developed rural areas, increased land values, and a healthier urban economy and greater population density (Mills, 1890; cited in Orsi 1975, 201). Having been introduced to the dangers of uncontrolled water usage by the periodic flooding of the Sacramento River and the hydraulic mining controversy, Mills believed that California's complex water problems could only be solved by a comprehensive and long range management program aimed at balancing the often conflicting requirements of flood control, irrigation, marsh drainage and inland navigation (Orsi 1975, 204).

The railroad also took the lead in introducing foreign crops, subdividing large land tracts into small farms, and fighting hydraulic mining interests in Sacramento (Orsi 1975, 201-207). In addition, it assisted in founding local granges, improving refrigeration technology, and generally promoting the quality of life in California through *Sunset Magazine,* its promotional monthly publication. The systematic collection and dissemination of scientific information about California soils, climate, pests and water development needs was undertaken by Southern Pacific's chief land agent, Benjamin Redding. Working with agriculturalists at the University of California, the railroad (a "University on Wheels") introduced California agriculture to thousands of farmers and rural school children throughout the country (Orsi 1975, 204).

Chinese, and later, Japanese labor also made rapid picking and shipping possible. The impact of these important immigrant laborers is expanded upon in the following chapter. Rail-dependent fruit growing districts evolved in the delta south of Walnut Grove for pears, along the southeastern slopes of the Coast Ranges for cherries and apricots, and the Vacaville area with a variety of fruits. Farmers in Yolo county had been growing fruit since 1855 but were stimulated with the opening of larger markets. The Putah Creek region near Winters built its reputation around early apricots and the Sierra Nevada foothills became fruit growing centers due to their suitable climate and proximity to the rail lines. Fruit growing was further stimulated in the first part of the twentieth century with new irrigation systems and the building of canneries. It was this factor that led to fruit growing along the Feather River and in the middle of the Valley at the turn of the century (McGowan 1961, 387).

The railroad also promoted land development by groups of new immigrants into selected areas. For example, in 1877 five-hundred families had settled on Central Pacific land in Colusa and Tehama counties. By 1890, French, Dutch and Spanish groups of up to fifty families each had arrived in California bound for railroad land in Northern California (Orsi 1975, 210).

One example of this process is the land development program of the Capay Valley Land Company, a firm created by the Big Four and their families in 1887 to purchase and improve a nine-thousand acre tract west of Woodland. They extended a branch railroad line to the area, improved roads, constructed irrigation facilities and divided the land into small farms and cooperative colonies. In these centers, the railroad built stations, warehouses, commercial buildings, and parks. By 1891, 1,700 acres of the company's land had been planted with 140,000 fruit trees (Orsi 1975, 212).

As towns were stimulated by rail access to markets for the sale of agricultural products, they were also helpful in stimulating regional lumber industries. Long flumes were built to bring logs to Chico and Red Bluff whereupon finished wood products would be shipped out by rail (McGowan 1961, 231).

Town Founding

The most vital decision that could be made concerning the success of a planned town was "location, location, location." The process of urban settlement in the West was, therefore, very much a competition for a site with a competitive edge. As was true in the more humid East, the initial siting of settlements in the Sacramento Valley had much to do with river access. Water transport of farm products and lumber to Sacramento and beyond was made possible with riverboats, a much cheaper and more reliable mode of transport than wagons. With this basic concept of geography in mind, town speculators chose such places as fords, ferry sites or junctions of streams for their town sites. The locations of Marysville and Yuba City are examples of the incorporation of these principles. However, other streamside speculative settlements in the Yuba,

Sutter, and Yolo County area were not as competitive and did not linger on the landscape. One of the earliest towns on the Feather River was Nicolaus which was settled by one of Sutter's associates, Nicolaus Allgier in 1842. Not really a town, Sutter's Hock Farm was also established in that general part of the Valley in the same year. By 1850, Fremont competed with Vernon at the junction of the Feather and Sacramento Rivers both losing out to the upstream cities. Other unsuccessful competitors included Eliza which was located three miles below Marysville, Linda (not the current settlement south of Marysville) which was located just upstream on the Yuba River, Plumas City at the mouth of Reeds Creek, El Dorado City across the river from Sutter's Hock farm, Kearny on the Bear River, Featherton at the Feather River, Honcut Creek Junction and Oakland between Featherton and Marysville.

It would be acknowledged later that high ground was also a critical location factor for town founding. One example of this is the replacement of Red Bluff over Tehama as trade center of the North Valley. Colusa is also credited with surviving several floods due to its slight elevation above the river. By 1850, more than a dozen settlements calling themselves towns were located on Sacramento Valley waterways. By 1860, the number had doubled. A few river towns became smaller or disappeared in this decade such as Benton City in Tehama County located, in 1847, on the Sacramento River near the mouth of Deer Creek (whose citizens all left for the gold mines in 1850!). Another such vanished town was Boston located just north of Sacramento on the river in 1849.

In order to avoid undue repetition, major early towns founded during the period of river transport are briefly discussed here. Readers who wish to know more about the founding and building of specific communities should consult the chapter references and the bibliography for more complete information. These towns include Colusa, Monroeville, Butte City, Knight's Landing, Tehama, Princeton, and Nicolaus.

The site of Colusa was named Salmon Bend in 1848 by teamsters hauling goods to the northern mines at Old Shasta. It was named this because it was the site of an early fish weir constructed by Native Americans. It was also an important site because it was one of the few places where livestock could be watered along the west bank of the river due to clearance of riparian vegetation. Other advantages of the site were deep water for river craft and a high and dry townsite next to it. Other factors that would insure the success of this town were its reliable river traffic access, its function as a county seat, and its busy ferry operation across the Sacramento River.

Butte City was founded in 1850 as a river shipping point. It developed significantly when a ferry was established there by the Marysville-Shasta Stage Line in 1875. The town of Monroeville, modestly named by its founder Uriah P. Monroe in 1850, exhibited a great deal of growth potential but exists only as a ghost town in the modern landscape. In its brief history, Monroeville could claim to be the head of all year navigation on the Sacramento River. It was also the county seat of Colusi (Colusa) County. By 1853, however, the county seat was moved and river navigation was expanded and extended as far as Red Bluff. Thereafter Monroeville functioned as a ferry across Stony Creek and resting place for oxen and mule teams on the "west side road" to the Old Shasta diggings.

Knight's Landing was also a ferry crossing on the Sacramento River. It was settled in 1843 and laid out as a town in 1853. Princeton combined locational advantages of being on the Shasta Road, a ferry site and a steamboat landing, but unlike Knight's Landing, it never had the advantage of rail access. Likewise, the town of Jacinto, in Glenn County, was a very busy river landing. The headquarters for the large Glenn Ranch have long since disappeared.

Tehama, founded in 1850, had locational advantages of being the first community in Tehama County. It was recognized as the head of river navigation, headquarters of a successful ferry operation, and was on an important road to the mining district. Nevertheless, it was surpassed by Red Bluff in the 1870s. Today, Tehama's main distinction is that it is the smallest incorporated city in California with a 1990 population of 300. Other river towns that have survived to the present day are Washington (now West Sacramento) in Sacramento County and Grimes, Princeton, and Meridian in Colusa County.

A few towns thrived during the river period without benefit of river access. One was Woodland, founded in 1855 as an irrigated agricultural center on Cache Creek. Others were Yolo, also on Cache Creek, St. John on Stony Creek, and Pentz in Butte County.

Another factor that affected the comparative successes or failures of nineteenth century California towns was the decision of where to locate public services and institutions. For example, although no towns in the region were created as county seats, such as was done in much of the Midwest, the early growth of those that did become county seats was certainly supported by that distinction. Public services could be located according to local need or according to an investor's political influence, thereby creating the need. Woodland, Oroville, Willows, and Colusa were stimulated with their status as county seat.

John Bidwell's efforts to locate the Normal School in Chico and his failure to capture the county seat are cases in point where institutional favoritism both helped and hurt a community. College City received its name and reason for existence by the location of the Pierce Christian College there from 1876 to 1894. Not much has happened in College City (population 300) since that time.

Davisville, now Davis, also benefited from its position as a home for higher education. It should be kept in mind, though, that most of the private colleges established in Northern California were very small, even by frontier standards and probably did not have a direct effect on much of the growth of community populations. The indirect effect of promising growth potential, real or imaginary, was probably a greater influence.

Other factors that had some effect on the competitiveness of the Valley's nineteenth century settlements were aggressive promotion by town leaders, location at the end (or beginning) of trails connecting it to the outside world, and historical inertia. The principle of *first effective settlement* or historical inertia recognizes that the first settlement in a district has decided advantages over the speculative nature of those who arrive later. Most of the larger towns and cities of the Valley today owe at least some of their success to these factors.

Towns that were located at entrances to the Valley on immigrant roads, or *gateway towns*, were Sacramento, Marysville, Chico, Roseville and Redding. Others which also had this distinctive locational advantage were Vacaville and Oroville.

Although *crossroads towns* are also worth mentioning, in most cases the town created the crossroad rather than the crossroad causing the town. Frontier roads primarily served as links between towns and other places. They were, therefore, an effect rather than a cause of town success. Most were created as a result of the initiative of one or more people and many times were the result of the same promotional effort that created and stimulated the towns. For the most part, routes of early roads were not determined by physical barriers or advantages on the land. Rather, they were the direct result of need and economic development.

Vina is just such a place. This small community was laid out away from river access but nevertheless became a successful agricultural settlement. It was eventually bisected by the railroad in 1871. Likewise, the town of Sutter in Sutter County developed without benefit of river or rail access. It was originally called Camp Bethel and was operated by Methodist churches throughout California. For a short time between 1887 and 1891, the town enjoyed a major land speculation boom. Platted and named by the Sutter County Land and Improvement Company in 1887, lots were sold, schools built, and plans for a railroad and canal were discussed (Hendrix 1980, 98-99). But, by 1893, the boom bubble had broken, the promoters had fled, and the town settled down into a stable population of about 500 people.

Some towns that owe at least part of their success to an advantageous road location include Anderson (formerly American Ranch) in Shasta County and St.

John in Glenn County. Anderson prospered and St. John disappeared due to competition from nearby Monroeville.

Other towns owe their reason for creation to placer gold mining. Although most mining towns were located in the foothills surrounding the Valley, a few were located on the outwash plain of tributary rivers such as Oroville and Hamilton in Butte County. Hamilton was even distinguished as a county seat from 1850-1853 but ultimately disappeared entirely (see Kilcollins 1993).

Optimism and subsequent town growth generated by the promise of rail service in the Sacramento Valley were not unlike events happening at other places in the American West. It seemed that every county, city, town, and individual wanted a rail stop at the front door. The decision-making process used in site selections for towns during the early years of the railroad era was, as one would expect, interrelated with the route location and economic development process. Sites of pre-rail towns, many times at river landings or road crossings were aided by the addition of railroad connections. Most of the towns shown in Figure 5.1 that also appear on the 1880 map fall into this category.

A general plan used by most companies to exploit a region's potential was to connect major cities, giving the smaller ones the option of "contributing" to the railroad (with cash or land donations) or being omitted from the route entirely (2). New towns were created by the railroads themselves or by companies under their control. This process influenced town founding from the Mississippi to the Pacific coast.

Notable towns created by the Southern Pacific or by speculators in immediate anticipation of it, in the Sacramento Valley included Nord, Gridley, Biggs, Nelson, Durham, Arbuckle, Corning, Delevan, Dunnigan, Esparto, Gerber, Kirkwood, Orland, Live Oak, Germantown (Artois), Sheridan, Williams, Willows, and Winters. Additional effects of the railroads on the fate of Valley towns included: (1) the stimulating influence of bringing in new populations and investment; (2) the isolation effect on older towns left off of the new rail routes; and (3) a similar starvation effect of rail route abandonment. All of these effects are found in some degree in the Sacramento Valley experience.

The town of Loomis exemplified the stimulation effects of the railroads. First settled as a mining camp, the town became a center of fruit growing after the Southern Pacific ran its tracks through the center of town. Towns that did not grow significantly may be partly accounted for by considering the reverse of the processes described above. This is to say that those towns not having a desirable river landing site, those not having institutional support, and those having little speculative potential did not have sufficient reason for survival in the face of competition. Overall, there were far more town failures than successes in the Valley during the late nineteenth century because there were more town sites than the local population, even with new immigration, could support.

It is not known how many of these paper towns were serious investments that failed and how many reflected rather passive wishes of local farmers to found and own a town. Filing fees for plat registration were actually quite small and many local residents could probably afford to "found" a town. Competition for extensive service areas does not seem to have been significant in the formative years of towns, as evidenced by the proximity of Marysville and Yuba City and other Feather River settlements.

Site selection and promotion of new towns was one of the most important processes in urbanizing the Sacramento Valley frontier. These towns became shipping points, trade centers, seats of government, and locations of institutions. They created the still necessary interface between primary producers and transporters, manufacturers, and users of those products.

Each Valley town can be seen in terms of the functions it performed, its location, its transportation access, its situation within the context of neighboring towns and other populations, and some elements of luck or pure chance. These variables make each place unique and interesting to the resident or visitor.

People

A Closer Look at Urban Ethnic Settlement: Jewish Nodes in the Valley

Residents of the evolving towns and cities of the Sacramento Valley after the Civil War were a colorful mixture of people of assorted ethnic and religious backgrounds. One such group were the Jewish immigrants who came to the region from the East Coast and Europe. Although most people think of California cities such as San Francisco and Los Angeles as the home of Jews, many of the smaller communities of the Sacramento Valley had significant Jewish populations after the 1850s. It is easy to forget that many of the Jewish immigrants who came to the United States in the nineteenth and early twentieth centuries came from rural places in Eastern Europe and so probably preferred life in smaller towns. Their adjustment to life in a predominately non-Jewish region offers a fascinating case study of ethnic accommodation to a new environment. Their story is, in a sense, the story of tens of thousands of other immigrants who came to northern California.

According to census listings, the majority of the Valley's Jewish residents were born in Germany and Russia, although most scholars believe that most of the Jewish residents of the region were natives of Poland (Stern interview, 1982, as cited in Levenson 1985, 55). Jews were undoubtedly attracted to relocating in the Valley because of its relative accessibility to San Francisco and the attractiveness of its quasi-rural lifestyle.

Residential and Commercial Expansion

As in other parts of the country, many of the early Jewish residents of the region opened commercial establishments in the area's rapidly expanding communities. Some started their entrepreneurial careers pushing peddler's carts up and down residential streets in Oroville, Marysville, Chico, and Redding. Others arrived in the area ready to invest in small businesses with money amassed during the Gold Rush or in eastern cities. One example of this was Morris Oser, the owner of a large and prestigious department store in downtown Chico who started his commercial career as a push-cart peddler in the mining camps. As early as 1867, the nine Jewish merchants listed in Table 6.1 had opened businesses in Oroville.

Close connections existed between Jewish residents of various communities in the Valley. Many bought and sold each other's businesses, relocating often according to business demands. One example of this was Edward Kusel who was in business in Sacramento, Marysville, Chico, and Oroville (Levenson 1985, 57). In addition, Jewish merchants often owned stock in businesses other than their own. For example, three of the initial owners of the Oroville Creamery Company, established in 1867, were Nathan Goldstein, I.E. Breslauer, and Max Brooks. Others opened fruit canneries such as the Rosenberg Brothers and Company Packing House in Yuba City (see Figure 6.2). Many were quite active in civic and political affairs of their new communities.

A Jewish presence was also firmly established in the town of Chico after the mid-1860s despite the town's reputation as a white, conservative, and very Protestant place. Although never as visible politically or socially as more activist Jews in Oroville, by the 1920s, numerous Jewish businesses had been opened in Chico. The dominance of Jewish names in the listing of all non-Anglo businesses in Chico in 1922 shown in Table 6.2 is indicative of their importance in the local commercial landscape.

Jewish Religious Expression

Jews who settled in the Sacramento Valley established themselves in their new homes but remained true to their faith by forming benevolent societies and

Figure 6.2. Rosenberg Brothers and Co. Packing House in Yuba City.
Reprinted with permission from the collection of the Community Memorial Museum
of Sutter County, Yuba City, California.

Table 6.1. Jewish Businesses in Oroville, 1867

Proprietor	Type of Business
Joseph Block	Grocery Store
S. Bromberger	Dry Goods and Clothing
Newman Dzergowsky	Clothing
Daniel Friesleben	Dry Goods and Clothing
A. Goldstein and Brothers	Dry Goods and Clothing
Edward A. Kusel	Photography
B. Marks and company	Dry Goods
S. Rosenbaum	Attorney
Joseph Rothschld	Tobacco

Source: Pacific Coast Business Directory, 1867 and Levenson 1985, 53-54.

conducting worship services. While virtually all of the Jewish residents of Valley towns were non-Orthodox in their beliefs, most did practice their religion regularly. Rarely able to carry out these practices on a daily basis, most pioneer Jews did what they could to preserve their religious ties. In a number of frontier towns, a lay leader stepped forward who for years organized and led communal worship and presided at marriage and burial services, which, in accordance with Jewish law, could be conducted by any knowledgeable Jew in the presence of two witnesses (Rocklin 1984, 30). One of the earliest of these lay leaders was Mr. Leo, brother of Reverend Ansel Leo of New York, who moved to the town of Shasta and founded the Shasta Hebrew Benevolent Society in 1857. According to the local paper (Giles 1949, 212):

At a meeting of the Israelites of Shasta, Mr. H. Leo was unanimously appointed president and S. Goldstone, secretary. Mr. Leo stated the object of the meeting to be the necessity of an immediate formation of a congregation to observe, in an appropriate manner, the Day of Atonement . . . to invite the Israelites of Red Bluffs to attend our religious meeting on Yom Kipper . . . taking into consideration the necessity of procuring a Hebrew burial ground.

Table 6.2. Non-Anglo Businesses in Chico, 1922

Business	Location
Driess Cut Glass	148 Broadway
Grawitz Bookbinder	4019 3rd Street
Oser's Department Store	240-244 Main Street
Greek Restaurant	834 Oroville Street
Bibbero and Levby Clothing	4444 2nd Street
Breslauer Clothing	4424 3rd Street
Feingold Clothing	827 Main Street
Pretzel and Jacob Clothing	805 Main Street
Koltanowski Clothing	243 Broadway
Rosenblum Clothing	4430 3rd Street
Vartabedian Hats	231 Main Street
Drouillard Milliners	624 Main Street
Kuhlke Milliners	314 Broadway
Chiapella Occulist	336 Broadway
Dreiss Diamonds	138 Broadway
Milano Hotel	1041 Cherry Street
Ono Koshiro General Merchandise	4242 4rd Street
Quistini and Mertagna Grocers	802 Main Street
Angal Meats	4430 9th Street
French-American Laundry	741 Broadway
Santee's Enameling and Painting	501 Flume Street
Goebel Pianos and Talking Machines	4420 2nd Street
Zink Photography	234 Broadway
Souza Vulcanizers	Main and 1st Streets

Source: Chico and Oroville Polk City Directory, 1922.

Weekly services were organized in other towns in the next decades. In 1877, the *American Israelite* reported that High Holy Day services were held in Marysville with Jews from Chico in attendance. Marysville Jews had organized a Hebrew Benevolent Society as early as 1853. This group, like similar ones in Oroville and Redding, organized High Holy Day events and maintained Jewish cemeteries in their respective communities. Chico's Jewish residents met regularly in homes and rented meeting halls as late as 1969 when their well organized Congregation Beth Israel purchased their own synagogue in Chapmantown, just southeast of the city's downtown.

In Redding, no Jewish formal organization for worship existed until 1976, when the Redding Jewish Community Center (later renamed the Congregation of Beth Israel of Redding in 1979) was founded by a group of approximately twenty families and individuals. The group has grown and is now affiliated with the Union of American Hebrew Congregations, the national organization of Reform Jews. The group's charter membership consisted of thirty-four adults in twenty-two households (Weissberg 1985, 3). As an example of the diversity of Jewish occupations now found in typical Valley communities, professions represented within Redding's Beth Israel membership include teachers, hospital administrator, lawyer, retirees, judge, mental health counselor, hairdresser, jewelry maker, mail delivery person, journalist, liquor and cigar store owner, archaeologist, psychiatric social worker, secretary, real estate owner, travel agent, and female log scaler (Smith 1986, 26-27).

Landscape

The total population of Sacramento Valley by counties is summarized in Table 6.3. This table reveals tremendous increases between 1850 and 1990 in every county. Table 6.4 provides a closer look at one county's racial breakdown for the years 1850 through 1900. These tables provide further evidence of the continuing demographic and landscape changes occurring in the Valley in the late 19th century. The next chapter details these ongoing changing patterns during the years following the turn of the century.

Table 6.3. Population of Sacramento Valley Counties, 1850-1990

County	1850	1880	1920	1930	1950	1970	1980	1990
Butte	3,574	18,721	30,030	34,093	64,930	101,969	143,851	182,120
Colusa	115	13,188	9,290	10,258	11,651	12,430	12,791	16,275
Glenn	*	*	11,853	10,935	15,448	17,521	21,350	24,798
Sacramento	9,087	34,390	91,029	141,999	277,140	531,498	783,381	1,041,219
Shasta	378	9,492	13,361	13,927	36,413	77,640	115,715	147,036
Solano	3,444	5,159	10,115	14,618	26,239	41,935	52,246	64,412
Sutter	*	9,301	12,882	13,866	19,216	29,517	38,888	49,625
Tehama	1,086	11,772	17,105	23,644	40,640	91,778	113,374	141,092
Yolo	9,673	11,284	10,375	11,331	24,420	44,736	49,733	58,228
Yuba	580	18,475	40,602	40,834	104,833	169,941	235,203	340,421

Source: Untied States Census of Population 1850, 1880, 1920, 1930, 1950, 1970, 1980, 1990.
*Census data not available.

Table 6.4. Butte County Population According to Race, 1850-1900

Race	1850	1860	1870	1880	1890	1900
White	3,541	9,737	9,197	14,270	15,864	15,733
Black	33	71	84	136	223	106
Chinese		2,177	2,082	3,793	1,530	712
Native American		121	40	522	319	201
Japanese						3
Native Born		7,509	7,428	12,488	14,141	14,349
Foreign Born		4,597	3,975	6,233	3,808	2,868

Source: United States Census of Population, 1850-1900 and Book, 1974, 100.

Chapter 7

Organization

As the last two chapters indicated, by the turn of the century, much of the Sacramento Valley had developed into a region of fertile farms and thriving communities. Domesticated landscapes fanned out across the vast plain north of the state's capital city at Sacramento. They encompassed tens of thousands of acres of newly irrigated land occupied by people from many parts of the world. Much, if not most of the population increases were the result of active work by land speculators who promoted and sold land for fulfillment of the dreams of residents of such places as Nebraska and Kansas, Utah and Idaho, as well as foreign areas.

The largest towns and cities in the Valley in 1910 are shown in Figure 7.1. Other smaller settlement nodes also existed at this time. As in today's landscape, some of these villages were tucked among rich agricultural fields and orchards, invisible to most travelers. Typical of these rapidly developing settlements was the community of Richvale in the heart of the Valley. This town was also unique among other places in the region in several ways because more than ninety percent of its earliest residents were natives of just one country—Sweden. Their story adds yet another dimension to the Valley's increasingly multicultural population and its impacts on the land.

People

Swedes in Richvale

Unlike most other Sacramento Valley agricultural towns, Richvale, first laid out in 1909, was not established until after the turn of the century. Surrounded by fertile, well drained soils, Richvale may have more closely lived up to the many promises made by developers and land companies in the Valley than any other community in the region. Numerous articles in glossy magazines such as

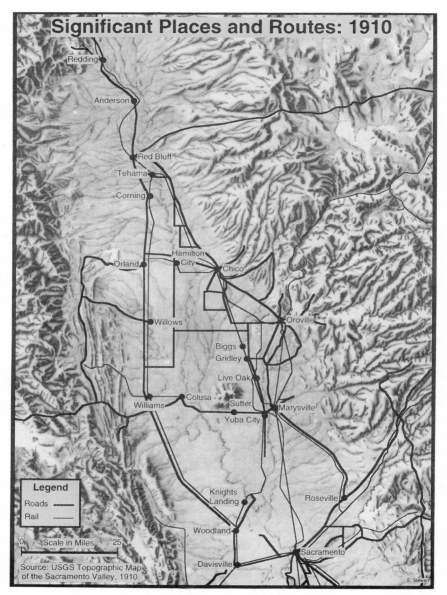

Figure 7.1. Significant Places and Routes, 1910.

Sunset and alluring brochures promised that prosperous towns would spring up almost overnight and wealth would be had by all who would come to settle this vast fertile and nearly "perfect" Sacramento Valley land.

Richvale was certainly a grand place for dreamers. Among the earliest buyers attracted to the area (formerly called Selby Switch) was Samuel Nunn, a Chico attorney, and four other Chico businessmen interested in investing in rural land for the establishment of new agricultural colonies. After purchasing land around Selby Switch in 1909, this investment group decided to call their proposed new town "Richvale" because of its promise of providing rich farm land. They likewise christened their new corporation the Richvale Land Company.

The optimistic team behind the establishment of the Richvale Land Company quickly bought and subdivided their land, laid out the town of Richvale, and began negotiations with the Sutter Butte Canal Company to bring much needed water onto their new property via a canal from the Cherokee Strip. By early 1911, the Richvale Land Company had completed the subdivision of several thousand acres into eleven colonies from just north of Richvale as far south as the town of Biggs. Having paid $10-$30 per acre, the investors planned to charge $100-$150 an acre to potential farmers who would be coaxed to settle the area and turn it into the garden spot of Butte County (Willson 1979, 28).

Toward this end, S.T. Axtell, vice president of the new corporation, made several trips to the Midwest to entice hopeful settlers into buying land in the Richvale area. Focusing his attention on experienced farmers in Nebraska and Kansas, Axtell enhanced his enthusiastic sales pitch with displays of newly printed photographs showing productive orange and olive orchards in Oroville and lush fields of pumpkins, alfalfa, corn and beans already established near Gridley and Biggs. Axtell's most important decision for the future success of the colony was enlisting the help of a Swedish immigrant real estate broker, Thomas Carlson, in Holdrege, Nebraska. Carlson organized and led tours of the Richvale area for prospective buyers. He strongly encouraged his Swedish neighbors and their families to be the first to travel to Richvale. His efforts contributed greatly to the establishment of a dominantly Swedish community in Richvale over the course of the next three years.

By 1915, using lumber supplied by the local distributer of the Chico Diamond Match Company, early Swedish residents with names like Lundberg, Dahlstrom, Carlson, Rystrom, Peterson, and Lofgren built houses, along with a grocery store, church, school, hardware store, blacksmith shop and hotel. The Biggs *Sunshine Valley News* listed new settlers arriving in the Richvale area nearly every week. These farmers, salesmen, well drillers, grocery store owners, brickmasons, carpenters, and homemakers traveled overland from Nebraska and

Kansas, arriving with as many of their possessions as they could carry with them by train and wagon in this pre-U-Haul era. By 1911, even the Greek laborers who had worked on the local Southern Pacific Railroad were fired and replaced by "white" (aka Scandinavian) laborers (*Sunshine Valley News,* May 5, 1911, 1). The list of property owners summarized in Box 7.A demonstrates the Swedish nature of the area by 1924.

Box 7.A
Property Owners Shown on Butte County Plat Maps
Richvale, 1924

The following list of names was tabulated from Butte County Plat Subdivision maps of Richvale found in California State University, Chico Meriam Library's Special Collections Division. Names were counted from all ten Richvale colonies. It is interesting to note that Swedish names were found in all colonies and did not seem to cluster in any one part of the area. All Scandinavian names (including Swedes, Danes and Norwegians) are underlined on this list.

Meikle, <u>Anderson</u>, <u>Grell</u>, <u>Olson</u>, Burnham, <u>Peterson</u>, <u>Lofgren</u>, Nataas, Graves, <u>Hanson</u>, <u>Hendrickson</u>, Bradley and Rolls, <u>Sunblad</u>, Simons, <u>Axtell</u>, Gocke, <u>Baker</u>, <u>Swensen</u>, <u>Haare</u>, <u>Johnson</u>, Dillon and <u>Robertson</u>, Ruenkler, Gutenfelder, Sipes, <u>Johnson</u>, Richards, <u>Carlson</u>, Reed, Pierce, Armstrong, Baldy, Downin, Kibler, Culver, Elliot, Dwyer, Emmanuel, King, <u>Burke</u>, <u>Nelson</u>, Culver, <u>Knutsen</u>, Deay, Evans, Rhoades, Plank, <u>Nystrom</u>, <u>Petersen</u>, <u>Lundberg</u>, <u>Olson</u>, <u>Lofgren</u>, Lantz, Reed, <u>Olsen</u>, <u>Broers</u>, Guttenfelder, <u>Hanson</u>, Harris, <u>Wileman</u>, <u>Fagerstone</u>, <u>Winter</u>, Mahill, Frouch, <u>Lindberg</u>, <u>Christensen</u>, <u>Dickerson</u>, Evans, Graham, <u>Hill</u>, <u>Bloom</u>, Lattemore, <u>Ingram</u>, <u>Olsson</u>, <u>Johnson</u>, <u>Magnerson</u>

Richvale's social and cultural connections remained distinctly Swedish in the early and mid-decades of the twentieth century. Swedish was the predominate language spoken in local homes and on the streets of the evolving town since very few of the earliest residents (who had only been exposed to German-speaking and other Swedish neighbors in Nebraska) could speak or understand English. Swedish cultural traditions and religious expression linger today with Swedish holiday celebrations and religious connections. Until the late 1930s, Swedish church services were held every other Sunday. Today's Swedish Evangelical Free Church continues this longstanding and important tradition in Richvale with the weekly services.

Not all was perfect for the early settlers in their new life in the Sacramento Valley, however. Despite promises of perfect soils and an ideal climate for producing a variety of fruits, nuts, and field crops, these early Richvale residents were in for a real shock when they arrived in the area. Richvale's adobe soils were a far cry from the well drained sandy loam advertised in other parts of Butte County. In addition, these newcomers originally had been shown photographs of fertile and productive land near Oroville and Gridley that was already under irrigation. Richvale's irrigation system was not even due for completion by the Sutter Butte Canal Company until 1912. These limitations dashed hopes of raising traditional garden and field crops.

But the new immigrants were unwilling to give up so easily. Having already been through many challenges in their adjustment to problems faced in their homeland and in the American Midwest, the Swedes were a hardy and versatile group of immigrants and they soon rebounded by switching their attention to the cultivation of rice. Their willingness to take a risk and try something completely new in an entirely new place set the stage for the development of the Sacramento Valley's most productive and profitable crop of the entire twentieth century—rice.

But they did not have an easy start with this new crop. Not only were Swedish farmers completely uninformed about rice growing techniques, it was a completely foreign crop to them. Except for the well loved holiday delicacy of rice pudding, rice was not a part of the Swedish diet. If it hadn't been for the establishment of the United States Department of Agriculture Rice Experiment Station near Biggs in 1912, early farmers might have given up on rice growing and returned to Nebraska.

The Biggs Rice Experiment Station, the first cereal research station established on the Pacific Coast by the Department of Agriculture, has remained a focal point for rice growers since its founding. It has long had a unique history of management since it is organized and run by a combination of the rice growers themselves and local, state, and federal government agencies. This longstanding cooperative agreements is codified in the their Articles of Incorporation spelled out in detail in Box 7.B.

Throughout 1911, rice was planted by a few hardy souls on Richvale adobe soils. By fall, these earliest crops of rice had matured and were ready for harvest (Ellen 1993, 19). By 1912 and 1913, the Richvale Land Company was nationally advertising the potential profit of growing rice in an effort to bring in new settlers. By the winter of 1914-1915, despite continuing problems with the experimental crop such as field flooding, inadequate or poorly timed water delivery, and other problems, rice had become the dominant crop in the Richvale and Biggs area and remained its most viable crop throughout the rest of the century. Thanks to the early efforts of these Richvale farmers, rice was well established in the Sacramento Valley by the end of the 1920s (see Figure 7.2).

Box 7.B
Biggs Rice Experiment Station Cooperative Agreement

The specific and primary purposes for which this corporation is formed are: To cooperate with the United States Department of Agriculture and the State Department of California and the inhabitants of the Sacramento Valley, California, in determining by experiments the best strain of rice and other crops adapted to the soils of the Sacramento Valley, and also to cooperate as aforesaid, in determining by experiments the proper and best methods of grading soil products, the marketing and transportation of crops, and the procuring of pure seeds, improved livestock, and the introduction of improved farming machinery; and to study and determine the proper methods of draining, irrigating, planting, cultivating and fertilizing lands in the Sacramento Valley and preventing and controlling plant and animal diseases in said locality, or elsewhere, for the mutual benefit and general welfare of its shareholders, members, and patrons who may be natural and legal persons.

Today, a distinctive Swedish economic and cultural imprint remains in the Richvale area. Major rice growing corporations such as the Lundberg Farms and other family corporations such as GRACO (Gieger, Rystrom, Anderson, and Company) and Hybrid Farms controlled by the Carlson family (descendants of T.A. Carlson from Sweden by way of Nebraska) have made their name and family fortunes in rice growing. Numerous street names in the community still bear Swedish names. For the astute observer, an overall sense of Scandinavian order remains visible on the landscape of this Sacramento Valley town.

Lundberg Family Farms is perhaps the best known company of local Swedish rice growers. Relative latecomers to the Richvale area, Albert and Frances Lundberg left their Western Nebraska farm in the 1930s with their four sons—Eldon, Wendell, Harlan, and Homer. The four brothers, who now operate the Lundberg Family Farms, were deeply influenced by their ecologically-minded father, who had observed the effects of over use of the soils during his Dust Bowl years farming in the Midwest. According to Harlan: "He didn't really fit in with the thinking of the time. . . . He always had the attitude that he wanted to make the soil better" (*A Partnership With Nature* 1994, 1). Influenced by their father, the Lundbergs have spent decades experimenting and investing in the develop-ment of farming practices that put their ecological principles to work. Box 7.C details the process of rice growing over the course of a year.

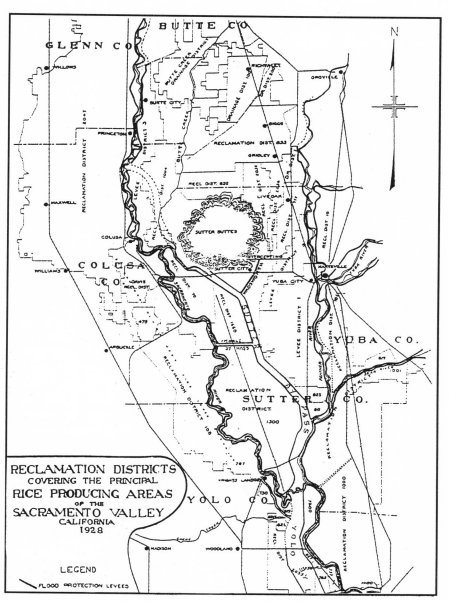

Figure 7.2. Source: Weir 1929, 34.

Box 7.C
Swedish Farmers in the Sacramento Valley

Rice planting occurs in April and May. On our Premium fields and organic fields we run a flail mower over the vetch, which chops the cover crop about six inches above the ground, creating a mat of organic matter on top of the soil. At this point on a Premium field, we chisel, disc, and level as conventional farmers do, preparing the soils for aerial planting.

On the Organic field, we use a special drill to plant the rice right through the vetch mat into the soil. We arrived at this method after many years of experimenting with planting techniques, such as planting rice in rows, injecting the seed into the ground with water, flying the seed with an airplane, and broadcasting the seed onto a dry field then irrigating. "We use the drill because this method controls the weeds best, which is a primary concern in Organic rice production," Homer states. "The hearty rice plant is able to germinate and come up through the vetch, while the weeds, without adequate light, do not get a good start."

Wehani, our russet-colored aromatic long grain, requires a special planting method—we broadcast the seed with a different type of dril and then apply water.

Many ducks and pheasants make their nests in our fields at this time of year. We look for the nests before working in the field, placing stakes around them to protect them from the equipment.

Source: A Partnership with Nature, 1994, 6.

Latter Day Saints

At about the same time as Swedes were arriving at the Richvale colonies, another neighboring community was developing its own land colonies and its own unique immigrant flavor. The town of Gridley, located in the very heart of the Heartland, is known today primarily for its kiwis and fruit orchards, and as the setting for the annual Butte County Fair. Few visitors realize the important role one early immigrant group, the Latter Day Saints, played in the development of the community.

Gridley, first known as Martinsburgh, was a quiet, pastoral place during Gold Rush years. Sheep roamed its open pastures as wheat ripened in annual cycles in nearby fields. It was also reported in the local paper in 1865 that "an extensive agricultural district producing wheat, barley, corn, potatoes, and other vegetables in prolific quantities" existed just south of the settlement near the crossroads hamlet of Martinsburgh (*The Butte Record*, March, 1865, n.p.). This traveler's stopover was superseded by the development of the town of Gridley after the railroad line was put through in 1869.

In a deal with the Central Pacific Railroad, George Gridley, the town's namesake, traded the site of the proposed railroad depot for a large acreage just west of town (McGie 1957, n.p.). The paper town of Gridley was surveyed in 1870 and laid out by a railroad employee at right angles to the northwest-southeast alignment of the tracks (*Book of Maps,* Number 1A, p. 66, June 3, 1871). It was an especially good time for railroad linkages to be established through Sacramento Valley agricultural towns such as Gridley since the demands of the Civil War made the successful shipping of wheat out of the region to more populated parts of the country in the East a matter of national necessity.

Subsequent decades enlarged the agrarian community significantly. Numerous successful businesses, a lumber yard and planing mill, schools, churches and social organizations, and even a small cannery were built before the turn of the century. But nothing equaled the establishment of a more expanded irrigation system and the subdivision of rural land around the community of Gridley in influencing sudden and unparalleled population growth in the area.

Life in Gridley was touted by speculators and land developers by an impressive system of promises for newcomers. Brochures like the one reproduced in Figure 7.3 hailed the area as California's "Land of Milk and Honey." This advertisement and others like it appeared regularly in the *Gridley Herald* between 1906 and 1908, enticing outsiders who believed that (as the ad states so convincingly): "A little farm, well tilled, is the ambition of about half the human race."

This new growth was fueled by the organization of the Butte County Canal Company in 1902. Its efforts made it possible for water to be brought directly to Gridley from the Feather River. This water, along with the "hustle" of the San Francisco-based California Irrigated Land Company who subdivided the Gridley colonies into ten, twenty, and forty acre parcels in 1905 launched a new movement west for thousands of newcomers. Advertisements were sent to Utah, Nevada, Idaho, and throughout the Midwest by this fledgling but hopeful development company. The first and largest group to respond to the ads for well watered, fertile land were experienced irrigation agriculturalists from Utah and Idaho, the Mormons.

Following the arrival of the first Latter Day Saint pioneer from Utah in April, 1906 and another from Dewsnup, Idaho in the summer of 1906 (to improve his health), twelve other members of the LDS church from Rexburg, Idaho arrived on a cold evening in November, 1906, and 150 more Mormon colonists followed them in the spring of 1907. Most concentrated in Colony #4.

Figure 7.3. California Irrigated Land Company Advertisement.
Source: *Gridley Herald*, Gridley, California, 1906-1908.

The *Gridley Herald* announced the arrival and settlement of more hearty and hopeful "Saints" from Utah, Idaho, and Arizona all through 1907. By 1912, Latter Day Saints had arrived in large numbers from these states as well as from Nevada, Canada, Mexico, and points farther east (The Reunion Committee 1980, 4). Notes from the journal of one of the sons of these early pioneers, Robert Fife, provides an interesting glimpse of images and perceptions of a typical Mormon of the region by this traveler from Metropolis, Nevada. A summary of his words is provided verbatim in Box 7.D.

By 1916, of the 2,634 Latter Day Saints living in the state of California, 619 were living in the Gridley area of Butte County. By the end of 1924, with the arrival of the last major migration from Metropolis, Nevada, Gridley had become the largest settlement of Mormons in the state.

These early colonists soon established a unique and binding sense of community in the area. The southern part of town literally became a Mormon colony. Called Liberty by its inhabitants, over half the street names in this part of Gridley today continue to bear Mormon names (Hendrix 1994, 3). A church was built at the corner of Sycamore and Vermont Streets in 1912. A few years later witnessed the establishment of a Mormon Sunday School in nearby Biggs and the organization of a Relief Society. The Walter Little family first experimented with the planting of Gridley's now famous peaches in the area. Their successes, along with the successful orchards of other Mormon farmers in the area, resulted in the construction of the Libby Fruit Cannery in Gridley in 1920.

In the 1940s, this religious community received a surge of new residents as missionaries to Canada brought brides back home with them from Saskatchewan, Manitoba, and Ontario. Their arrival added energy and numbers to church membership patterns in the area. Today's new Stake Center on Spruce Street in Gridley establishes the presence of the large number of Mormons still residing in the area.

Although other groups of colonists settled in the community in the coming decades, Mormons have retained their social, religious, and cultural distinctiveness over the years and helped create a sense of community in Gridley that still possesses traditional values and conservative politics that linger well into the 1990s.

To understand the geographical distribution of LDS settlers in the Sacramento Valley, Box 7.E is provided as a summary of church-related boundary decisions over the years. As explained in this box, church structure directly relates to this religious group's population base.

Box 7.D
A Mormon Pioneer in Gridley Speaks
1924

The following excerpt is taken from the journal of Robert Fife, son of one of Gridley's early Mormon settlers. Mr. Fife's father had been born in Ogden, Utah and, along with several thousand other Mormons, had resettled in a place called Metropolis, Nevada when he was quite young (for a dramatic description of conditions in this part of Nevada, see Dale L. Morgan's The Humboldt: Highroad of the West, Lincoln: University of Nebraska Press, 1985, pp. 326-337). After hearing about the "Promised Land" of Gridley, California, the elder Mr. Fife took a train from Metropolis to the Sacramento Valley. Riding in an open car down the Feather River Canyon, Fife arrived in Marysville about 10:00 in the morning. Traveling north to Gridley to be near other Mormons, Fife recalls:

My father couldn't believe what he was seeing. Fruit was everywhere. Dad thought this was Paradise. He had seen enough. This, surely was the land of plenty and he wanted his family to partake of it.

Impressed with the productivity and promise of his new home, Fife later traveled back to Metropolis carrying samples of fruits and vegetables grown in Gridley with him. His efforts to impress his friends and family proved costly to their Nevada community, however. Will Fife eventually encouraged eighteen families to come to Gridley from Metropolis, thereby eliminating the Mormon presence in this part of Nevada entirely! By 1912, Gridley had the largest community of Latter Day Saints outside of Utah.

Japanese Settlement

Euro-American agricultural colonists were not the only newcomers to the Valley during the years before World War I. Although, as related in Chapter 5, most of the region's Chinese had been forced out by the turn of the century by severe anti-Asian laws and attitudes, another group of Asians, the Japanese, soon moved in to fill the labor gap. Although the earliest Japanese settlers in California arrived as part of the Wakamatsu Tea and Silk Colony in El Dorado County in 1869 and others came from Hawaii after working on sugar plantations, the great majority did not arrive in the American West until several decades later (*Five Views* 1988, 161-162). Many Japanese left their homeland around the turn of the century to escape extreme poverty. Others ventured out of Japan in the aftermath of the Russo-Japanese War in 1904-05. Table 7.1 compares Japanese, Chinese, and Native American residents in Valley counties between 1900 and 1920.

Box 7.E
The Geography of LDS Church Structure
in the Sacramento Valley

The Church of the Latter Day Saints organizes its members by dividing them up into geographical areas. A Ward (similar to a Catholic parish) may include everyone within city limits or include those living in half a county. Wherever the lines are drawn, the location of a person's house determines their assigned Ward. (Some Wards in metropolitan Utah are only a few blocks wide and deep!) A Ward consists of about 299 families. If it exceeds 388+ families, it will be divided into two Wards and the process begins again. When an area has 5-6 Wards, it becomes an organized Stake (the word Stake refers to the stakes used to anchor the Tabernacle of the Old Testament). When a Stake reaches 18-21+ Wards, it then usually splits into two Stakes.

The first Stakes organized in the Sacramento Valley were the Sacramento and Gridley Stakes, both organized in 1934. The Gridley Stake had Wards in Corning, Nevada City, Yuba City, Oroville, Gridley, and Liberty. This Stake had about 1,500 members.

The Church then continued to expand until the Gridley Stake had to be divided into two in 1972. The combined membership of the new Gridley and Chico Stakes was approximately 6,500.

The Yuba City Stake now includes about 122,600 members. This Stake is made up of Wards from Loma Rica, Colusa, four Wards in Yuba City, two Wards in Marysville, and a Hmong Branch.

Butte County is currently divided into two Stakes. The northern Stake is called the Chico Stake and includes Wards in Williams, Orland, three Wards in Paradise and six Wards in Chico with a total membership of 4,050. The original Gridley Stake now includes four Wards in Oroville, three Wards in Gridley, and two Wards in Liberty.

Source: Hendrix 1994, 2-4.

Japanese migration and settlement in California continued without interruption until 1907-08 when agitation from hostile politicians, white supremacists, and labor union activists culminated in the passage of the "Gentleman's Agreement" (*Five Views* 1988, 162). This act blocked further immigration by Japanese workers; however, their wives and children were still allowed to enter the United States for purposes of settlement. Many arrived at the port of San Francisco as "picture brides" for men already living in California. This new law significantly changed the demographics of the state's Japanese population as increasing numbers of women and children and decreasing numbers of new male entries tipped the scale in favor of families instead of single young men as in earlier years. Female Japanese immigrants accounted for forty percent of all

Table 7.1. Native American, Chinese, and Japanese Populations in Sacramento Valley Counties, 1900-1920

County	Native Americans			Chinese			Japanese		
	1900	1910	1920	1900	1910	1920	1900	1910	1920
Butte	201	298	225	712	572	289	365	295	423
Colusa	121	169	112	274	218	167	53	140	275
Glenn	24	32	24	227	129	130	14	33	122
Sacramento	24	62	53	3,254	2,143	1,954	1,200	3,874	5,800
Shasta	862	750	610	102	88	25	20	42	3
Solano	2	1	7	903	811	669	870	824	1,017
Sutter	20	18	12	226	79	42	155	134	373
Tehama	99	94	125	720	309	161	143	98	95
Yolo	28	32	42	346	198	175	410	789	1,152
Yuba	24	16	46	719	493	359	56	336	355

Source: United States Census of Population, 1900, 1910, and 1920.

arrivals between 1910 and 1920, three-quarters being wives of residents of Hawaii or the United States (Thomas 1952, 7).

By the turn of the century, Japanese laborers had become important contributors to the agricultural sector of the Sacramento Valley. As early as 1891, three Japanese came to work in a pear orchard in Biggs. By 1893, the United States Immigration Commission reported that several other Japanese were employed as hop pickers in the Marysville district (Itamura 1971, 29). At least three hundred Japanese farm workers were employed by the Durst Hop Ranch near Wheatland in 1906 during the harvest season (Nakamura Interview, 1969, as cited in Itamura 1971, 29). Others were employed at the Reed Ranch in Yuba County (managed by a Japanese immigrant) and by other smaller operations set up in mid-Sacramento Valley counties. It is estimated that in the year 1909, Japanese farm workers made up more than fifty percent of the state's agricultural employees. Many of these single, young male workers traveled between fields and orchards in the Sacramento Valley and the Imperial Valley staying in Japanese-owned and operated boarding houses.

Between 1900 and 1909, Japanese laborers began to purchase small farms and plant vegetables, vineyards, and orchards. Communities of exclusively Japanese land owners developed in California's Central Valley including one in south Sacramento in the town of Florin, and two in the San Joaquin Valley. These Japanese land owners became especially well known for their production of strawberries in the Sacramento area and their early experiments with rice farming in Butte County. Here, at the Biggs Rice Experiment Station a few miles from the newly arriving Swedish farmers at Richvale, Japanese immigrant Kenju Ikuta first demonstrated that rice could be produced commercially in the area (*Five Views* 1988, 166).

As the recent seminal work on the Japanese in Butte County by historian Archie McDonald (1993) conveys in such rich detail, Japanese in this Valley county formed an important part of both the rural and urban scene. Many opened small businesses, such as Mr. Kubo's grocery store in Gridley (1903), Ogen and Terada's laundry in Oroville (1905), and Jodo's restaurant in Chico (1906). Early Japanese residents of Butte County also operated boarding houses, pool halls, and barber shops to meet the local Japanese community's needs (McDonald 1993, 28). According to city directory listings, more Japanese businesses were added over the next two decades. These included new restaurants, a general merchandise store, laundries, a fish and poultry market, and numerous other businesses in widely dispersed Butte County towns.

Fruit and vegetable farmers also cultivated land outside the city limits of these Butte County communities. At least nine Japanese families rented land from the Morehead ranch just west of town, growing strawberries and other products for local consumption (McDonald 1993, 56).

Although Butte and Colusa counties also had sizable numbers of Japanese residents by 1910, the main center of Japanese cultural and economic activities north of Sacramento was the multicultural town of Marysville. Japanese immigrants living in Butte, Glenn, Colusa, Sutter, and Yuba counties traveled to Marysville to Japantown, located at the site of the town's old Chinatown to renew friendships, make religious connections at the Marysville Buddhist Church, and shop for specialty goods at Japanese markets (see Figure 7.4). City directory listings for pre-World War II Japantown businesses in Marysville and Sacramento are shown on Table 7.2. This summary illustrates the importance of these two places and reveals a highly developed commercial network of services for Japanese residents throughout the Sacramento Valley.

This well organized and highly visible Japanese community in Yuba and Sutter counties was the direct result of in-migration of new Japanese from the same prefectures and villages as earlier residents. Intense "chain migration" resulted in over forty percent of the 149 Japanese families in the area in 1940 originating from just two prefectures in Japan—Hiroshima and Kumamoto. Of the families with Issei family heads (Japanese-born immigrants) from Hiroshima, eighteen percent were from the same small village (Itamura 1971, 31). Table 7.3 summarizes the specific place of origins of all Issei family Heads in Yuba and Sutter counties in 1940. As with other immigrants settling in the Sacramento Valley, this table establishes without a doubt that word of mouth was the best advertisement luring newcomers into the area throughout most of the region's settlement history.

The Buddhist Church in Marysville became a focal point for the Japanese community soon after it was organized in 1908. After meeting in members' homes for many years, the congregation finally leased a building at B and 2nd Streets for services in 1918. After a fire destroyed this building in 1930, the energetic congregation began making plans for the construction of their own Buddhist Church in the heart of Japantown. This new church was dedicated in 1931. It has since sponsored annual celebrations, language and culture classes, and even athletic teams and remains an important symbolic linkage among Japanese residents of the North State.

These close-knit Japanese communities in the North State were severely disrupted by the onset of World War II as thousands of Valley Japanese were evacuated from their homes in 1942. The signing of Executive Order 9006 had divided the state's Japanese population into 108 areas on the west coast for resettlement in distant camps. During the spring and summer of 1942, over

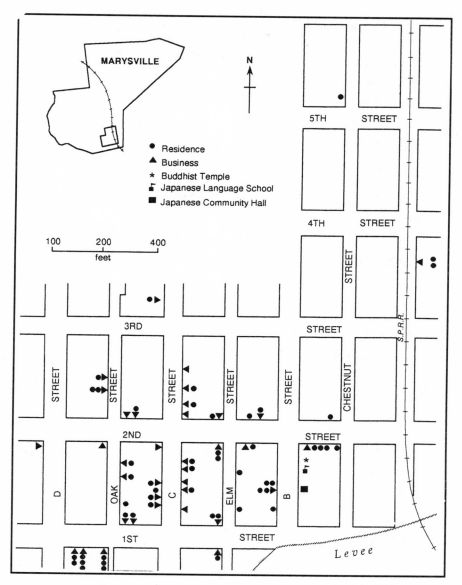

Figure 7.4. Marysville's Japanese Town, 1941.
Source: Redrawn from Itamura 1971, 41.

Table 7.2. Japanese Businesses in Sacramento and Marysville, 1940

Type of Business	Sacramento	Marysville
Auto Garage	1	4
Auto Repair	2	
Banks	1	
Barbers	15	3
Barber/Pool Hall		1
Beauty Shops	2	2
Billiards	4	1
Boarding House		2
Boarding House/Grocery Store		1
Boarding House/Pool Hall		2
Boarding House/Tofu Shop		1
Clothes Pressers and Cleaners	6	1
Clothes Dealers	6	
Confectionery/Ice Cream	1	
Contractors	10	
Dressmakers	2	2
Druggists	5	1
Dry Goods	7	1
Fish Dealers	5	
Florists	3	
Fruit Dealers	9	
Furniture Dealers	1	
Gasoline Stations	1	
Grocers, Retail	33	5

Table 7.2. Japanese Businesses in Sacramento and Marysville, 1940

Type of Business	Sacramento	Marysville
Grocers, Wholesale	1	
Hardware	1	
Hotel		2
Insurance Agency		1
Jewelers	2	
Laundries	8	2
Lawyers	2	
Liquors	6	
Massage	2	
Men's Furnishings	2	
Newspapers	1	
Notions	2	
Photographers	2	
Poultry	1	
Produce	1	
Radio Sets	2	
Real Estate	1	
Restaurants	20	1
Shoe Dealers	2	
Shoe Repairs	8	1
Soda Fountain		2
Soda Fountain and Appliances		1
Sporting Goods	2	
Taxi Service		1

Table 7.2. Japanese Businesses in Sacramento and Marysville, 1940

Type of Business	Sacramento	Marysville
Vegetable market		2
Watch and Jewelry Repair	2	
Total	187	40

Source: Sacramento City Directory, 1940, Hardwick, 1986, p. 119 and
New World Sun Japanese Directory, 1941; Frank Nakamura, James
Nakagawa, and Dan Nishita, Personal Interviews, August, 1970, adapted
from Itamura, 1971, p. 39.

110,000 persons of Japanese ancestry, two-thirds of whom were natural born citizens of the United States, had been evacuated to internment camps in the interior of the United States.

Sacramento Valley organizations such as the Native Sons, the Farm Bureau, the American Legion, and even the Joint Immigration Commission spoke in favor of the removal of both the Issei and Nisei (second generation Japanese born in the United States). The following detailed historical account of the official statement of the Joint Immigration Commission captures the venomous reaction against the Japanese in the state (tenBroek 1954, 78-79):

> Had the warnings been heeded—had the federal and state authorities been on the alert, and rigidly enforced the Exclusion Law and the Alien Land Law, had the Japanese propaganda agencies in this country been silenced, had legislation been enacted, denying citizenship to the offspring of an alien ineligible for citizenship; had the Japs been prohibited from colonizing in strategic locations, had not Jap dollars been so eagerly sought by the white land owners and businessmen; had a deaf ear not been turned to the honeyed words of the Japs and pro-Japs, had Japan been denied the privilege of using California as a breeding ground for dual citizens, the treacherous Japs probably would not today be at war with the United States.

The original plan for the evacuation of all Japanese from the west coast was not intended to limit their movement once they were outside prohibited zones. With this plan in mind, two assembly centers at Manzanar, California and Parker, Utah were first constructed by the army to house these evacuees until they could move to the midwest and east coasts and find employment and housing (Itamura 1971, 65). But extreme pressure from politicians and the

Table 7.3. Origins of Issei Family Heads in the
Yuba/Sutter Area, 1940

Prefecture	Number	Percentage
Hiroshima	81	54
Kumamoto	24	16
Wakayama	9	6
Yamaguchi	6	4
Kochi	6	4
Others	23	16
Total	149	100

Source: New World Sun Japanese directory, 1941; Shiro
Hatamiya and Dan Nishita, Personal Interviews, 1907; Adapted
from Itamura 1971, p. 33.

general public changed the original plan. Instead, Japanese residents of the west coast were forcibly detained in concentration camps guarded by army troops. Fifteen assembly centers were built to organize the Japanese before their departure to the camps. Twelve of these were in California—two in the Sacramento Valley in Marysville and Sacramento. The final destination of the wartime Japanese were relocation centers scattered throughout the American West.

Japanese in the Valley were divided into various evacuation districts. Civilian Exclusion Order #69, dated May 12, 1942, designated that all persons of Japanese ancestry residing in Colusa County and all of those portion of Yuba and Sutter counties lying west of State Highway 99E were to be evacuated by May 18, 1942 (Itamura 1971, 84). Similar orders were passed for other parts of the Valley, effectively fragmenting the region's Japanese community into several pieces. Most of the Japanese from Butte County (except those living on the Morehead Ranch west of Highway 99) and those who lived in the area east of Highway 99E in Yuba and Sutter counties were sent to the Tule Lake Relocation Center. Residents living in areas west of Highway 99, on the other hand, were sent to the Amache Center in faraway Colorado. This decision of the United States government to divide the Japanese community in the North State was the first serious disruption in the cultural and ethnic cohesiveness of the Japanese community in the region.

In Butte County, further wartime atrocities against the Japanese occurred. All stock and land owned by the Butte Land Company, a Japanese-owned corporation with rice lands near Nelson, was seized by the United States government in 1941 and sold to a Caucasian rice farmer (Tolan Committee Report, 10094, as cited in McDonald 1993, 74). Other Japanese residents of the area had about five days to settle their personal business, dispose of their land and possessions, and obtain immunizations required before their departure. In their haste to get organized before being removed from their homes, most orchard owners were able to transfer their property into friends' names or find someone to take care of their business while they were away. Smaller land owners, such as truck farmers, however, found it much more difficult to find local residents to take over their labor-intensive farming operations. Japanese families in places like Gridley, Oroville, Marysville, and Yuba City hastily stored their possessions in places like the Marysville Buddhist Church, rented garages, and in sympathetic friends' basements and storage sheds.

The Marysville *Appeal-Democrat* printed the following poignant letter from a local Japanese resident to his friend on its front page on the day the large group of residents left on the Southern Pacific Railroad for Tule Lake (Tsuji 1967, 4):

> It is my hope that, because we are evacuated, the rest of the American people will not look upon us as being unworthy of United States citizenship. Many of our fellow American Japanese are serving with Uncle Sam's armed forces, and many who are now being evacuated from certain zones will be called to serve our country! We will serve to the best of our abilities. We American Japanese can demonstrate our loyalty to the United States by cooperating willingly in moving from the areas so vital to our national defense.

This letter says it all. Most of the area's Japanese went along peacefully and without resistance to the federal government decision to relocate them to detention camps because they believed it was the patriotic thing to do. The unfounded belief by many other residents of the area that the Japanese were a threat to national security was never proven by one incident during the history of the entire war. As additional evidence of their loyalty to the United States, many fought valiantly in the war. Pentagon records indicate that the Japanese 442nd Regimental Combat Team was the most decorated unit in the history of the United States Army. According to General Joseph Stillwell in 1945 (Bosworth 1967, 214):

> The Nisei bought an awful big hunk of America with their blood. You're damn right these Nisei boys have a place in the American heart, now and for-

ever. And I say we soldiers ought to form a pickax club to protect Japanese Americans who fought the war with us. Anytime, we see a barfly commando picking on these kids or discriminating against them, we ought to bang him over the head with a pickax. I'm willing to be a charter member. We cannot allow a single injustice to be done to the Nisei without defeating the purpose for which we fought.

Not all local residents agreed with this statement of support for those who were returning from relocation camps and from the war in 1945. Many residents of the Sacramento Valley (and elsewhere in the West), tried to keep the Japanese from reclaiming their land or reestablishing themselves in any way in the area. Hostile signs in store windows proclaiming "No Japs," threatening phone calls and letters to former residents, acts of terrorism and violence—all were tried to keep the former residents of the Valley away from their former homes. These hostile activities and attitudes, along with a severe post-war housing shortage, made a return to the area extremely difficult.

Despite pressure and threats to stay away, many families did find the courage to return to Yuba, Sutter, and Sacramento counties after the war. Most resettled in areas far removed from original residential districts, however. Japantowns in both Sacramento and Marysville were observably diminished in size and density after the war since many African-Americans and Chinese had moved into the available housing there during wartime years. Japanese business owners in these districts along with vegetable farmers, for the most part, did not return after the war. Of the fifteen Japanese families living in the Gridley-Biggs areas before the war, four returned and are all engaged in agriculture (McDonald 1993, 135).

The post-war years also brought many new Japanese residents who had lived elsewhere in California before the war, into the Sutter County area. The majority of these newcomers bought land and developed it into large tomato fields. As the maps of Japanese distribution in the Yuba Sutter Area in 1940 and 1950 in Figure 7.5 illustrate, although there were not too many fewer Japanese in the area after the war, their distribution patterns had changed somewhat due to the arrival of these new tomato growers who favored Sutter County land over Yuba County acreages.

By the early 1950s, the vast majority of the Japanese residents of the North State remained heavily concentrated in the city of Sacramento, with smaller clusters in the Marysville-Yuba City area. A few Japanese families and individuals also reside in other urban areas in the North State such as Chico, Oroville, and Redding. Census totals for Japanese residents as compared to other ethnic groups living in each of the counties of our study area, as shown earlier in this chapter on Table 7.1 illustrate these demographic trends in the region. As

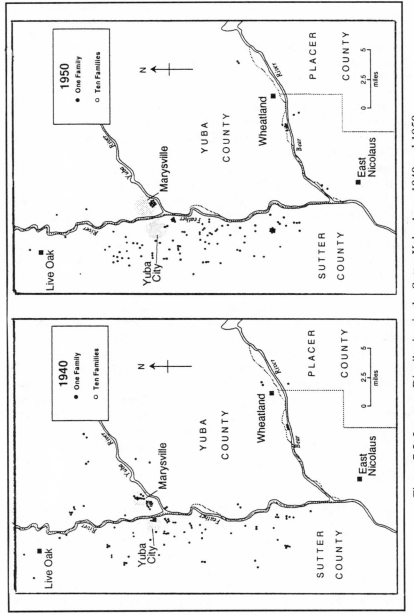

Figure 7.5. Japanese Distribution in the Sutter-Yuba Area, 1940 and 1950.
Source: Redrawn from Itamura 1971, 38, 116.

this table indicates, there were dramatic changes in the nature and diversity of population distribution in the Sacramento Valley in the years between the world wars. The experiences of three of the largest of these groups of newcomers, African-Americans, Sikhs, and people from the Midwest are an important part of the following chapter.

Economy

Planned Agricultural Colonies

The arrival of Mormon, Swedish, and Japanese farmers in the Valley formed only a small percentage of the many thousands of newcomers arriving between 1900 and 1920, setting in motion a tremendous "land boom" in the early twentieth century. Paralleling an earlier pattern begun in southern California as described by Glenn Dumke in *The Boom of the Eighties* (1944), improved irrigation and water control systems, the breakup of huge tracts of land formerly held by the region's "wheat barons," and improvements in transportation all made the North State more accessible to immigrants who contributed to this exciting era of land development.

And exciting it was! Real estate agents traveled to many parts of the country advertising the perfection of life in the Valley. Promises of new gold to be found in California—this time in the form of productive soils, a perfect climate, and incredible crop yields—were sounded far and wide. It was a dynamic time, a time of hope and prosperity for many thousands of new dreamers who arrived on the trains almost daily to seek their fortunes from the soil.

It was primarily the work of newly organized land and water development agencies that brought the boom to a head. Their efforts to subdivide land into affordably-sized units and provide water for new properties resulted in successful settlement on a number of small acreages. Companies such as the West Sacramento Land Company in Yolo County, the Sacramento Valley Colonization Company in North Sacramento, the Italian-American Land and Colonization Company between Marcuse and Tudor, the Los Verjels Land and Water Company just north of Marysville, the Sacramento Valley Irrigation Company in Glenn County, and the Maywood and Kirkwood colonies in Tehama County attracted new arrivals from all over the country. Even the state of California got into the act, buying land for two model colonies in the Central Valley, one at Durham in Butte County.

Most of these colonies succeeded, some failed, but in the end, the schemes and dreams of various land development companies changed the look of the Valley forever by planting seeds of development wherever they set their sights.

The results of this influx show up dramatically in census records. According to McGowan (1960, 186):

> The population of the valley increased from 156,000 in 1900 to 198,000 in 1910 and to 246,000 in 1920, a population gain of about sixty percent during these two decades. Butte and Sacramento led in these statistics during the first decade. Butte's population jumped from 17,000 to 27,000, while Sacramento went from 46,000 to 67,000. However, during this second decade several other counties felt the impact of colonization. Glenn's population increased from 7,000 to 12,000, Solano's from 27,000 to 40,000, Sutter's from 6,000 to 10,000, and Yolo's from 14,000 to 17,000. Four counties, namely Placer, Yuba, Colusa, and Shasta showed no population gain between 1900 and 1920.

Orange Vale

Most travelers driving east from Sacramento on their way to South Lake Tahoe on Highway 50 recognize the name Orangevale as a rapidly growing suburb on Sacramento's northeast side. Few realize that Orange Vale, as it was originally called, was once a well established agricultural colony famous for its citrus crops. Layed out originally as the Cardwell Colony in 1887, Orange Vale was planned as a series of north-south and east-west streets divided into eight ten acre plots. Two-thirds of each lot was to be planted with fruit trees, two acres were to be used for grain, one for alfalfa, and one and a quarter for house and barn (Castro 1993, 2).

The Orange Vale colony grew slowly at first. Settlers could purchase a farm for $1,250. The colony's first family came from Canada in 1889 and the first crop was harvested the following year. A promotional brochure, published by local developers, was distributed all across the country. It pictured the beautiful snow-capped Sierra to the east and dramatically told of the area's warm weather and ideal rivers.

The peak of Orange Vale's citrus crop occurred in 1925. Things were beginning to look up. Then, a cold wave swept through the area in 1932, killing most of the orange trees. By 1940, there were only 473 acres of oranges left (Castro 1993). Today, almost all the orange orchards have been replaced with subdivisions. Its largest through street, Greenback Lane (so named because it was the area's first paved road to be paid for entirely with cash), allows people of

Orangevale to reach either Highway 50 or Interstate 80, major east-west transportation routes.

Despite the hurried pace of development in Sacramento's northeast corridor, Orangevale still maintains some of its rural charm. Horse shows are regular events and, much as in the past, the community still hosts a yearly "Pow Wow Days." These activities notwithstanding, most visitors and some residents who more often perceive the community with images of shopping at Sunrise Mall and other commercial developments in the area find it difficult to remember the frontier origin of this agricultural colony.

West Sacramento

As these population surges illustrate, certain counties were more affected by land development efforts than were others. In Yolo County, for example, the work of the West Sacramento Land Company succeeded in bringing in newcomers from as far away as Russia. Efforts by the state legislature to make this part of east Yolo County attractive and stable for subdivision had begun as early as 1891 when the region's first reclamation district was formed. The area's location within walking distance from employment opportunities in downtown Sacramento, along with its fertile agricultural land, and water availability, made this part of Yolo County especially desirable for land speculation. Accordingly, the West Sacramento Land Company was incorporated in 1907 and included wealthy San Francisco investors like the Lilienthal, Sloss, deSable, and Hammon families (West Sacramento Company historical file, 1907). This group of investors had originally promoted and supported the development of the Pacific Gas and Electric Company and also were interested in promoting the interurban railway that was being built to connect the Sacramento Valley to the San Francisco Bay area (Hardwick 1986, 241).

After the worst flood in the history of the Sacramento River in 1907, virtually all of the area west of the river ended up underwater. After three years of financial problems caused by costly reclamation efforts, the West Sacramento Land Company was incorporated into a new company called the West Sacramento Company in 1910. At that time, they controlled 1,120 acres of land. Lobbying efforts by wealthy investors in the company motivated the state legislature to officially create an East Yolo reclamation district in 1911 to reclaim swamp and overflow lands. The construction of landscape-changing levees, pumping stations, and canals was finally completed by 1915 after years of intensive and expensive labor.

A second reclamation district was established in East Yolo in 1910 to reclaim the area around Bryte, near the bend in the Sacramento River just west of the town of Broderick. The West Sacramento Company's report of 1912 listed three million cubic yards of fill used to build the expensive system of levees along the Yolo Bypass and the river near Bryte (West Sacramento Company Historical File, 1912). By 1916, most of the work along the river was complete. Thousands of elm trees had been planted along Jefferson Boulevard and numerous weeping willows put in along the banks of Lake Washington, while acres of stumps and brush were accumulated to protect new vegetation along three and a half miles of riverfront levees. Seventeen square miles of land had been made permanently dry. By 1917, the completion of the Yolo Bypass finished the expensive task of reclaiming East Yolo land for residential and commercial development.

Promotion of land sales in the newly drained community of Bryte began in earnest after the first effort to reclaim the land. Letters were sent all over the country. Real estate agents visited primarily West Coast cities to hype their new colony. Of particular interest were letters, in Russian, sent to the San Francisco Russian community in 1912 by the Sacramento Land Company (West Sacramento Company Historical File, 1912). In some cases, lots were purchased, sight unseen, on land still not completely reclaimed for settlement. Sales agents also visited Russians in Eureka in 1914 to sell East Yolo land (Hardwick 1986, 286).

Once several Russian families became established in the area, a chain migration effect began, and by 1914, a significant concentration of Russians had settled in this East Yolo colony. Naturalization records indicate that a typical pattern of migration brought Russians from their homeland to San Francisco to Bryte. Most were drawn to the new settlement in West Sacramento by its quasi-rural ambience and proximity to California's capital city.

In the decades after the 1917 revolution in Russia, the number of Russian people settling in Bryte increased. They were joined by a significant number of Portuguese and Italian families as well. Today, the same neighborhood, now part of the newly incorporated city of West Sacramento, is home to many thousands of new post-Soviet era Russian immigrants who are drawn in by promises of the good life and religio-ethnic connections, much like their predecessors in the original Russian colony. Over the years, a distinct Russian imprint evolved in the area that lingers in the late 1990s.

Corning's Maywood Colony

Into this land of opportunity came two more Sacramento Valley residents with a vision of land development. In Tehama County, Charles Foster and

Warren Woodson purchased 3,100 acres from early settler George Hoag for $25.00 an acre in 1891, eventually acquiring 4000 acres. Dividing their immense property into small plots of affordable land, these enterprising land developers soon disseminated an advertising scheme touting their Maywood Colony that reached from coast to coast.

Maywood Colony
California Fruit Land—Within the Reach of All—
Easiest Terms Ever Offered

We have just purchased and platted 3000 acres of good land into 10, 20, and 40 acre tracts each of which faces to an avenue of 40 feet in width. The tract is situated in the southern part of Tehama County, lying between the California and Oregon Railroad and the Sacramento River and adjoining the flourishing town of Corning. The soil is especially suited to the successful production of the raisin grape, peach, apricot, almond, fig, pear, plum, and prune. . . .

Using advertisements like these and others heralding Horace Greeley's 1859 quote, "Fruit growing is destined to be the ultimate glory of California," Woodson traveled all over the country promoting his "promised land." He eventually established Maywood Colony offices in New York, Boston, and Chicago. Because the promises of land speculators in the American West were often mistrusted by many people in other parts of the country, Maywood promoters ran ads in Christian periodicals on the East Coast. They even hired a minister to work in their Corning office on a commission basis to communicate directly with religious organizations back east (Hultgren 1982, 29). As increasing numbers of urban people were attracted to Corning, the partners developed the Maywood Addition in town as well. These new 160 acres were divided into city blocks and included a central park and cooperative cannery and packing house to provide employment for the new residents.

In the mid-1890s, Foster and Woodson decided to try growing olives on their land. They soon discovered that the best soils of the Corning area produced high yields of small olives, but that their land's poorer soils produced a smaller yield but larger olives. Soil quality, in addition to the Valley's climate with its cool winters which were needed to encourage blooms and dry summers for bringing olives to maturity, encouraged newcomers to plant more and more olives. Eager residents of the new colony soon discovered that jack rabbits and locusts, which feasted regularly on all their other crops, had no appetite for olives (Hultgren 1982, 30-31). By the turn of the century, Corning had become the center of olive growing in all of Northern California, a distinction it still enjoys in the 1990s.

Oroville Citrus Colonies

The Maywood Colonies were but one part of similar efforts taking place in other parts of the Valley. In Butte County, two "citrus colonies" were also being promoted in the Sierra Nevada foothills just east of Oroville. As early as 1885, Butte County was reported to have 'at least 9,000 orange trees (*Oroville Weekly Register,* Nov. 15, 1888, 1). This same newspaper reported in 1900 that this citrus growing district contained 3,300 acres of producing citrus trees (July 28, 1900, 1). How did oranges come to be such an important crop, especially in a region located at the northern limits of potential citrus production?

Enter land speculators who believed that anything was possible in the fertile Sacramento Valley. At the urging of E.W. Fogg of Oroville, the Citrus Grower's Association was formed in 1885. The group soon purchased land in Thermolito just east of town, and brought in orange tree seedlings from Riverside in southern California. The Association also set up a nursery in Oroville to demonstrate and advertise the new crop (Hoiland 1975, 27-28). This effort, along with the prominent presence of Butte County orange growers at the first citrus fair (sponsored by the Northern California Emigration Society in 1885 to attract people to "golden opportunities" provided in the Golden State) drew attention to the fledgling colony. Later, in 1887, Butte County hosted its own event held inside large tents, attracting visitors from as far away as San Francisco and Sacramento. According to Hoiland (1975, 29-30):

> All types of Butte County produce were exhibited but citrus predominated. It sounds as if the interior of the tent must have been a bizarre sight. Oroville exhibitors built intricate arrangements of oranges, lemons, and dried fruits in the form of pyramids, beehives, cornucopias, and mining implements. At the far end the folks had built out of fruit an eight by twelve model of a Gothic cathedral.

Meanwhile, business leaders in Oroville and Colusa founded the regional Sacramento Valley Development Association in the early 1900s to continue the effort to attract new settlers to the Sacramento Valley (Mansfield 1918, 338). Founded by two newspapermen, Will Green of *The Colusa Sun* and W.A. Beard, editor of the *Oroville Mercury,* the organization published the *Sacramento Valley Monthly* extolling the virtues of irrigation projects and potential crop production in the region. They also sent representatives to agricultural fairs all over the country to set up exhibits on Butte County citrus production and give away free samples of Oroville oranges (McGowan 1961, 403).

Along with the efforts of these developers was the promotion of two citrus colonies near Oroville in the late nineteenth century. The peak year of the Thermolito colony was in 1892 when about fifty owners lived on 3,000 acres. After foreclosures during the panic of 1893 and eventual suspension of the articles of incorporation in 1905, this citrus colony was disbanded (Hoiland 1975, 34). Few traces of this hopeful colony remain today.

Not far away, the Palermo Land and Water Company had been organized by several Oroville residents and San Francisco investors who first advertised their new Palermo Citrus Colony in various newspapers in 1888 (*Oroville Weekly Register*, January 26, 1888, 1). Enlisting the help of the Southern Pacific Railroad who eventually ran excursion trains to visit the colony and with the strong backing of wealthy investors from the Bay Area, Palermo got off to a strong start in its early years of development. On May 30, 1888, a special first class round trip excursion from San Francisco to Palermo was offered at a cost of $3.00. The purpose of this successful trip was to auction five and ten acre parcels of land in the Palermo Colony (Jones 1982, 1).

Most of the owners of Palermo land, in contrast to Thermolito, were absenee landlords. With the diversified investments of these owners then, this colony did not suffer as much in the financial panic of 1893; the Palermo Corporation continued on until 1945 (Frederick 1969, 50). The manuscript collection in Special Collections of Meriam Library at California State University, Chico houses the *Register of the Palermo Land and Water Company* which contains a more complete history of this development venture in the Sacramento Valley (see Jones 1982).

In the 1990s, the now historic, but important, Oroville citrus industry is barely visible in the local landscape. A combination of climate setbacks along with governmental decisions largely ended the success of orange growers in the area. Damaging freezes in 1932, 1949, and 1972 decimated the productivity of the trees. These events were compounded by government decisions on pricing and distribution first enforced by the Agricultural Marketing Agreement Act of 1937. Most of the oranges grown in the Sacramento Valley in the 1990s center instead on land east of Orland in Glenn County where more fertile soils, affordable water, and vast expanses of level land encouraged large scale production. Oranges grown in this area are packed and marketed through the large James Mills Growers Service Company in Hamilton City, an affiliate of Sunkist Corporation.

The State Lends a Hand: The Durham Land Colony

Unlike other colonies in the Valley which were developed by land speculators and local property owners, the Durham Colony, located one mile east of
the town of Durham in Butte County, was organized, funded, and implemented
by the state of California. The legislature appropriated $260,000 in 1917 to
sponsor two such colonies, one in the Sacramento Valley at Durham and the
other in the San Joaquin Valley. State officials bought the land, subdivided it,
determined how large each farm would be, installed irrigation canals and drainage
systems, organized cooperatives and a social and cultural center for the colony
and suggested specific locations for farm sites (McGowan 1960, 189).

The Durham site had been selected for its low price, soil quality, ease of
preparation for irrigation, and access to transportation systems already in place
(Pisani 1984, 444). It offered lots in various sizes from 8 to 300 acres and also
featured 26 two-acre farm plots. When settlers first arrived, they found roads,
irrigation ditches, barns, houses, and fences ready. Much of the land had already
been seeded to pasture. The goal of the land colony was to promote orderly and
systematic settlement, rather than a loose collection of individuals scattered
throughout irrigation districts.

Despite careful planning and hopeful beginnings, however, it was not long
before all was not well with the new project. Colonists soon felt isolated and
began to complain about the remote location of their new home. In addition,
surrounding communities began to criticize the special treatment these newcomers were receiving from the government. By 1924, it had become apparent
that the Durham Colony was not working out as everyone had hoped for a
variety of reasons.

First and foremost among the many problems with the Durham plan was its
location. Because the elevation of Butte Creek was higher than the surrounding
land in several places on the property (due to inflows of hydraulic mining debris
in former decades), poor drainage was an issue from the very beginning. As early
as 1858, it had been recorded that Butte Creek regularly overflowed its natural
levees, inundating the surrounding area (Trussell 1969, 225). This environmental
challenge was compounded by poor crop choices, soil limitations, and the
decision to divide the land into small plots that were two small to survive
economically.

In 1929, land owners at the Durham Colony convinced the government to
let them take over their own land and make management decisions regarding
irrigation, drainage, crop choices, and binding legal matters. After so many
problems and losses, the state of California was only too happy to comply with
their request. Unfortunately, the disastrous farm depression after World War I left

many residents with little hope of prosperity (Peck 1966, 84-86). Because the state had not made terms of their responsibilities clear to early settlers, it became vulnerable to claims for legal retribution (Peck 1966, 112). Numerous law suits were filed by property owners against the state in subsequent years and, by 1931, California had withdrawn all support for the struggling attempt at colonization near Durham (Cleary 1931, 10).

The Evolution of Regional Transportation Networks

A critical part of the grand vision of establishing orchards and truck crop operations was the speculative sales of small tracts of land. The success of these orchard tracts depended upon getting fresh grown products to markets quickly and the ability of rural inhabitants to get to urban areas for employment while their new orchard trees grew to productive size. The coming of the electric railroads at the turn of the century enabled urban people to be more mobile and rural people to become more urban.

Railways

Electric rail service for the Sacramento Valley was discussed as early as the turn of the century but, as with the earlier steam railroads, finding capital for such investments was difficult. A pioneer effort in the provision of electric trains was undertaken by the Diamond Match Company. In 1903 it built a trolley system in the Chico area to service its workers. Construction finally began on a regional line in 1905 that answered to many names including the Sacramento Northern Railroad and the Northern Electric Company. The first part of the line connected the Diamond Match facility at Chico to Oroville in 1906. Company officials then immediately began planning for a link-up with Marysville or Yuba City and by the end of the same year they did so with a route from Oroville junction, six miles to the west, through East Biggs and Live Oak to Yuba City and Marysville. With completion of the Chico to Marysville line, a branch line to Hamilton City was completed in 1907 but it operated for only seven years before it was discontinued due to lack of use. The extension from Marysville to Sacramento in 1907 was very successful because it made possible a continuous trip from Chico to Oakland by connecting with other lines in the capital city.

Two branch lines were added to the Northern Pacific system in 1911. The first was from Yuba City to Colusa and the second was from Sacramento to Woodland. Other lines were contemplated or planned but by the beginning of

World War I competition from other lines, financial difficulties and the appearance of the automobile limited further expansion of the system. The Sacramento Northern and its subsidiaries were purchased by the new and aggressive Western Pacific Railroad in 1921. The last of the electric trains in the Sacramento Valley would be discontinued in 1945.

The Western Pacific Railroad successfully competed with the giant Southern Pacific system by building its transcontinental connection through the Feather River Canyon in 1909. It connected Oroville, Marysville, Sacramento, and Oakland with other parts of the far west often paralleling SP lines. The Western Pacific was consolidated with the Great Northern, Northern Pacific, and Burlington Northern in 1926 and virtually all parts of the Valley were connected with rail service by at least one line.

Peak railroad mileage in the United States was reached in the early 1930s and likewise the rail coverage of the Valley was most extensive during this time. Gradually from about 1940 to 1960, lines were abandoned or consolidated in response to the increased popularity of autos and trucks. The shift to highway transportation was stimulated by improvements in local and state highways and the creation of the Federal highway system.

Roads

Roads throughout the Sacramento Valley in the 1870s were merely cleared tracks that connected farms with river landings and rail stops. But, as the production of perishable fruit crops made travel times more important, most counties undertook road maintenance and improvement programs. By the early 1890s, auto and bicycle users promoted hard surface roads. A report by the new State Bureau of Highways recommended that the state build a highway system that would span the length of the state connecting all the county seats. The plan suggested a west-side highway from Sacramento through Woodland to Red Bluff and an east-side route through Pleasant Grove, Marysville, Oroville, and Chico to Red Bluff. The plan remained on paper until a new Highway Commission undertook serious construction of concrete based highways in 1914. The various connected highway projects throughout the Valley included a major elevated link over the Yolo bypass in 1916 thereby avoiding the perennial floods that separated Sacramento from Davis, Vacaville and the Bay area. The Yolo causeway was eventually replaced with a parallel one in the 1960s. Passage of the Federal Aid Road Act in 1919 provided even more money for road building and by the 1930s, the U.S. Highway system was essentially in place.

Environment

Impacts on Wildlife and Fishery Resources

For thirty years after the Gold Rush, there was no control or any kind of monitoring of environmental losses in the Sacramento Valley. Debris from hydraulic mining destroyed fish habitats, agricultural conversion drained waterfowl habitat, and most of the larger game animals were killed outright. Fish were hauled out of the river easily, caught in gill nets, fyke traps, or seines (Reynolds et al. 1990). During spawning runs, salmon were killed by the hundreds to be used as animal food or fertilizer. During the Gold Rush many Chinese, Greeks, Italians, and Portuguese turned from mining to fishing using skills brought with them from home. They sold fish to miners with no environmental or other kind of regulation by the state. By 1852 the sediments from the mines—not overfishing—nearly destroyed the salmon runs in the Sacramento River and its tributaries.

The last wild elk in the Valley were seen in 1870. A few sightings of grizzlies were reported as late as 1880 although most had been killed by 1865. Most early descriptions of the Valley in winter time included amazed comments about the abundance of waterfowl. Flocks of tens of thousands of geese, ducks, swans, cranes, and other migratory birds were reported as pests because they damaged grain fields. The birds were hunted as if there were an inexhaustible supply until their populations were almost exhausted in the early years of the twentieth century. Many farmers employed "goose herders" who were charged with keeping these wild birds from eating grain crops by continually shooting at them. Many goose herders supplemented their incomes by selling goose feathers by using large bore shotguns. They brought down hundreds of birds.

Salmon were the first of the Valley's wild resources to receive protection. By the 1870s, an important commercial fishery had developed and a State Board of Fish Commissioners had been created. Fresh and preserved fish had been sold in San Francisco and Sacramento throughout the days of the Gold Rush and a fish cannery had been established in Sacramento in 1864 (McGowan 1961, 355). By the 1880s, there were twenty canneries operating along the Sacramento River (see Reynolds et al. 1990). The first salmon hatchery was placed at the junction of the Pit and McCloud Rivers in 1872 which turned out to be successful in increasing downstream fish populations. Two others were opened in the 1880s and approximately ten million pounds of chinook per year were harvested between 1880 and 1883 (McEvoy 1986). But the number of fish caught, packed and shipped out by rail exceeded production by such a large difference that by

1886 the canneries were closed due to a lack of fresh fish. In 1880 alone, nine hundred boats with two thousand men took over ten million pounds of salmon out of the delta (McGowan 1961, 356). In 1993, it was estimated that 95 percent of the historic Central Valley salmon habitat had been lost due to hydraulic mining, water diversion projects, and flood control efforts (see Reynolds 1993).

The decline of the fishery forced the beginnings of resource management in the mid-1800s. Closed seasons were implemented, fine mesh shrimp nets were prohibited and more support for hatcheries was provided. With probable good intentions, this period was also a time when several new varieties of fish were introduced. Striped Bass, carp, shad, and catfish were planted with mixed results. The success of Striped Bass led to a commercial fishery until 1955 and a thriving sport fishery thereafter, although some say, at the expense of several million young salmon. Catfish and carp also impacted native fish populations by eating the eggs of Sacramento Perch and Tule Perch. Largemouth Bass provide excellent sport fishing in Valley lakes and ponds but they too are voracious eaters of native fish and amphibia.

In spite of the implementation of fishing license requirements, closed seasons, hatchery production, and habitat improvements, the numbers of andronamus fish in the Sacramento River system continues to decline (Reynolds 1993). Several reasons are offered including upstream logging, state and federal water diversions, local agricultural pumping, urbanization, and poaching. Chapter 9 discusses more recent plans and projects that have attempted to restore water quality and fisheries to the Valley's rivers and streams.

In the latter part of the nineteenth century, deer were the only game that survived in enough numbers to still be thought to be inexhaustible. A glove factory which used thousands of deer skins a month was established at Red Bluff. Again, extraction of the resource far exceeded the reproductive rates of the animals. By 1900, several protective regulations had to be adopted. With protective laws requiring licenses and tags, seasonal and sex prohibitions and other management techniques, the area's deer populations remained rather steady until the 1990s. Now urbanization, thereby reducing the winter range, and restrictions on hunting of mountain lions, a deer predator, are named as the reasons for declining populations. Auto-deer collisions also exact a heavy toll on deer.

Market Hunting

The decline of waterfowl at the turn of the century was largely attributed to market hunters and farmers trying to protect their grain crops from hungry geese. Historic photographs of hunters amidst hundreds of dead birds testify to the original abundance of the resource and the reason for the rapid decrease in its population. The largest bag of waterfowl reported from a reliable source was in 1902 when 783 geese were shot by four hunters in two days near Willows (McGowan 1961, 364). When rice was planted in place of wheat after 1912, ducks were the targeted invaders. It is reported by McGowan that "one occasion over ten thousand ducks reached San Francisco in a single day" and that unofficial estimates indicated that five hundred thousand ducks were marketed in the 1910-1911 season (McGowan 1961, 365). Quail and pheasants were other game birds favored by the market hunters for sale in San Francisco.

A local historical journal quoted "old timers'" memories of market hunting as follows:

> About 1884 commercial slaughter of geese had begun. Market hunters with sawed-off shotguns and trained horses sneaked up on the geese dawning from 60 to 180 at a shot. San Francisco offered a ready market for the geese at .75 to $1.25 a dozen. It was supposed that a limit bag of ducks would be beneficial in stopping the slaughter of birds. That this is a fallacy is provided by the market traffic in birds which goes on persistently and systematically. It is no exaggeration to state that 10,000 ducks have been sent into this city (San Francisco) in one day, not often, but frequently. Two hundred limit bags of fifty each is not a big invoice when large numbers of hotels, restaurants, clubs, swell boarding houses, etc. in this city, that are ready buyers of wild game, is taken into consideration (*Wagon Wheels* 1953, 2-3).

Finally, in 1918, the Federal Migratory Bird Act was passed to restrict the killing of migratory birds by market hunters. Game wardens were in the field by 1902 to enforce game regulations but it would be well into the 1940s before they became an effective deterrent to large scale poaching. Stories of these early efforts are told by Warden Terry Hodges in his book *Sabertooth; the Rip-Roaring Adventures of a Legendary Game Warden* published in 1988. Today, state wardens are active in habitat protection, pollution control and environmental education as well as code enforcement duties.

The years before and during World War II were difficult for Valley residents because of economic depression and drought. Despite these challenges, this period of time, however, was also a time of increasing population and rather steady and stable growth. The next chapter discusses new in-migrants who arrived in the region between 1920 and 1940 and details their changing impacts on the land.

Chapter 8

New Dreamers

The years after World War I brought new prosperity to Sacramento Valley farmers and city dwellers alike. As shown on the map in Figure 8.1, towns increased in size and number, linked by new transportation routes for trains, cars, and trucks. Along with this growth within the region came improved access to other parts of the state and nation. This, in turn, encouraged the migration and settlement of ever more diverse groups of people including some from "the outside world" (such as the Sikhs from India) and some from within the borders of the United States (such as African-Americans).

Later, as the decade of the 1930s witnessed increasingly difficult economic challenges, others came to the North State in search of new ways to survive the hardships of the nation's Great Depression Families from the Midwestern states of Oklahoma, Arkansas, and the Texas panhandle established new homes in the Valley, adding new ethnic and religious diversity to the region.

People

Sikhs Find Their New Punjab

Not long after the settlement of Japanese, Latter Day Saints, and Swedish farmers in the Sacramento Valley, another group of hopeful agriculturalists found their way into the fertile region. This group, the Sikhs, originated in the Punjab area of northern India. They first came to North America in 1904 by way of Vancouver, British Columbia, traveling southward into Washington, Oregon, and California (LaBrack 1982, 29).

Sikhs are often confused with Hindus who also came from India. Although there are Hindus in the Sacramento Valley, Sikhs by far make up the most populous group of East Indians in the region and are, therefore, emphasized in

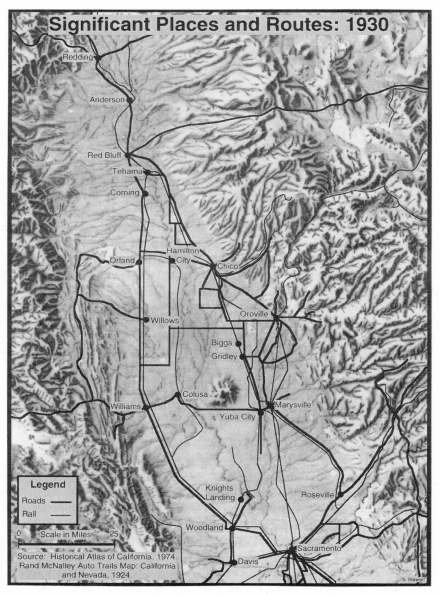

Figure 8.1. Significant Places and Routes, 1930.

this chapter. A few arrived in the Valley before World War I but the majority had found their way into the Marysville-Yuba City area by the early 1920s.

Despite their common Indian place of origin, it is important to note here that Sikhs are distinctly different from Hindus. Sikhism originated in the Punjab amid the religious upheavals of fifteenth century India. Although there are many types of Sikhs, the most visible group in the Sacramento Valley are keshadharis, or "long-haired" Sikhs. Followers of this group display the five symbols of Sikhism by wearing the 5 ks: kes (long hair), kanga (comb), kacha (short pants), kara (iron bracelet), and kirpan (sword). Although even strict believers in this type of Sikhism are permitted to wear modern clothing in the 1990s, they do not believe in cutting their hair or beard. Thus, many Sikh men are noticeable in the local landscape because of their large turbans (designed to keep long hair in place) and beards.[1]

Although the total number of this Asian group in California never equaled the number of Chinese or Japanese, anti-Asian attitudes and laws applied to East Indians equally. Between 1900 and 1910, nearly 5000 Punjabis settled in California. Between 1911 and 1920, more than 2000 more came to farm California soils (Scheuring 1987, 52). Most of these early arrivals settled in the Sacramento, San Joaquin, and Imperial valleys.

From the very beginning, the broad, open Sacramento Valley felt like home to Sikhs selecting the North State for settlement. They were especially comfortable with the fertile area near the Sutter Buttes between Biggs and Yuba City-Marysville. Many old timers still reminisce that the Valley's vast, treeless plain in the shadow of the Sutter Buttes reminded them of the flat Indian Punjab in the shadow of the Himilayas. This uncanny resemblance to Northern India along with the promise of high quality soils, large land holdings, and the high per acre yield of crops caused many Sikhs to envision a bright future on Valley farms. As one longtime Sikh resident recalled, "California seemed enchanted" (LaBrack 1982, 32).

Most Sikhs initially came into the Sacramento Valley to work in the rice fields near Biggs. They soon became a part of multicultural labor gangs, living in work camps and cooking their own food. Das locates the following sites of Sikh settlement in the area (1924, 18-19):

> The Hindustanees . . . are found congregated in two different sections; first, the fruit growing sections of Folsom, Orangevale, Loomis and Newcastle; and second, in the rice growing districts of Marysville, Colusa, Tudo (Tudor), Willows, Chico, Butte City, Nelson, Gridley, and Briggs (Biggs).

LaBrack's extensive study of Sikhs in the Yuba City area suggests that this ethnic group seemed to prefer lands adjacent to streams and rivers where flood plain soils led to certain types of crop production. His analysis lists three locational considerations, all based on agriculture, that shaped Sikh distribution patterns in the Sacramento Valley (LaBrack 1982, 32):

- Land two miles on either side of the Feather River most suitable for some varieties of specialty fruit orchard cultivation;
- Land one mile father, or three miles from the river suitable for row crops, nut trees, prunes, etc.;
- Lands another mile beyond, or four-plus miles from the river, that supports only grain-related or range activities.

Through hard work in local fields and orchards, a few Sikhs were soon able to save enough money to lease farmland. After 1915, many leased large tracts of land. Tracts of less than ten acres suitable for growing peaches, prunes, walnut, and almonds were most favored. By 1919, Sikh farm lands in Butte, Glenn, Colusa, Sacramento, Sutter, and Yuba counties comprised sixty-one percent of the total land owned (1,273 acres) and fifty-one percent of the total land leased (44,585) acres) (LaBrack 1982, 41). Table 8.1 details East Indian land occupancy rates in Sacramento Valley counties. Percentages are comparisons with the rest of the state of California.

Table 8.1. East Indian Land Occupancy in
Sacramento Valley Counties, 1919

County	Owned	Leased	Total	Percent
Butte	775	4,200	4,975	5.6
Colusa	0	10,240	10,240	11.6
Glenn	0	13,915	13,915	15.7
Sacramento	75	2,529	2,604	2.9
Sutter	423	6,901	7,324	8.3
Yuba	0	6,800	6,800	7.8

Source: La Brack 1982, 41 and Kurtz 1984.

Sikhs continued to migrate into the Valley at a fairly steady rate until the early 1920s. At the end of World War I, as the number of immigrants entering the United States increased drastically, the United States government passed a series of laws designed to limit entry of certain groups. The Asiatic Barred Zone Immigration Act of 1917 (which made it impossible for most East Asians who left the United States to reenter) and the 1924 Immigration Act (which established small quotas for the entry of certain groups, including East Indians) basically shut down most possibilities for the continued entry of Asian immigrants into California. Some were able to enter California as illegal aliens by way of Mexico, a trend that continues today. Most who were already residing in California stayed in the years following World War I even though their lives were often very difficult economically.

Following the passage of these restrictive immigration laws, the decades between the wars were generally a time of slow growth for almost all foreign-born immigrant groups in the Sacramento Valley. The most successful Sikhs in the area during these decades consolidated their small land holdings and converted almost all of it into orchard crops. Unable to secure citizenship or own land due to restrictive laws, many listed property holdings in the names of their American-born children.

Sikhs from other parts of the state increasingly resettled in the Yuba City-Marysville area as orchards became more and more successful in the region. LaBrack lists the following six factors encouraging this conversion to orchards after 1924 as (1986, 43-44):

- Small amount of land needed to produce an adequate return;
- Probability of some type of dwelling (shack, shed, or laborer's quarters) on the orchard property;
- Lower labor costs than for other types of crops;
- Financial and physical help from fellow Sikhs;
- Majority of the work, depending on the size of the orchard, could be done during the morning or evening hours thus allowing for dual employment;
- Suitability of the type of work, location, and climate for Sikhs.

After World War II, as laws limiting immigration into the United States eased, new inflows of Sikhs arrived in the Yuba City-Marysville area. By 1959, Sutter County had become the largest East Indian (Sikh and Hindu) community in the United States (Shepherd 1993, 19). Today, there are at least 8,000-10,000 Sikhs living in the Yuba City-Marysville area, enough to support three temples (Weaver 1986, A1). Unlike many other ethnic groups who cluster in one part of their new community, Sikh housing is dispersed throughout the urban area as shown on the map in Figure 8.2.

Because of the relative density of the Sikh population and the well organized Sikh religious and social network, Yuba City-Marysville has, in fact, become a

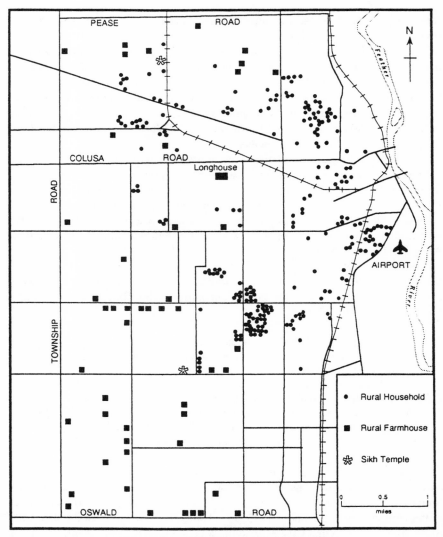

Figure 8.2. Sikh Housing in Yuba City.
Source: Redrawn from Kurtz 1984, 106.

safe haven for new arrivals from northern India. It is viewed by most as a place to begin their new life in the United States. Many stay on, working their way into the local economy much like the first generation of Sikhs did in the early 1900s. According to Mohinder Ghag, a Yuba City farmer, even those Sikhs who eventually move elsewhere come to Yuba City first. In his words (Weaver 1986, A-1):

> Everybody come here and settle here before they search out. That is because the Sikh religion calls on its believers to share what they have. In Yuba City, that means there is a free lunch available every day at all three temples. No one is turned away.

Despite this caring welcome by supportive people from their homeland, many Sikhs find life difficult in the North State. Along with the sometimes hostile attitudes towards "those foreigners" by local residents, a life filled with deprivation and hard work too often awaited Indian newcomers in the early years of Sikh settlement. Many arrived as undocumented workers, hoping to find a new life in the United States where "the money is like leaves on a tree." Instead, they often found themselves in a situation like the one described by a resident of Sacramento in Box 8.A.

This story recounts the dramatic and often miserable conditions that have shaped many newcomers' lives in California. Despite these struggles of illegal aliens from northern India, however, many Sikh families in the Yuba City-Marysville area have been able to sponsor relatives from India and provide them with work and shelter once they arrive. According to a more optimistic study of Sikhs in the Valley (LaBrack 1982, 49):

> Rural Sikh family life, with its agrarian orientations and division of labor, has remained well-suited to a labor intensive crop. The use of family labor and lower living costs has been crucial in holding down 'production costs.' As the Sikh community of the northern Sacramento valley has grown, it has become increasingly apparent that the costs of maintaining immigrant families are well below comparable costs for non-Sikh farm families of equal size.

The distribution of Sikh-owned orchards in the Yuba City-Marysville area as shown in Figure 8.3 illustrates that many have been able to succeed in the orchards of the Yuba City-Marysville area over the past several decades. There are several reasons for this. First, it is possible to make a profit in the orchard business without a large investment in machinery. Because joint family labor is

---

Box 8.A
A Sikh Story

This account of a typical Sikh experience in the Sacramento Valley was summarized in a recent article in the *Sacramento Bee*, Weaver 1986, A-14:

Asking not to be quoted by name, this man said that he sold everything he had in India to pay the price for being smuggled into the United States through Mexico. He got a job picking peaches and prunes in Live Oak, just north of Yuba City. The farmer let him live with other undocumented workers in a house near the orchard.

Each day, someone would pick them up early in the morning for work and return them to the house in the evening. They were told to stay inside.

"At times, the owner would lock the door from the outside. He would threaten them that immigration was looking for them . . . When they see a padlock on the door, they just go away," he said. "They had orders not to open the door regardless of who was there."

The farmer would keep their front door padlocked from the outside for hours or days at a time. Sometimes they would sneak out a window if the door was locked. One day, after he had left the house, another worker tried to start a fire in the stove. The house caught on fire. Two of those inside were burned critically.

---

practiced routinely, most direct expenses can be kept low. Over half the costs of bringing an acre of fruit or nuts to the canner is in direct labor costs, such as thinning, pruning, and picking operations. Members of a Sikh family usually greatly reduce these costs by doing it themselves (Kurtz 1984, 89).

Orchard production of peaches, prunes, walnuts, and almonds have made it possible for Sikh immigrants and their families to succeed in the competitive economy of the North State for the past several decades. Sikhs now produce eight percent of Sutter County's agricultural goods and twenty-two percent of the cling peaches in the United States (see Table 8.2). One Sikh farmer is the largest producer of cling peaches in the United States (Kurtz 1984, 114).

Evidences of the Sikh presence in the Sacramento Valley are expressed not only in these economic patterns, but also in the area's religious landscape. The first Sikh temple in Yuba City opened its doors in 1970. This impressive building has two large kitchens and a dining facility as well as a large meeting room. This original temple remains an important cultural focal point for the local Sikh community. In 1980, a second temple was opened on Bogue Road to accommodate the expanding Sikh community. The recent construction of a third temple has increased the visibility of the Sikh cultural landscape in the mid-Sacramento Valley even more in recent years than in the past.

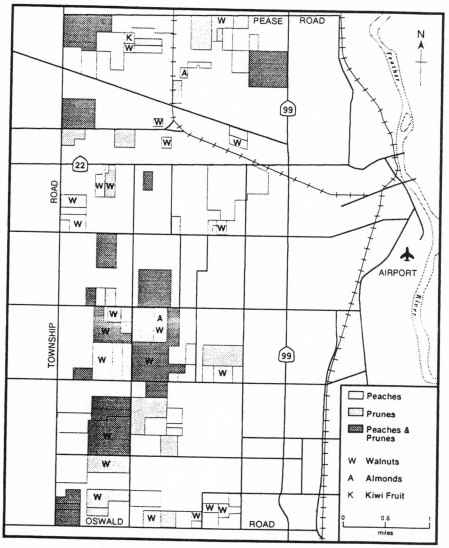

Figure 8.3. Sikh-Owned Agricultural Land Near Yuba City.
Source: Redrawn from Kurtz 1984, 116.

African-American Patterns

Despite a common perception by urban Californians that the Sacramento Valley is a hostile region for non-white residents because of its rural and small town (and somewhat *provincial!*) mentality, small pockets of African-American settlement do exist in the state north of the city of Sacramento (see Table 8.3).

Table 8.2. Sikh Fruit and Nut Products: Acreages and Percents

Crop/Crops	Acreage	Percent of Total
Peaches	1,326	29.6
Peaches and Prunes	1,179	26.3
Prunes	723	16.1
Peaches, Prunes, and Walnuts	453	10.1
Peaches and Walnuts	310	6.9
Prunes and Walnuts	261	5.8
Walnuts	173	3.9
Kiwi and Prunes	35	0.8
Almonds	15	0.3
Kiwi	10	0.2
Total	4,485	100

Source: Kurtz, 1984, 115 and Sutter County Assessor's Office, 1984.

They are, for the most part, located in rural communities where African-Americans have a long history of contributing to the local economy. In Northern California, more than half the Black residents live in four areas: Oroville, Marysville, Weed, and Honey Lake. The African-American community in Oroville is discussed here, as well as several other significant sites of early African-American settlement in the region—Red Bluff in Tehama County and Guinda in Yolo County. Mention is also made of Black contributions to life in Marysville, Wheatland, and Chico.

Table 8.3. African-American and White Populations in
Sacramento Valley Counties by Gender, 1850

| County | African-American | | White | | |
	Males	Females	Males	Females	Total
Butte	32	1	3,441	100	3,574
Colusa	0	0	77	38	115
Sacramento	195	17	8,277	598	9,087
Shasta	0	0	371	7	378
Solano	33	4	449	94	580
Sutter	20	0	3,300	124	3,444
Yolo	7	3	953	123	1,086
Yuba	60	6	9,392	215	9,673

Source: United States Census of Population, 1850.
Note: Only these counties were tabulated in the year 1850.

The earliest Black residents of the Sacramento Valley found their way into
the region during and after the Gold Rush. Traveling west as did other hopeful
miners, these earliest African-Americans did not establish any significant settlement nodes in the Sacramento Valley. A small number, however, did cluster in
two places—downtown Marysville and in Tehama County about eight miles
south of Red Bluff. The earliest African Methodist Episcopal Church north of
Sacramento was holding services in Marysville as early as 1863. It was affiliated
with Sacramento's Bethel African Methodist Episcopal Church, the first Black
church built west if the Mississippi River (*Five Views* 1988, 61). An African
Methodist Episcopal church was also dedicated in the town of Chico as early as
1870 (Shover 1991, 17).

Many school districts in the North State did not have enough black children
to offer them a separate classroom. In Sacramento, Chico, and Marysville, however, a state-supported Black school was in full operation (*Five Views* 1988, 63;
Shover 1991, 19). Local scholar Michele Shover's research on African-
Americans in the Chico area revealed the following interesting information about
school attendance rates in these segregated classrooms (Shover 1991, 21):

In considering this aspect of black Chicoans' experience, it should be noted that school census figures repeatedly indicated that about half of Chico's black children attended no school. This was a widespread pattern not reserved to the black community. For instance in 1882-1883 over 700 Butte County children attended no school. Whites composed the greatest share of these.

At about the same time, a somewhat surprising event connected with African-American settlement was occurring in Tehama County. This story revolves around the arrival in this frontier town in 1864 of none other than the widow and children of John Brown. The family of this well known abolitionist, who gave his life in support of freedom for slaves, settled in Red Bluff in an attempt to start a new life. After six months of difficult overland travel by covered wagon, Mary Brown and her two daughters and son quickly became a part of the community.

Her son, Salmon, who had set out from his native New York state with six Spanish Merino sheep, arrived with only two still alive. Nonetheless, he soon purchased five acres of land south of the town of Tehama to begin his sheep herding efforts. According to an article in the Red Bluff paper, the people of the area were suitably impressed with Salmon Brown's stock (*Red Bluff Independent*, May 25, 1865):

Fine sheep—wool growers, and those who are interested in fine sheep, can have the pleasure of examining the best fleece of wool in the country (we guess) by calling at the Independent office. The fleece was clipped from a Merino ewe which had a lamb this spring, and weighs 16 lbs. Its mate, a fine Merino black, sheared 28 lbs. The sheep are owned by Salmon Brown, son of John Brown, the martyr, and were brought across the plains last season.

The breeding stock John Brown's son brought with him to Tehama County helped improve the quality of sheep raised in this area which is now well known for successful sheep raising (Phay 1986, 25).

Meanwhile, a massive fund raising effort was organized to raise money for the construction of a home in Red Bluff for Mary Brown. In support of this effort (and to show support for the cause of abolition of slavery by John Brown), the *Independent* stated: "The East educated his children, the West is called upon to provide a home for the widow and daughters" (*Independent*, June 5, 1865). Successful fund raising efforts and support of the community made it possible to present Mary Brown with a small frame house in 1866 located on the corner of

Main and Willow streets in Red Bluff. The house still stands today, although it has been moved to 135 Main Street.

Sarah and Annie Brown both became teachers in schools in Tehama County, one at Oat Creek School, eight miles south of Red Bluff. The significance of this to the subject at hand is the school's location in the heart of a small cluster of African-American families living in the area. According to research accomplished by William Phay (1986), Annie probably boarded with a well known Black resident of the area who had children enrolled at Oat Creek School, Perfection D. Logan, while she was employed as a teacher there (Phay 1986, 28).

Another interesting and little known story of African-American settlement in the Sacramento Valley took place at the western edge of Yolo County near the town of Guinda. The Guinda Colony Tract, first laid out in 1887 on the west side of Cache Creek, attracted a number of Black families who established small ranches and built the only church ever constructed in the Capay Valley (Larkey and Walters 1987, 53). The Methodist Episcopal Church, built in 1895, was replaced by a new building in 1960.

It is impossible to locate the site of this historic Black settlement about 25 miles northwest of the town of Davis on today's maps because its name, "Nigger Heaven," was eliminated by the Bureau of Land Management in the mid-1970s for reasons of political correctness. Despite its absence from maps and disappearance from the modern landscape, the African-American community in this part of the Valley is remembered somewhat emotionally by many Black and White oldtimers still living in Northern California.

Although there is abundant evidence that African-Americans were forced to homestead the poorest land in a remote area overlooking the town of Guinda, both blacks and whites were quite successful in developing the area. They devoted their efforts to grazing cattle and sheep and planting apricot and peach orchards. Most had secured title to their land through the Homestead Act and virtually every African-American resident of the area had a history of slavery. Some, like Greenberry Logan, had won their freedom early and had fought in the Civil War (Milich 1987, 25).

The site of this early African-American settlement in the western Sacramento Valley in Yolo County is now almost invisible to the untrained eye. All that remains today are a few tombstones, a well and cistern, an old fence, and 2,000 acres of relatively undisturbed land. On what was once the main road leading to the summit stands a sandstone boulder, "Owl Rock," on which residents over the years have etched their names. Owl Rock represents the last physical evidence of this early settlement (*Five Views* 1988, 67).

A nucleus of African-Americans also settled in Oroville after the turn of the century and was well established by the early 1930s. While most scholarly work on the migration patterns of this ethnic group have emphasized the importance of economic opportunities as magnets for settlement, the African-American community in Oroville is an exception to this rule. Although Oroville's economic base provided sporadic employment opportunities from minerals in the early days, and later from agriculture, lumbering, and food processing, this ethnic community was actually the result of other factors.

It was the promise of inexpensive and available land and rural living, along with a slow paced lifestyle that was most attractive about the area. Since the majority of African-Americans in Oroville originally came from the American South or from urban California, the attraction of a small town with a great deal of open space was irresistible. The highest percentages of responses on a survey conducted among local African-American residents of Oroville in the late 1960s reported that their location in the community was due to environmental and social factors. Proximity to friends, a desirable social and cultural atmosphere, and the region's attractive physical landscape were all cited as the most important attributes of the Oroville area (Johnson 1969, 90).

Despite Oroville's sporadic and uncertain economic situation, the population of African-Americans in the area increased 235 percent between 1930 and 1960 (compared to a total overall population increase of approximately 120 percent) (Johnson 1969, 49). Most settled in a small subdivision on the southeast edge of town isolated from the rest of Oroville by a busy street. Over 90 percent of these ethnic residents live in single family homes today rather than in apartments.

Other visible evidences of the presence of African-Americans in Oroville are the large number of Black churches in the area. Businesses owned by this ethnic group are also visible in the local commercial landscape. They include restaurants, dry cleaning firms, and barber and beauty shops. Many African-Americans in the Oroville area also work as professionals in local firms and in school district offices and classrooms, in government employment, and in local lumber mills. Despite these economic success stories, however, the high unemployment rate for south Oroville continues to loom as a large problem for the local economy.

A closer look at one final example of the importance of early African-American settlement in the Sacramento Valley is presented in Box 8.B. This summary of the activities of Edward Park Duplex's contributions to Wheatland's commercial and political scene reminds us of the often unrecognized role African-Americans have played in the development of the region.

Box 8.B
One of the Best Known African-Americans in the North State

The Hairdressing and Shaving Saloon shown in this photograph has been in continuous use as a barber shop since 1875, just one year after Wheatland's incorporation. The building, also known as George's Barber Shop, still stands in Wheatland. It appears that this building's exterior has remained the same as it was in 1875.

The original owner of the business, Edward Park Duplex, a black man who would become mayor of Wheatland, opened a hairdressing and shaving saloon at 415 Main Street in 1875. Duplex had been a barber in Marysville for 20 years before moving to Wheatland.

Duplex's Hairdressing and Shaving Saloon was located several doors from the Central Hotel in the heart of the business district and was a locus of Wheatland's civic activity. Here, leaders exchanged information on matters facing the town's development, while receiving tonsorial services. According to an advertisement in the *Wheatland Free Press*, may 29, 1875, "the shop paid particular attention to cutting ladies and issues hair, to honing and setting razors, and Duplex's celebrated Eau Lustral Hair Restorative, together with a choice selection of oils and pomades, kept constantly on hand."

Duplex was elected mayor of Wheatland April 11, 1888 by the Board of Trustees, and may well have been the first black person to hold such a high office in the western United States. by the time he occupied the mayor's office, Duplex had more than one-quarter century's experience as a businessman and civic leader. In 1855, he was the Yuba County representative at the first California's Colored Citizens State Convention in Sacramento.

Source: Adapted from *Five Views 1988, 91*

New Midwesterners Arrive

Many of the engineers, college professors, government workers, and ministers in today's Valley towns are the children and grandchildren of another large group of migrants who settled the region from the Midwest in the years between the wars. Today, the Valley's distinctive white subculture is, in many ways, a reflection of the conservative values of the thousands of people from Oklahoma, Missouri, Arkansas, and Northwest Texas who were drawn into its agricultural towns in the 1930s. Although this group was a diverse, heterogeneous group from many different parts of the Midwest, they all came to be known as "Okies."

Consider these facts about the importance of this group of hardy settlers:

• About half the population of one town in Arkansas lived in the Yuba City Farm Security Administration Camp at the same time;

- The Valley was such an important destination point for Midwesterners that one of the first two migrant workers' camps built by the federal government was constructed in the Marysville-Yuba City area (Stein 1973, 39);
- The town of Live Oak, at the foot of the Sutter Buttes, was home to an entire town of Pentecostals from the Midwest (Work Projects Administration, Federal Writers Project, *Labor History of Oklahoma* (Oklahoma City) 1939, 33-42);
- In Winters in Yolo County, a migrant camp with three hundred men, women, and children was established south of Putah Creek (Larkey and Walters, 1987, 83);
- According to the 1940 census, Yuba County's total population increased half again over the population it had in 1930.

As we have seen in previous chapters, a surge of new people moving to the Sacramento Valley was nothing new. From the earliest replacement of Native populations by Euro-Americans and Chinese in the 1850s, the area had long been populated almost entirely by outsiders. Some, like the Chinese and Japanese had largely been driven out by the 1930s by harsh legislation and discriminatory treatment; others, such as the East Indians and African-Americans had stayed on despite challenging social and economic conditions.

But the arrival of this largely white population from Oklahoma and other Midwestern states set in motion the first anti-immigrant hysteria directed at white newcomers in the region. Prior to their settlement in the Valley, groups such as the Swedes and the Latter Day Saints (Mormons) had been encouraged to migrate to the area by glossy advertisements and the wooing of real estate agents hired by land colonies. Now, for the first time, an incoming white group was to experience much of the same harsh treatment experienced by non-white groups. According to Walter Stein, chronicler of the Midwestern experience in California (1973, x):

> This is particularly surprising since the migration of a little over a million Americans to California during the depression was, in fact, much smaller in absolute as well as proportional terms, than the increases in population in either of the decades that straddled the depression years, increases which were assimilated into the state with relative ease.

Despite popular misconceptions, it wasn't just drought and the resulting Dust Bowl conditions that drove this group of settlers out of their homeland and into the state of California. Although the dramatic, desiccating dust storms were a disaster for much of the Great Plains, a number of push and pull factors actually encouraged their resettlement. A 1940 study outlining conditions forcing people out of the state of Oklahoma summarized these push factors as a combination of (Tolan Committee Report, 1940):

- Mechanization of cotton and other crops made the tenant system unworkable; farm laborers had become unemployed when they were forced off the land by tractors and other machines;
- Federal regulatory agencies had leveed high freight transport rates on Oklahoma manufactured goods, thereby making it impossible to compete in any other arena than agricultural production in the state;
- Drought, intensified by soil depletion; farmers had cultivated and recultivated, harvested and reharvested 'until many of their best fields had been depleted of their fertility, some of them hopelessly' (Testimony of Carey McWilliams, La Follette Committee Hearings, Part 59, 21, 889);

Overall, rural poverty was cited by this committee report as the primary reason people were forced to leave their homes. It is interesting to note that this report never even mentioned the depression. This national challenge was apparently just the final straw that forced agricultural people to leave their homeland. One farmer who had to leave his farm for the reasons cited above poignantly recalled (Packard 1935 as cited in Stein 1973, 9):

I put mine in what I thought was the best investment—the good old earth—but we lost on that too. The finance company caught up with us. Managed to lose $12,000 in three years. My boys have no more future than I have, so far as I can see ahead.

In a similar voice, a native of Arkansas, living in the Federal Migrant Camp in Marysville wrote on his registration form (Voorhis 1938, as cited in Stein 1973, 11):

Wife, husband, six children. Natives of Oklahoma. Do not like migrating . . . had a 200 acre ranch in Oklahoma. Raised cotton. Had nice home. Still have fine car. Were doing well and had money in the bank.

A complex set of interrelated pull factors brought the displaced Midwesterners into California. Promises of economic prosperity undoubtedly headed the list. Many had seen circulars advertising jobs for cotton pickers and other agricultural laborers (although historical evidence has established that most of these handbills were actually put out by cotton growers in Arizona). One Oklahoma farmer wrote that the attraction to California was "just like thousands of other folks—circulars all over the country, crying for help in the beautiful state of California" (Taylor, July 1935, 351). Anticipating a decrease in the number of laborers from Mexico because of the depression, many land owners in Arizona and some in California believed these displaced farmers would be ideal as replacements.

Much more important than these fliers and brochures advertising the bounties of the Golden State, however, were the all important links provided by letters home. As was common with other immigrant groups in other times and places, word of mouth proved to be the state's most effective drawing card. Enthusiastic reports of their improved lifestyle and economic situation quickly spread through the mail and by word of mouth east along Route 66, attracting others to the West in search of a better life for themselves and their families.

Unlike many other immigrants who had settled in the Sacramento Valley, new arrivals from the Midwest came with their families and planned to permanently relocate in the region's farming communities. Many who eventually ended up in places like Yuba City, Olivehurst, Winters, and Live Oak had first worked in the cotton fields in the Imperial and San Joaquin Valleys, working their way north. West Sacramento's "Little Hooverville" provided a launching place for permanent settlement farther north. West Sacramento's pea camp provides one dramatic example of the large number of new arrivals into the area in the 1930s. It is shown in the historic photograph in Figure 8.4. This crowded tent city had been established by unemployed, single men during the early days of the depression, but had become an "Okie" town by 1939 (*New York Times*, March 6, 1940).

Migrants from the Midwestern states arrived with a strong set of family values already in place. These tight connections within their families and communities back home forged bonds between residents in Sacramento Valley communities as well. Ethnographic work by Sociologist Carl Withers established that close connections existed between the people of a small town, Plainville, in the Missouri Ozarks with a small town in the Sacramento Valley. By 1940, so many newcomers had resettled in Olivehurst that (Withers 1950, 25):

A Plainviller arriving in the Sacramento Valley finds a complete replica of his social situation (kin, neighbors, intimacies, security system) back home. As a visitor and news bearer from home he is warmly received in the homes of kin folks or old neighbors. He need spend no money for food or shelter until he finds a job.

Religious institutions held the new community together along with as these

Figure 8.4. Hooverville, West Sacramento, 1939.
Courtesy of the California History Section, California State Library, Sacramento, California.

family and community bonds. By the early 1940s, nearly every town in the Central Valley boasted at least Nazarene, Assemblies of God, and often several other Pentecostal churches (Gregory 1989, 202-203). The town of Olivehurst again provides evidence of this transplanted Midwestern religious landscape. According to Gregory (1989, 203):

> By 1942, the Yuba County town with its predominately Okie population boasted eight religious institutions, only one of them, a Methodist community center, affiliated with a mainstream denomination. The others, meeting in everything from private homes to a converted dance hall, bore the following names: Nazarene, Free Pentecostal, Pentecostal Holiness, Faith Tabernacle, Church of God (two of them, different sects), and Jehovah's Witnesses.

Olivehurst continues to be home to an abundance of churches in the late 1990s. Just like in the 1930s, most of them are evangelical charismatic denominations.

These tightly connected social and religious networks proved extremely beneficial to the emotional survival of newcomers from the Midwestern states since their arrival was deeply resented by many other residents of Valley towns. The vast majority of these new settlers had arrived in a state of disparate social and economic dislocation. With their Midwestern patterns of speech and relatively unsophisticated appearance, this group of newcomers became an easy target for hostile discrimination during these stressful economic times. The entire economy of the Sacramento Valley was in state of flux and residents were nervous and tense about their economic survival. Adding to the challenges of the national economic situation, California's complex agricultural system was being transformed by mechanization and huge government-controlled water projects. As such, the social and economic fabric of the entire region was unraveling, making this most recent group of newcomers the perfect target.

Adding to the challenges posed by the economic problems of the era and the region was the background of the new residents. Almost all were white, Protestant conservatives who believed in the importance of maintaining the right of the individual. Life in crowded worker's camps where group behavior was strictly watchdogged by government employees took precedence over the rights of the individual family.

Geographer John Fraser Hart summarized the attitudes and values of a typical resident of the American Midwest (Hart 1972, 271). His list of sentiments and values of Midwestern farmers summarized in Box 8.C provides additional insights into the personal challenges faced by people with this cultural

```
┌─────────────────────────────────────────────────────────────┐
│                        Box 8.C                              │
│            Sentiments and Values of a Typical               │
│                  Midwestern Farmer                          │
│                                                             │
│   ° Each farmer should own the land he farms;               │
│   ° Each farm should be large enough to provide a decent living; │
│   ° The farmer and his family should do most of the work;   │
│   ° They should receive a fair price for their products.    │
│   These sentiments then result in the following value system: │
│    ° Hard work is a virtue;                                 │
│    ° Anyone who fails to make good is lazy;                 │
│    ° A man's true worth can be determined by his or her income; │
│    ° A self-made man is better than one "to the manor born"; │
│    ° A family is responsible for its own economic security; │
│    ° The best government is the least government.           │
│   Source: Hart 1972, 271.                                   │
└─────────────────────────────────────────────────────────────┘
```

background who found themselves living in government-managed camps in the 1930s.

According to many Midwesterners currently living in the Sacramento Valley, Hart's list leaves out one very important aspect of this subculture's belief system. "Family Values" were emphasized in every interview conducted with people originating in Arkansas, Oklahoma, and Texas when gathering data for this section of the book. According to Angela Morris, a former resident of the Midwest (Interview, 1995):

> It is the family that matters most to us. When I used to go to the corner store to buy a loaf of bread when I was a kid, I'd just say, 'I'm Jean's grand-daughter' and they'd give me the bread without questioning me at all or asking for payment. We depend on each other a lot. Families are still the most important thing in our lives, even nowadays.

In earlier days, conflicts arose for Midwesterner in the Valley because of differences in traditional Midwestern values and the unacceptable lifestyle of the labor camps. Because of their growing dissatisfaction with the demands of grower-bosses and conflicts within traditional value systems, labor union organizers had a great deal of success in reaching workers who lived in these labor camps. Despite strong anti-union attitudes among residents of agriculturally-dominated Sacramento valley towns, therefore, active union branches were successfully established in Marysville, Gridley, and Winters. In the Winters camp, a full labor boycott was averted only a bumper apricot crop which made it necessary for growers to depend on workers from the camp (Stein 1973, 254). Between 1937 and 1939, a number of rather serious occurrences were staged by union organizers. One of these, a strike and complete work stoppage in the fruit orchards of Marysville and Winters, led to the arrival of strikebreakers in cars with Oklahoma licenses (*Marysville Appeal-Democrat*, July 10, 18, 26, 1939; May 13, 1939).

Despite these many challenges of life in the Sacramento Valley in the 1930s, by the time World War II began in the early 1940s, labor union activities of farm workers were accepted and even supported by most local residents. Many are now unaware of the continuing importance of this subgroup in the culture and lingering evidence in the local landscape of Sacramento Valley communities. Whether it is the region's preference for country western music, its conservative political and personal values, or its many "down home" style coffee shops featuring breakfast menus of biscuits and gravy, grits, and chicken-fried steak, the many contributions of this group of residents cannot be overemphasized.

These evidences of the important role of people from the Midwest in shaping today's life and landscape in the Valley provide yet another example of the blending of diverse cultures and lifeways in the region over the past one hundred and fifty years of its development. As with many other groups, strong connections to the land they left behind still linger in the minds and hearts of Midwesterners. One only has to read the advertising pages of a local issue of weekly newspapers such as the "Pennysaver" to observe the continuing pull of their homes in the Midwest:

> Cheap land for sale; fifty acres of beautiful Oklahoma land available at low cost.

These ads abound on Valley newspaper Want Ad pages. And, according to numerous interviews with local Valley residents, the magnetic draw of "returning home" has already lured many thousands of retired Midwesterners back to the land from whence they came. According to one Valley resident who moved to California from Winniewood, Oklahoma:

> It is more than just going home to us. It is safe there. There is less crime and land is cheap. It is so green there too, you know, the way farm land is supposed to look. It is all there still just waiting for us, waiting for us all to finally come back home.

Economy and Environment

Controlling the Water: The Central Valley Project

In 1921, the California legislature authorized the State Engineer to determine a comprehensive plan for the conservation, control, storage, and distribution of water in California. The primary purpose of the project was irrigation for farmers in the Sacramento and San Joaquin Valleys. The plan was also to include the costs and feasibility of constructing dams, canals, reservoirs, and other works for the redistribution of water from the wet months to the dry ones. A creative component of the plan was the sale of power generated by Shasta Dam, in effect collecting a subsidy for agriculture from electricity (Worster 1985, 241). After the state engineer submitted his report in 1923, appropriations were passed and the final plan was adopted in 1931. In 1933, the Central Valley Project was approved by the state of California. The next problem was to finance it.

It was clear that the project could not get under way unless the federal government made funds available through the Roosevelt administration's "New Deal" program. In 1935, the War Department recommended the construction of Shasta Dam, the keystone of the Central Valley Project.[2] That same year, the Bureau of Reclamation took over responsibility for the CVP. By the early 1950s, the dam was essentially completed and Shasta and Keswick dams on the Sacramento River and Folsom Dam on the American River were in place to generate power, control floods, improve navigation and, most importantly, provide irrigation. In addition, the Red Bluff Diversion Dam and the Tehama-Colusa Canal were constructed to carry water down the west side of the Sacramento Valley. The Corning Canal was also constructed in the 1950s. Figure 8.5 shows the major components of the project.

The project now consists of seven major reservoirs, including Shasta, Trinity, and Folsom, two of the ten pumps which divert delta water to the south, and thousands of miles of canals that supply an average of 7.5 million acre feet of water annually to 18,000 farms and 3 million urban residents. Even during the completion stages of the CVP, state water resource managers and various groups of water users were seeking ways to control and move even more water. A California-owned and operated water project, similar to, but even larger than the CVP, was envisioned. This huge project, the California Water Project, is discussed in detail in the following chapter.

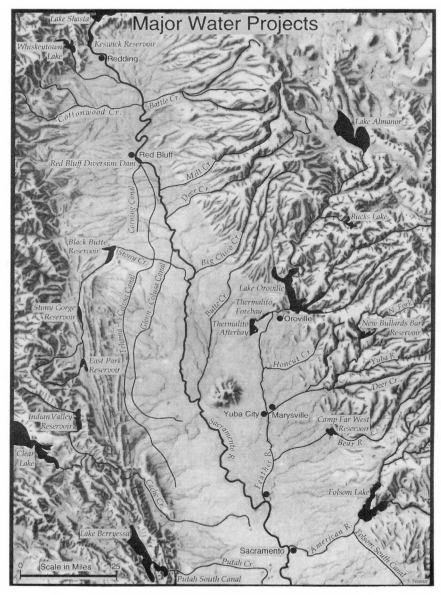

Figure 8.5. Major Water Projects in California.

Transportation Improvements

As discussed in the previous chapter, new roads were constructed in earnest in the years between the world wars to provide intra-regional linkages and to connect remote Valley towns with the outside world. As early as 1911, state authorities were trying to determine the best route for a highway to Oregon. A popular planning notion was to route the new highway on both the eastern and the western sides of the Sacramento Valley. This plan was also being considered for Oregon's Willamette Valley. Ultimately, this plan was adopted in both states.

Figure 8.1 at the beginning of this chapter maps original routes of Highways 99 East and West in the Sacramento Valley from Sacramento to Red Bluff. At Red Bluff, the two routes were again joined and continued to Redding and beyond. Improvements to both routes continued through 1952 when new links would replace older ones (which then reverted to county roads). Evidences of these older highways and their attendant relic gas stations, motels, and diners may be seen in Chico, Orland, Corning, and other Valley towns. Remnant places such as the "99 Club" bar located on Park Avenue in Chico's southside, for example, is one not-so-subtle reminder of this pattern.

Endnotes

1. An interesting sidelight regarding the wearing of these large turbans is their symbolic significance (as well as their practicality). Ancient gurus required the wearing of the turban partly to prevent non-Sikhs from being treated as Sikhs in times of persecution and also to prevent the less courageous followers from deserting or merging with crowds when difficulties arose (Kurtz 1984, 34).

2. There are numerous detailed sources about the Central Valley Project. One of the most interesting because it was written during its construction is Works Progress Administration's *The Central Valley Project* published by the California State Board of Education in 1942. One of its more optimistic predictions was that "by restoring reliable water depths, Shasta Dam will give new life to steamboat and barge traffic on the Sacramento River" (p. 122). Other descriptions and analyses are in de Roos, Harding, Hundley, Worster, Kelly, and McGowan cited in the bibliography of this book.

Chapter 9

Boom Years

Most of the towns and cities of the Sacramento Valley grew dramatically in the years following World War II. Nodes of economic and social activity in the region gathered momentum in the early 1950s as newcomers from the San Francisco Bay Area, Sacramento, Southern California, and other parts of the United States joined with thousands of new arrivals from Latin America, especially Mexico. The map shown in Figure 9.1 locates significant places and routes in the Valley in 1970. New arrivals from Mexico made significant contributions to the region's census figures and also to its economy and culture in these post-war years. Their impact continues today.

People

Mexicans and Other Latinos

Except for Mexican vaqueros who left their mark as cowboys in the American West, very few Mexicans worked on California farms prior to 1900 (Scheuring 1988, 26). Yet, people of Mexican descent now make up California's largest "minority" group. For the past several decades, as vividly illustrated in Figure 9.2, the United States has received more people from Mexico than from any other foreign country. The 1990 census established that people from Mexico and other countries in Latin America now make up at least 25.8 percent of the population of California. About 75 percent of California's farm workers today were born in Mexico and many of the rest are Mexican-Americans (Scheuring 1988, 27).

Declining economic conditions and political instability at home and the proximity of the border with the Southwestern United States has long encouraged people from Mexico to leave their homeland, some on a temporary basis, to

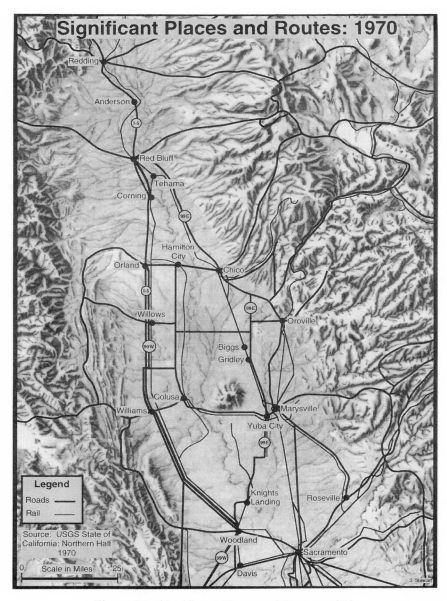

Figure 9.1. Significant Places and Routes, 1970.

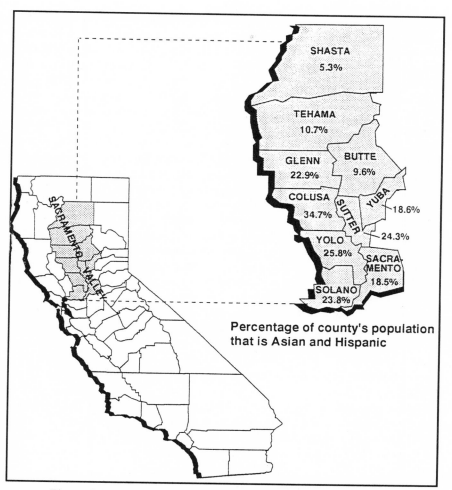

Figure 9.2. Recent Immigrants to the Sacramento Valley, 1990.
Source: U.S. Census of Population, 1990.

find work elsewhere. These factors, combined with the magnetic attraction of economic opportunities north of the border and the encouragement of the United States government during the war years motivated displaced and sometimes desperate Mexicans to come to California. By 1960, there were at least 1.4 million Mexicans and Mexican-Americans living in the state.

As we have seen in previous chapters, agricultural development in the fertile Sacramento Valley had provided employment for a large number of foreign-born workers throughout its history. In the late nineteenth and early twentieth centuries, Chinese and Japanese laborers filled this need. Then, East Indians and Filipinos were imported to work in the fields and orchards of the North State. But after 1910, and especially during the years of the First World War, workers from Mexico began to arrive in large numbers. By the 1920s, with hometown workers returning from the war (and many seeking a new life away from the farm), and the arrival of new immigrants from Europe and India slowed by restrictive legislation, many growers in California and Texas soon became dependent on affordable and available workers from Mexico.

The Mexican Revolution of 1910 also pushed thousands of Mexican families out of their turbulent homeland. Most hoped to return home when the instability of this major political and economic upheaval ended. The revolution accelerated the extreme poverty already plaguing parts of Mexico. By the early 1920s, survival at home had become so difficult that people were forced to seek a new life elsewhere. Nearly one-half million Mexicans entered the United States during the 1920s, some 11 percent of total United States immigration during that decade (*Five Views* 1988, 212).

The years of the Great Depression dramatically reversed the movement of Mexicans north into California. As displaced American farm workers surged into the Central Valley from the Midwest, Mexican workers were pushed out of agricultural employment. Many returned to Mexico. Tabulated immigration from Mexico fell from nearly 500,000 in the 1920s to only 32,700 during the 1930s (*Five Views* 1988, 215).

Severe economic pressures and increasingly negative attitudes about workers from Mexico resulted in the passage of a federal Repatriation Program. This law encouraged local, county, state, and federal agencies to apply pressure on Mexican farm workers for their "voluntary" return to Mexico. Some were deported outright.

Although this ethnic group played a dominant role in agricultural development in other parts of the state before World War II, Mexican workers and their families did not find their way to the North State in large numbers until after 1940. The Sacramento Valley's location farther north than other agricultural areas of the state made it relatively inaccessible to migrant farm workers. This distance factor, along with the Valley's large population of Midwestern farm workers in the 1930s, discouraged the settlement of large numbers of Mexican workers until the early 1940s. Their settlement in the Valley during the war and in the years immediately after, was a direct result of the passage of a pivotal piece of legislation by the United States government.

This bilateral agreement encouraged Mexican workers to come to the United States to work in agriculture for a limited period of time. It was signed by the United States and Mexican governments and in effect from 1942 to 1963 and was later extended to 1968. The decision to permit an unlimited number of Mexican workers to enter the United State was made during a time of increased need for agricultural goods during the wartime years and a decreased availability of local workers. The so-called "Bracero Program" was to be terminated at the end of the war. It continued well into the 1950s, however, encouraging Mexicans to move into the state in increasingly large numbers. The peak was reached in 1956 when more than 400,000 braceros ("strong-armed ones") came to the United States legally (Wollenberg 1970, 145).

The ending of the Bracero Program witnessed the beginning of Cesar Chavez's dedicated efforts to organize farm workers into a union. Chavez's commitment, hard work, and personal charisma finally succeeded in doing what no one had been able to do before—organize an effective and active labor union to protect the rights of farm workers throughout the state. The passage of California's *Labor Relations Act of 1975* was a tribute to Chavez's efforts and helped guide labor policy among farm workers in the Sacramento Valley. Although problems continue to plague the relationship between workers and growers statewide, the United Farm Workers of America union has provided a powerful point of departure for generations to come.

Meanwhile, the resettlement of Mexicans continues in earnest. Several laws have been passed to restrict this flow northward. The first attempt to keep illegal arrivals from entering the United States has since become known as "Operation Wetback." It was passed into law in 1953. This early effort attempted to stop the movement of workers not part of the legal Bracero Program into the United States. In 1964, the Bracero Program, originally designed to support wartime agricultural production, was terminated. These two changes were compounded by the passage of the first immigration law in our history which placed limits on the number of immigrants allowed into the United States from countries in the Western Hemisphere. It was passed by Congress in 1965.

The majority of Mexican-born residents in Sacramento Valley towns like Hamilton City originated in one of six states in north central Mexico. Over 80 percent of all Mexicans in California, in fact, come from this core sending area. Even though they come from extreme poverty and the stigma of being mestizos, these immigrants are not assisted by the United States government as is widely believed unlike many other refugees. This makes it very difficult for families to stay here legally for any length of time.

Most Mexicans who came to the Valley initially to work in its fields and orchards came from the San Joaquin and Imperial Valleys. Many were seasonal workers, arriving in the region during spring and summer harvests, returning south in the fall and early winter months. Most who came with family members settled near large ranches where employment opportunities were maximized. Hamilton City, located along the western banks of the Sacramento River in Glenn County is typical of this pattern.

The most prominent feature in the economic landscape of Hamilton City is the huge Holly Sugar plant which operates around the clock during harvest season (see Figure 9.3). Known for the constant noise of pulp grinders, the sewage-like smell of sugar being refined, and the congestion of diesel trucks lined up to deposit their loads of sugar beets, Holly Sugar provides the livelihood of the majority of the Latino residents of not only Hamilton City but also Orland and other small towns in Glenn County today.

But the real character of Hamilton City is found in its people. Over sixty percent of the town's population is now Mexican-American. A count of surnames in the Hamilton City High School Yearbook for the years 1940 through 1990 revealed 0 percent Mexican surnames in 1940 increasing to over 50 percent today. The Mexican neighborhood on the eastside of town forms a particularly visible ethnic enclave. Houses and yards here are distinguishable by the preponderance of cactus gardens and hedges, lack of fencing, and less symmetrical planting designs. Hamilton City also has an active social life based on ethnic connections. One local resident described it like being a part of "one big family with a party nearly every night." The community is also served by several Mexican-owned stores and cafes which serve as popular gathering places for Latino residents of Glenn and Butte counties.

A major migration of Mexicans into Colusa County also has occurred during the past thirty years. Remarkably, between 1950 and 1970, there was an increase of 293 percent of persons born in Mexico moving into Colusa County (Moles 1979, 23). Most have settled in the county as permanent residents. Many have found gainful employment in occupations not related directly to farming. However, most continue to work as farm managers or field workers for large land owners in the area. The reasons for this are both economic and cultural.

As mechanization after World War II forced many white agricultural employees to leave their rural land (and forced many out of the Sacramento Valley), minimum wage workers still needed on many large ranches became unavailable. Thousands of newly arriving Mexican migrants moved into Colusa County to

Figure 9.3. Holly Sugar Corporation, Hamilton City. Photo by author.

fill this labor gap. As long-term residents moved away, employment opportunities were created in low-paying jobs for the relatively unskilled migrants (Moles 1079, 25).

As a result, Colusa, like many other communities in the Valley, now has a bilateral socioeconomic hierarchy based on divisions in race and ethnicity. Two groups, with divergent social interests and economic values, now live in Colusa —large land owners and/or farm managers and farm laborers. As a result, the community and county now find themselves providing support services for residents largely unable to amass enough capital to purchase their own land. This has resulted in Colusa evolving a local economy not made up of farmers, but of farm laborers (Moles 1979, 25). Problems associated with this imbalance of power common among long-term and more recent ethnic groups in the Sacramento Valley are discussed in more detail in Chapter 11.

Many other towns in the region are rapidly becoming equally Latino-ized in the 1990s. A strong Mexican cultural flavor can now be felt in places like Gridley, Oroville, Colusa, Marysville-Yuba City, and even Williams. The town of Williams now has a population almost one half Mexican-American and Mexican. Most are resettling in this small town just west of Interstate 5 from cities in the San Francisco Bay Area and Los Angeles. They, like most other newcomers in Valley towns, come looking for work in an environment free from crime and traffic problems, attracted by several low income housing projects currently under construction on the northwestern edge of town.

A unique aspect of Latino life in the somewhat inaccessible Sacramento Valley is their continued connection with metropolitan California, especially Los Angeles, and with their homeland "south of the border." This reflects the lingering importance of family and social connections, and also linguistic ties. Spanish-language videos, music, and other cultural linkages hold communities together up and down the state. Thus, the tendency of many outsiders to view the North State as remote and isolated does not hold true in the Latino experience. Clothing styles, musical tastes, and popular video selections may be the same among Spanish-speaking residents of rural towns like Hamilton City and Williams as they are in faraway Los Angeles.

It may be seen from these examples that Mexican-born and Mexican-American residents of small towns in the North State are a part of a huge transnational community (see Kearney and Nagengast 1989). In a similar way, other Mexican enclaves in the state are interconnected with their homeland in Mexico and with other ethnic communities in the western United States. As compared to the experiences of other immigrant groups living in the study area, the ease of travel across the border and the relative nearness of their homeland encourage these continuing connections. The following experience of Mexicans in Redwood City who originated in Aguililla in western Mexico, for example, from research conducted by Rouse is much the same as the situation in a typical Sacramento Valley Mexican enclave (Rouse, n.d., 11 as cited in Kearney and Nagengast 1989, 17):

> Through the constant movement back and forth and the concomitant circulation of money, goods, and services, Aguililla and its various satellites have become so closely linked that, in a sense, they now form a single community, one that I refer to as a 'transnational migrant circuit.' It is the circuit, rather than a segment of western Mexico, that now constitutes for most Aguilillans the significant environment in which they organize their lives. Within this framework, the creation and maintenance of family ties has been a complex affair. Many Aguilillan families are divided between the two countries; family members are constantly separating and reuniting; and relationships between people more than a thousand miles apart are often as significant as those between people living side-by-side.

This binational lifestyle sets Mexican residents of the Sacramento Valley apart from other immigrants who came to the region with a desire to adapt quickly to local cultural values and lifestyles. As increasing numbers of women and children have migrated out of Mexico with their husbands in recent years (or joined their spouse after he has found employment here), these plural roles as both "Mexicans" and "Californians" have become more and more complex. Added to this complex ethnic mix are the vast differences in values and culture between recent arrivals from Mexico and those who have resided in the region for an entire generation or longer.

Efforts to provide support for this challenging ethnic and socioeconomic situation have been expanded significantly in recent years. Increasing pressure has been exerted on local communities to create more opportunities for Spanish-speaking students in public schools. As these important bilingual education programs have been expanded and popularized among other non-Spanish speaking residents of Valley school districts, a wide variety of other Latino political and social networks and organizations have also been established within the region. These ethnic connections and their impact on future developments in the Sacramento Valley are discussed in more detail in Chapter 11.

Mid-Valley Mennonites

Halfway between Hamilton City and Colusa in the mid-Valley town of Glenn, are members of a strict religious sect with European connections, the Mennonites. First settling in Glenn County during the Depression, the religious beliefs of these hardy pioneers originally grew out of the Anabaptist movement that advocated adult baptism and followed a radical, literal interpretation of the Bible. Mennonites have a long history of persecution and subsequent migration. Fleeing religious intolerance in their homelands of Switzerland and the Netherlands, their resettlement eventually stretched throughout Europe, Russia, and North America. The earliest Mennonites to settle in California established a church and community in 1887 near Paso Robles. They arrived in Glenn County in the Sacramento Valley during the Depression.

Glenn County is now home to two distinct groups of Mennonites. The first group, the Mennonite Brethren, has a small congregation in the Capay District in the northern part of the county. These Mennonites actively participate in mainstream society.

During the 1910s and 1920s, Mennonite Brethren were among the first farmers to migrate from the Midwest to the Central Valley. Settling first in the Reedley area in the San Joaquin Valley, they later "discovered" (via a Mennonite land speculator) the abundant, cheap land in Rancho Capay in Glenn County. This promising land had easy access to water from the nearby Sacramento River for irrigation. The first Mennonite in the area bought land and promoted it in Reedley. This resulted in the first six Mennonite families moving to the Sacramento Valley later that same year. Later groups followed suit, including a group from Corn, Oklahoma, the birthplace of nine Brethren still active in the congregation today.

The other group, the Church of God in Christ (or the Holdeman Mennonites), is much more conservative. This group is clustered around the small town of Glenn and live quite isolated from the rest of the community. Settlement in California by this group of Mennonites began in the winter of 1911-12 when several families from Alberta, Canada and the states of Kansas and Washington came to explore settlement opportunities in the fertile and inexpensive Central Valley. They first established a church in Winton in the San Joaquin Valley. As their congregation expanded and many bought land in nearby Livingston, they established a new church there in 1943.

This Winton congregation provided the families that eventually formed the Glenn Mennonite community. In 1950, one Winton family, threatened by the construction of the proposed Castle Air Base, traveled north to find a more isolated place to practice their conservative lifestyle and religion. They bought a farm in Glenn County and began a trend that eventually brought numerous Holdeman Mennonites from Winton and from southern California, Kansas, Oklahoma, and Oregon. Today their congregation numbers about 250 people and they attend services in the newly constructed church located on the western banks of the meandering Sacramento River.

About half the Mennonite households in Glenn County are engaged in farming and the other half in truck driving. Among the diverse crops grown in the area are corn, rice, sugar beets, safflower, beans, walnuts, and almonds. A few Mennonites also work as carpenters and mechanics.

These conservative Mennonites value a traditional lifestyle and strict behavior. They prefer not to have their picture taken, and filter out outside influences from their children's lives as much as possible. Children attend a religious school, television and radio are prohibited, and all are encouraged to remain distant from society if at all possible. Women and girls wear homemade dresses (all made of a similar pattern) and they do not wear make up or jewelry. They cover their hair with a black cap after baptism and wear an additional scarf during church services. Men have beards, wear conservative clothing, and never wear ties. In contrast to their traditional clothing tastes and requirements, Mennonites in Glenn do drive modern cars and trucks and use modern machinery in farm operations.

Mennonite homes stand out in the local landscape of Glenn County because of their ultra-tidy appearance. Yards and gardens are particularly neat and well tended and are usually bordered by picket fences or flower beds. Many of the houses are quite spacious to accommodate large families and frequent visitors from out of town as well as providing room to host traditional Sunday dinners for family and friends.

Economy

Carey McWilliams foresaw the potential for postwar development in California in *California The Great Exception* published in 1949. In this now classic book, McWilliams discussed the Sacramento Valley's limiting factors for growth including problems of flooding and the need for better irrigation systems. At the time his book was published, a massive water transfer and flood control project was in the planning stages by visionaries and various state agencies.

Controlling the Water: The California Water Project

As discussed in the previous chapter and summarized in Figure 8.5, water control systems became increasingly important to the Valley's economic development in the mid-twentieth century. One major effect of the Central Valley Project (CVP) was to promote large scale, high profit, agriculture along with the disappearance of family farming as a way of life (Pisani 1984, 451). The CVP provided interest free loans under the Reclamation Act of 1902 as well as power distribution, sales of water to towns and cities, and direct federal subsidization of the cost of massive dams and canals. There was, therefore, a built-in motivation to do more of the same with a similar state project utilizing the Feather River and its tributaries. In 1958, Governor Pat Brown took responsibility for the state water project, stating: "I wanted this project to be a monument to me" (Hundley 992 , 270).

Conceived as a flood control *and* a water supply and redistribution project, this first state sponsored water development project in the United States was also the largest inter-basin water transfer project ever built at one time. Construction soon began on the *California State Water Project* and proceeded steadily, with water reaching Alameda County in 1962, the San Joaquin Valley six years later, and crossing the Techachapis in 1971. By year's end, the West Branch Aqueduct was completed to Castaic Lake and by 1973, with the filling of Lake Perris in Riverside County, the first phase of the state project had been completed. Water poured into southern California at a rate that would have completely filled the Rose Bowl stadium in Pasadena every hour and a half (Hundley 1992, 287).

Upon completion of the project in the 1970s, the California State Water Project included dams on the upper tributaries of the Feather River at Frenchman, Antelope Valley, Dixie Refuge, Abby Bridge, and Grizzley as well as the massive Oroville Dam and Reservoir with its forebay and afterbay. Other components of the project are the 444 mile long California Aqueduct and its several branches, a series of pumping stations, the San Luis Reservoir, Castaic Lake, and Perris Reservoir. Dependable water supplies from the State Water Project facilities now total about 2.3 million acre feet per year (Department of Warter Resources 1987, 24). About one half of this water comes from Lake Oroville and the rest is developed from other flows into the Sacramento-San Joaquin delta.

In addition to the project's main objective of providing irrigation and municipal water to most of the population of the state, it also provides flood control, recreation sites, and electric power. In addition, its facilities are important in regulating stream flows into the Sacramento-San Joaquin Delta. These very components, however, have also created problems and issues that planners are coping with in the 1990s. They include inducement of growth in urban areas, loss of water quality in the delta, depletion of ground water, and endangerment of some species of native fish. An additional concern is the liberalization of restrictions on the transfer of water rights. If carefully planned and carried out, a free market in which water would go to the highest bidder could prevent misuse and waste but as Norris Hundley observed (1992, 393):

> Such a market reallocation will be difficult to realize so long as agriculture remains heavily subsidized, and even if one should develop, its impact on wildlife and the environment could be devastating if the public failed to demand adequate protection.

The Sacramento Valley's water supply now moves through an integrated complex of natural and engineered conveyance systems. Water is both imported and exported from the region. On the import side, the Clear Creek Tunnel carries roughly 881,000 acre feet annually from Lewiston Lake on the Trinity River into Whiskeytown Reservoir. Since 1876, Pacific Gas and Electric has imported 2,000 acre feet annually from Echo Lake in the high Sierra to the South Fork of the American River. Including the Central Valley Project flows, about 6 million acre feet of the outflow from the Sacramento River region is exported to regions to the south and west through local, state, and federal conveyance facilities.

Ground water provides about 22 percent of the water supply in the region. Well yields in the alluvial basin of the Valley vary from less than 100 to over 4,000 gallons per minute. Ground water recharge in the basin is primarily from river and stream seepage or infiltration of applied agricultural water. Additional recharge occurs as rainfall and snow melt percolate into the basin. In drought years, ground water extraction exceeds recharge. It is not yet known what level of continuous withdrawal will irrevocably deplete the aquifers.

The last remaining component of the California Water Project, the Peripheral Canal, was defeated by the state's voters in 1982 but has not been pulled from the drawing boards. This proposed canal would better regulate flows within the delta but it also contained the hidden consequence of creating the ability to send even more fresh water to the south. As this book goes to press, federal and state agencies are drafting yet another plan that will, it is hoped, combine the responsibilities of several agencies and simplify the complex task of delivering needed water to a growing number of users.

Full implementation of both the Central Valley Project and the California Water Project created major improvements in controlling and preventing floods. With proper timing of outfalls from the major reservoirs, it is now possible to maintain capacity for peak flood events as well as supplies of stored water for export.

Economic Expansion and Population Growth

While the post-war boom in the Valley was nowhere near the magnitude of growth in Southern California, it was quite noticeable to long-time residents. The net increase in California's population from 1950 to 1970 was 89 percent. Most of the impact was viewed as positive because it created jobs and a market for inexpensive housing. Many of the new jobs were in primary economic activities such as agriculture, forestry, and mining in the surrounding foothills. Service sector jobs were also created in education, health care, and retail sales. New housing was built on the edges of existing cities and towns prompting annexations and rapid population increases. The average growth rate for Valley counties from 1950 to 1970 was 72 percent. The average growth rate for its major cities was 79 percent. The fastest growing cities during this period were Anderson, Vacaville, Davis, Woodland, Wheatland, Rocklin, and Roseville.

Upon completion of Shasta Dam and US Highway 99 to Oregon, Redding was ready and able to become a full service regional node for the North State. It continued to function as the county seat of Shasta County and as a regional headquarters for several state and federal agencies. Redding's location made it an ideal hub for several improved highways to the east, north and west and it continued its long term function as a retail center for those who lived or found recreation in the surrounding mountains on three sides. By 1970, Redding could make uncontested claim to be the economic center for all of northeastern California (although Reno now competes for trade from Modoc and Lassen Counties). A profile of the city of Redding, now the Sacramento Valley's largest city north of the city of Sacramento, is featured in Chapter 11.

Changes in Transportation and Accessibility

The decade of the 1970s ended with the completion of Interstate Route 5 (I–5) and the Sacramento Valley's removal of a century of isolation from the rest of California and the nation. By 1980, the region was not only known as a distinct place by local residents, it was economically connected with the Sacramento urban region, the San Francisco Bay area, the Reno-Sparks area in Nevada, and southern Oregon and beyond by new and improved transportation linkages. The region also became increasingly more self-sufficient as an economic unit, especially in the retail sales and services sector. Table 9.1 provides a summary of social and economic characteristics of some of the smaller towns in the Sacramento Valley in 1960. These smaller nodes of economic activity and local culture, along with the region's largest cities, such as Redding, Chico, and Sacramento were destined for very dramatic changes in the 1980s and 1990s.

Table 9.1. Social and Economic Characteristics of Selected
Sacramento Valley Towns, 1960

Subject	Gridley	Colusa	Corning	Live Oak[a]	Orland	Willows
Nativity and Parentage						
Total population	3,343	3,518	3,006	3,518	2,534	4,139
Native	3,093	3,351	2,907	3,196	2,465	3,996
Native parentage	2,678	2,840	2,583	2,662	2,085	3,500
Foreign/mixed parentage	415	511	324	534	380	496
Foreign born	250	167	99	322	69	143
Years of School Completed						
Persons 25 yrs old and over	1,958	1,909	1,768	2,216	1,508	2,340
No school years completed	35	60	—	33	—	22
Elementary						
1 to 4 years	112	96	74	72	39	63
5 and 6 years	150	78	88	148	49	66
7 years	73	82	105	124	51	111
8 years	396	186	347	470	279	357
High School						
1 to 3 years	415	379	360	510	341	527
4 years	432	586	423	595	466	800
College						
1 to 3 years	244	254	234	181	182	214
4 yrs or more	101	188	137	83	101	180
Median school years completed	10.5	12.1	11.3	10.5	12.0	12.0

Table 9.1. Social and Economic Characteristics of Selected
Sacramento Valley Towns, 1960

Subject	Gridley	Colusa	Corning	Live Oak[a]	Orland	Willows
Employment Status						
Male 14 yrs old and over	1,114	1,180	1,069	1,260	885	1,449
Labor force	788	941	752	919	680	1,105
Civilian labor force	784	941	752	911	680	1,105
Employed	707	912	715	859	625	1,033
Unemployed	77	29	37	52	55	72
Not in labor force	326	239	317	341	205	344
Female 14 years old and over	1,292	1,218	1,123	1,385	980	1,410
Labor force	461	545	358	386	358	493
Civilian labor force	461	545	358	386	358	493
Employed	404	493	321	342	333	476
Unemployed	57	52	37	44	25	17
Not in labor force	831	673	765	999	622	917
Male employed	707	912	715	859	625	1,033
Female employed	404	493	321	342	333	476
Industry						
Employed	1,111	1,405	1,036	1,201	958	1,509
Agriculture, forestry, and fisheries	131	167	85	170	63	246
Mining	—	32	—	—	—	50
Construction	86	86	76	144	75	85
Durable goods manufacturing	21	9	183	157	22	83
Nondurable goods manufacturing	85	66	122	129	89	70
Transportation, communications and other public utilities	58	70	45	66	53	117

Table 9.1. Social and Economic Characteristics of Selected
Sacramento Valley Towns, 1960

Subject	Gridley	Colusa	Corning	Live Oak[a]	Orland	Willows
Wholesale and retail trade	322	345	193	239	292	337
Finance, insurance, and real estate	76	56	57	31	57	69
Business and repair services	24	29	22	40	33	31
Personal services	88	105	68	61	89	138
Entertainment and recreation services	13	21	—	16	12	16
Professional and related services	157	257	134	89	137	179
Public administration	39	117	28	16	31	88
Industry not reported	11	45	23	43	5	—

Source: United States Census of Population, 1960, I, Part 6, pp. 399, 401, 403, 408.
[a]Live Oak was unincorporated in 1960.

Chapter 10

Seekers and Finders

The 1970s and 1980s were decades of major, and at times uncontrolled, growth in the Sacramento Valley. Increasing economic development resulted in the creation of new employment, stable prices of farm and forest products commodities, and an improved quality of life for many local residents. This improved lifestyle, in turn, was expressed in an increased involvement in recreational opportunities, higher standards of living for most residents, the construction of new shopping malls and massive warehouse-style commercial establishments, and the in-migration of newer residents with a change in life style as their motive for moving to the Valley.

Among these newcomers were new immigrants from Southeast Asia, New Age-inspired *alternative lifestylers* from various parts of the country, and retirees who were drawn in by the benefits of a lower cost of living and small town amenities. Another form of immigrant, the *equity immigrant* (who may be most clearly defined by a large savings account and cash to invest upfront in new Valley housing and land), makes up the final group of newcomers discussed in this chapter.

With in-migration and economic growth came a set of environmental concerns already familiar to the more urban parts of the state. Air and water pollution, decreases in agricultural lands, and deteriorating water supplies and wildlife habitats were becoming all too familiar issues. Environmental groups began to collaborate with other local residents to begin planning for growth impacts that would minimize damage to natural environments.

The 1970s and 1980s were indeed a heady time in the Valley. Growth seemed assured, economic prosperity blossomed. But it was also a time for reflection, a time for finding a way to both hold onto the past and plan for the future.

People

Southeast Asians

The most recent ethnic immigrant group to try their hand at farming and community life in the Sacramento Valley originated in Southeast Asia. Families from Vietnam, Laos, Cambodia, and Thailand began settling in the North State in the 1980s and continue into the 1990s. Table 10.1 summarizes this drastic increase in the total number of people from Southeast Asian residing in Sacramento Valley counties.

Table 10.1. Total Southeast Asian Refugees in Sacramento
Valley Counties, 1980, 1990, 1991, and 1992[a]

County	Total		New Arrivals		Oct 1992 Total	Percent of 1992 Total
	Oct 1980	Oct 1990	1990-91	1991-92		
Butte	130	2,225	214	163	2,602	0.5
Colusa	2	6	0	0	6	[b]
Glenn	150	218	19	66	303	0.1
Sacramento	4,508	28,834	875	1,047	30,756	5.9
Shasta	33	1,621	0	28	1,649	0.3
Solano	371	1,014	60	30	1,104	0.2
Sutter	3	364	0	1	365	0.1
Tehama	23	36	0	0	36	[b]
Yolo	106	1,604	25	5	1,634	0.3
Yuba	23	2,460	121	128	2,709	0.5

Source: Estimates of Refugees in California Counties and the State 1994, 5-6.
[a]Includes net secondary migration between California and other States for Southeast Asian refugees from 1980 to 1989.
[b]Less than 0.1 percent.

Many who came from Cambodia and Laos were farmers before resettling in the United States. Most lived elsewhere outside their homeland before finding their way to communities north of Sacramento. The exception to this pattern are recent Hmong and Mien refugees who have been sponsored by local Christian groups in Redding. They continue to relocate to this North State community monthly directly from refugee camps in Thailand. Some Mien and Hmong have also lived in other places before coming to the Valley. Earliest clan leaders who have shaped migration patterns north of Sacramento came to the region directly from Fresno, Merced, and from Oregon and Washington. Table 10.2 shows the tremendous impact of various Southeast Asian language groups on public education in a sample Valley county.

Table 10.2. Number of Students Speaking
Southeast Asian Languages, Glenn County
Public Schools, 1990

Grade	Language	
	Hmong	Lao
Kindergarten	21	6
1	38	7
2	15	11
3	19	12
4	9	7
5	7	6
6	7	3
7	5	3
8	1	6
9	4	3
10	5	4
11	3	3
12	2	0
Total	136	71

Source: Department of Education, Language Census
Data 1990 and Helzer 1993, 50.

Southeast Asian newcomers are a diverse group who originated from many different environments in their homelands. Vietnamese are the largest population from this part of the world who now live in the United States. At least 450,000 Southeast Asians (including Vietnamese, Cambodians, Laotians, Hmong, Mien, and Thai) now live in the state of California (U.S. Census of Population 1990). About half are secondary migrants from other states. Many are refugees who are drawn to California because of the state's liberal welfare policies. Beginning in the late 1980s, many Southeast Asians specifically chose a Central Valley location because they hoped to establish themselves in farming (Allen and Turner, 1988, 196). Family reunification, rural life style advantages, a search for economic well being, and environmental amenities are other reasons for their resettlement here (see Helzer 1993).

Many Southeast Asians who have relocated to the Sacramento Valley have clustered in small towns in Glenn, Butte, Sutter, Yuba, and Shasta counties. The Southeast Asian experience in three of these communities—Willows, Redding, and Oroville—is discussed here. As Asian neighborhoods in these Valley towns gain in their ethnic population, cities in the San Joaquin Valley such as Merced and Stockton, are actually losing Southeast Asians in the late-1990s. Mien are most common in Redding (about 1500 total Southeast Asian population in 1994) and in Oroville, and Hmong are the most numerous Southeast Asian groups in Chico and in Willows.

A complex combination of push-pull factors have encouraged the resettlement to the Sacramento Valley of refugees from rural parts of Southeast Asia (see Helzer 1993, 59-64). They include:

- Fear of crime and personal safety in large urban areas;
- The high cost of living in cities such as Sacramento, Los Angeles, and San Diego;
- Competition with other ethnic groups in urban neighborhoods in California;
- The existence of a respected clan leader or other relative in the new community.

For these reasons, highland groups such as the Hmong and Mien have especially favored resettlement in Sacramento Valley communities. Many come in search of a rural place with available land to farm and also to search for a non-urban environment for their families somewhat like the one they were forced to leave in their Laotian homeland. They, like other Valley *dreamers*, hope to buy a piece of their own land for truck farming to supply local markets. The high cost of purchasing agricultural land in the Valley, instead, has forced most to turn to raising vegetables in large community gardens. A photo and brief description of one of these intensive gardens in Redding is contained in Box 10.A.

Although many thousands of people from Vietnam and Cambodia have clustered in the city of Sacramento and communities along the Highway 99 corridor in the San Joaquin Valley, relatively few have found their way north of the state's capital. Reasons for this include their attraction to more urban parts of the state where employment opportunities are better, their tendency to relocate where other members of their families already have settled (note that Weimar,

---

Box 10.A
Hmong and Mien Community Gardens in the Sacramento Valley

According to geographer Jennifer Helzer (1993, 1994), Hmong and Mien gardens provide one of the North State's most visible Southeast Asian "ethnic signatures." She describes a typical garden as (Helzer 1993, 67):

Garden sites are typically dotted with makeshift wooden sheds,most often used for storage and for temporary greenhouses in the winter. Chicken pens are also common features of the landscape and like the garden sheds, are built from scrap lumber, corrugated plastic or metal, and chicken wire. Smaller chicken coops were also found at some residences located outside neighborhood settings. The prevalence of these unique landscape signatures are representative of ongoing attempts to preserve Hmong and Mien cultural traditions. In fact, many neighborhoods and apartment complexes have taken on the appearance of former villages.

Ethnic gardens adjacent to Hmong-dominated apartment buildings were likewise described by a reporter for the Sacramento Bee (December 1, 1984, CL-3) as:

Barefoot gardeners, some with babies on their backs, tend tiny vegetable patches squeezed between cement sidewalks and stucco walls. Tiny cages containing dovelike birds are perched on railings outside the apartments.

---

just east of Sacramento, was one of the United States government's first refugee camps for newly arriving Vietnamese in the mid-1970s), and their tendency to desire a more urban lifestyle. Since the mid-1980s, the Sacramento area has supported numerous Southeast Asian markets, restaurants, and video stores, most owned by Vietnamese residents of the Valley (See Hardwick 1986, 167-168).

Unlike other ethnic groups in the region, most Southeast Asians who have settled in the North State favor apartments over single family homes. Because of the importance of family and clan ties and their strong desire to keep relatives together, both Hmong and Mien, in particular, much prefer apartment living where a large number of family members can reside in close quarters. This attraction to apartment rentals formed the initial magnet for the earliest Southeast Asians who now live in the small town of Willows.

The county seat of Glenn County, Willows, is located in the heart of the Valley just west of the Sacramento River. The primary economic activities of this small town are based on agricultural processing and distribution. Willows is a typical Valley town with a primarily white, homogeneous population. Most residents have had limited experience or contact with refugee groups, especially Asians.

The first Southeast Asians to move to Willows were Laotians who were sponsored by a local church group. They arrived in the late 1970s. Many of these earliest Asian residents of Glenn County have since returned to larger California towns and cities south of Sacramento. They have largely been replaced by Hmong in the 1990s.

The first Hmong families to relocate to the community of Willows were attracted by a local apartment owner who had close linkages with the Hmong community via his other properties in Fresno and Stockton. This ambitious entrepreneur flew several clan leaders to Willows to show them the advantages of settling in the area. He also agreed to pay moving costs for families willing to move north. The Pine Ridge Apartments near downtown Willows are currently more than 75 percent Hmong-occupied; there are at least six hundred people belonging to this ethnic group now residing in the Willows area (Interview with Less, 1993 in Helzer 1993, 51).

A fascinating and quite successful effort to assist these newest Willows residents to adjust to American life (and participate fully in the farming lifestyle they came to the area to practice) is currently underway in the community of Willows. This agricultural co-op program, sponsored by the local police department, is a model of community refugee interaction and support. It is discussed in detail in the next chapter as a case study illustrating potential projects useful in other places in the future that may reshape the Sacramento Valley life and landscape.

The town of Willows by no means has the largest population of Southeast Asian refugees in the Sacramento Valley. Chico has at least a thousand Hmong mostly residing in its south side Chapmantown neighborhoods. Oroville, county seat of Butte County, has a significant number of both Hmong and Mien residents. As shown on the map in Figure 10.1, Hmong families are scattered throughout the community while the majority of Mien tend to cluster in apartments and small homes along north side Mono and Nelson avenues. Formerly residents of Portland, Sacramento, Yuba City, and other communities in central

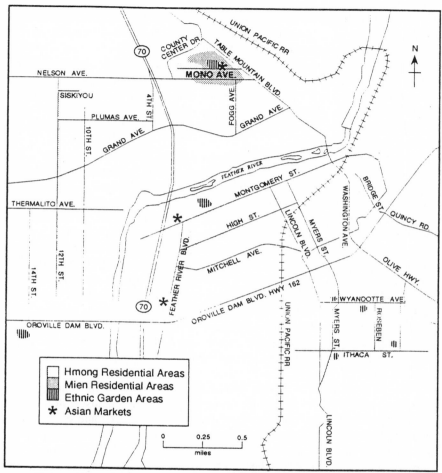

Figure 10.1. Hmong and Mien Cultural Landscape in Oroville, 1993.
Source: Redrawn from Helzer 1993, 57.

California, many have now reassembled in the town of Oroville in an attempt to unify their group. Approximately four hundred Mien and at least seven hundred Hmong live in the Oroville area at the present time (Helzer 1993, 56-57). Members of three or four distinctive clans dominate each group (Kelly Interview, 1993).

Another node of Southeast Asian setttlement in the Sacramento Valley is located in Redding, county seat of Shasta County. According to public school language reports, the largest Asian group in this community is Mien, followed by Hmong. There were also four or five Vietnamese families and two Cambodian families living in Redding in the mid-1990s (Chao interview, 1994). It is interesting to note that there was a much larger Cambodian community in Redding about five years ago, but most have moved north to the small rural community of Yreka near the California-Oregon border. More Vietnamese are expected in the near future.

Hmong and Mien families in Redding are unique because most came to this North State community directly from refugee camps in Thailand. These new arrivals have been sponsored by Redding's very active social service agency, the Southeast Asian Christian Ministry. Others have joined their clan members and relatives from earlier nodes of Hmong and Mien settlement in Oregon and Washington. Linked by the transportation corridor provided by Interstate 5, these recent immigrants are connected with not only their family and friends living in the Pacific Northwest, but also with their fellow clanspeople in San Joaquin Valley communities and in southern California. Redding's location midway between Hmong and Mien centers of population north and south makes it a popular and accessible destination for these secondary migrants.

The experiences of the Mien woman described in Box 10.B are typical of recent Southeast Asian immigrants now living in the Sacramento Valley. Her story is one of a young woman's survival caught somewhere between two often opposing cultures.

Box 10.C summarizes some of the many socioeconomic and cultural challenges faced by these newest of Valley residents. Their adjustment to life in Northern California has not been easy. Faced with negative and even hostile treatment by mainstream residents of the area and a lack of an internal understanding of their new cultural milieu have caused frustration and depression for many. As local school districts, health care agencies, and government programs continue to expand that provide support for these Southeast Asian refugee groups, opportunities for their successful adjustment to American culture should improve in the coming years.

The settlement of dozens of different groups in the Sacramento Valley as discussed in previous chapters of this book has significantly altered life for us all. Without experienced immigrant farmers like the Hmong and Mien, the Germans, French, Portuguese, Italians, Swedes, Sikhs, Japanese, Chinese, Latinos, and African-American and Anglo settlers from the American Midwest and South, agricultural development in the region would have been slowed

Box 10.B
The Story of a Mien Woman in Redding

Lai was five years old when her family left Laos in 1975. Six years later, she arrived in Seattle, Washington. After initial resettlement, her family moved to Merced, where she met her husband. Although she wanted to continue her education at Merced College and eventually go to a university, she felt pressure to marry. After marrying, her husband's family moved to Redding, and in keeping with Mien tradition, Lai and her husband followed. As a married woman, Lai regrets not being able to go to parties anymore. She says it is difficult to make friends, but that she has one American friend in her English class. Lai says she likes "the American way" better. Sometimes she wants to "let out the anger" and express her feelings, but is reminded that it is not the "Mien way" to discuss problems with strangers. Lai says her dream is to live away from her inlaws, finish school, and get a good job. She feels her daughters will not have the same difficulties she had in adjusting to life in this country. Perhaps their American names (Susie, Jennifer, and Julie) are an indication that there is little to look forward to as a traditional Mien woman.
Source: Saephanh, 1993 as quoted in Helzer, 1993, p. 78.

Box 10.C
The Adjustment Process

The first years of adjustment were especially difficult, partly because the refugees had not planned to move permanently to America. The sense of loss at leaving home and family in Vietnam was combined with the pressure to adjust to the strange ways of Americans. Moreover, many of the men in the 1975 wave had the additional difficulty of initial loss of job status; those who had been managers, professionals, or businessmen, found that the only jobs available to them here were low-paying jobs as laborers, busboys, dishwashers, and janitors. Since those early years, many have been able to move into positions that pay better and use their talents and skills more effectively. Some of these people became professionals, but the largest number have opened small businesses. Others, however, especially the more recent arrivals in the 1980s, have lacked the skills that would have prepared them for good jobs here and have found only dead-end jobs, with few prospects for advancement. Accepting welfare has seemed better than taking jobs with low pay and no future.
Source: Allen and Turner, 1988, p. 191.

considerably. The survival skills and agricultural know-how of these various groups has contributed to the development of both agriculture and urban life in numerous ways throughout the past one hundred and fifty years. As data from the recent census counts so vividly illustrate in Table 10.3, by 1990, small but increasingly significant numbers of ethnic minorities now live in Sacramento Valley communities. At the same time, former immigrants and their descendants continue to make up a large percentage of the Valley's population. Without them, the diversity and quality of life and landscape in the Sacramento Valley would most certainly have been compromised.

Three additional groups of newcomers arrived in large numbers in Sacramento Valley towns and cities between 1970 and the mid-1990s. They include *Alternative Lifestylers, Retirees,* and *Equity Immigrants.* These most recent of Valley newcomers generally share three common traits: Most are defined by the following characteristics:

- Predominately white;
- Middle or upper middle income;
- Former residents of East Coast or California urban areas;
- Searching for an improved environment in a quasi-rural place with perceived lifestyle amenities including a slower pace of life, less crime, clean air, and open space.

Alternative Lifestylers

The late 1960s and early 1970s witnessed the arrival of a self-identified group of seekers into the Sacramento Valley, young people with dreams of freedom, spiritual fulfillment, and environmental perfection. Small towns like Chico, along with the volcanic canyons rimming the eastern side of the mid-Valley and rugged foothills east of Oroville, in particular, offered these new arrivals a chance for a new vision of their futures—a chance for a new life filled not only with clean, nonpolluted air and pristine water, but also with freedom for exploration and a chance to recreate their own personalized and very individualized image of "the good life."

Amenities in communities like Chico ranged from environmental to social to political. This town provided:

- An extremely affordable cost of living, especially when compared to the Bay Area or Southern California;
- The availability of an abundance of small rental houses with large backyards for vegetable and flower gardens;
- A warm, snow-free climate but which possessed enough seasonality to

Table 10.3. Ethnic Minorities in the Sacramento Valley, 1990

County	Total Population	Black (%)	Hispanic (%)	Asian (%)	Indian (%)	Total Ethnic (%)
Butte	182,120	1.2	7.4	2.8	1.8	13.4
Colusa	16,275	5.9	33.4	2.2	2.1	43.5
Glenn	24,798	5.5	20.0	3.3	2.1	30.9
Sacramento	1,041,219	9.3	11.7	9.3	1.2	31.5
Shasta	147,036	0.6	3.8	1.8	2.7	9.0
Solano	340,421	13.5	13.4	12.8	0.9	40.5
Sutter	64,415	1.6	16.4	9.4	1.5	28.9
Tehama	49,625	0.1	10.3	0.6	1.9	13.4
Yolo	141,092	2.2	20.0	8.4	1.2	31.8
Yuba	58,228	4.2	11.6	8.4	2.9	27.1
Total	2,065,229	7.5	12.0	3.7	1.4	29.3

Source: *United States Census of Population, 1990.*

satisfy the nostalgic yearnings of those who had left their "establishment" lifestyles in the east and Midwest;

• A relaxed pace of life and a sense of community and caring so important to these footloose sojourners;

• A wild, seemingly mystical and accessible area of canyons, free flowing streams, and forests located in immediate proximity to town;

• An increasingly radical political environment, fostered and nurtured by the influence of the university and its well-educated graduates who had stayed in the town they came to love during their college years;

• A sense of place that resembled beloved Oregon to the immediate north (but with the economic advantages provided by its location within the state of California);

• A huge, free park located within the heart of the community, that provided much desired daily contact with nature.

In short, Chico was seen as the perfect place for visionaries who came seeking dreams of freedom of thought and spirit. According to Dawn Selene, Chico practitioner of Chinese holistic medicine (Selene interview, 8/94):

> Chico is well known up and down the West Coast as a place where you can go to afford to get back to the land. I came from San Diego eighteen years ago because it was such a great place for me and my boys. My kids and I loved Bidwell Park most of all; we just loved the freedom of being able to ride our bikes wherever we wanted to go.

Many others found freedom and contentment in Chico and stayed, ultimately reshaping the community's values to fit their own notion of true fulfillment. Early institutions were organized to loosely reflect the common values and goals of these alternative lifestylers. Groups such as SunArts were organized in the early 1970s to educate and illuminate young people seeking a fuller and freer life. This organization offered meditation classes, spiritual discussion sessions, and art classes.

SunArts was only one of numerous groups organized around the principles of freedom of expression, spiritual growth, and personal fulfillment. Some, such as the followers of the teachings of various spiritual "gurus" came and went as times changed. Others still exist, continuing to work to address community problems and needs. A sampling of these include two organic suppliers, Chico Natural Foods and S & S Produce; The Bridge, organized at Chico State College to address a wide variety of social and counseling needs in the community in the early 1970s; Butte Environmental Council; Rape Crisis Center; California State University, Chico's Child Development Lab (precursor to the Montessori

School-concept now popular throughout the country); Catalyst; Feminist Women's Health Center; and the Church of Religious Science. These ongoing organizations as well as numerous less structured groups continue to play an important role in shaping Chico's sense of community. They also provided a vision of a better tomorrow that helped guide the community through the rapidly changing decades of the 1970s and 1980s, acting as mediating institutions that eased the challenges of rapid cultural, socioeconomic, and spiritual change common throughout these sometimes turbulent years.

The importance of organic farming in the Valley in the 1990s is also a reflection of the long-term influence of these health conscious and environmentally sensitive alternative lifestylers on the local economy. According to the *Organic Farming Directory* (1995), the California Certified Organic Farmer's Association currently has two active chapters in the Sacramento Valley. The *North Valley* group includes producers in Tehama, Glenn, Butte, and Shasta counties while the *Yolo* chapter is headquartered in Capay and includes all growers living in the Yolo County area. Members are listed by name, address, and crops grown in the *Certified Organic Membership Directory and Product Index*, published most recently in 1994. Tabulations from this publication indicate that the North Valley chapter has 55 total growers producing organic crops on 8,154 acres. The Yolo chapter is a bit larger with its 56 members and 10,528 acres (*Certified Organic Membership Directory and Product Index* 1994, 2).

Farmers' markets are popular Saturday morning and week night gathering places in several communities in the agriculturally-rich Sacramento Valley. Towns and cities such as Redding, Davis, and Chico all have well organized outdoor markets throughout the year. Membership lists produced by the Chico Certified Farmer's Market include growers living both in and outside the Valley and include Gridley, Orland, Oroville, Petaluma, Chico, Hamilton City, Durham, Paradise, Capay, Corning, Placerville, Yuba City, Glenn, Live Oak, Marysville, Biggs, and Nord.

According to several community leaders interviewed for this book, the arrival and settlement of several thousand of these "alternative lifestylers" over the course of the past three decades has created change in the community that continues in earnest today. Organic food production is only one of their visible influences in the local landscape. Other examples include the opening of the Mediation Center of the North Valley, founded in 1990 to facilitate the resolution of legal difficulties without participation in the adversarial process of the courtroom. Even more recently, the influence of this group of alternative thinkers was seen in the creation and dissemination of a new *General Plan* for Chico, a visionary document that will guide Chico's growth in the future. This resource-based plan is designed to guide future expansion in one of the Sacramento Valley's most rapidly growing communities. It includes encouraging compact growth through in-filling, discouraging expansion into new areas, increasing density overall, and creating connectivity between open spaces.

In summary, this group of recent migrants into the Sacramento Valley has created change that has influenced the evolution of growth and culture in towns such as Chico, and more recently, Redding. Their influence may be observed most noticeably in the abundance of the following in these communities: alternative medicine practitioners (e.g. rolfers, massage therapists, chiropractors, the Alexander technique, acupuncturists); arts and crafts organizations and businesses (e.g., Orient and Flume Glass Works); counseling services; and environmental organizations (e.g., Butte Environmental Council, Streaminders).

Perhaps one of the most visible impacts of this particular group of Sacramento Valley newcomers is a newly constructed co-housing project on 4.75 acres of land near Bidwell Park. Plans for this participatory community, known as Valley Oaks Village, include twenty-eight homes attached in groups of two or three clustered around a community center with 60 percent of the land left in open space, and gardens, play areas, and pedestrian walkways linking each of the homes. The purpose of this innovative development, as stated in their informational brochure, provides a perfect summary description of the values of "alternative lifestyles" in the 1990s (*Valley Oaks Village: A Co-Housing Neighborhood*, 1994, 1):

> Valley Oaks Village, Chico's co-housing development, seeks to create a neighborhood of people of diverse ages and backgrounds who share an interest in finding alternatives to the social isolation and inefficient land use associated with current approaches to housing and urban development. Our neighborhood is based on the Co-Housing approach, which combines the autonomy of private dwellings with the advantages of living in a cohesive community.

Retirees

During the past three decades, selected towns and cities in the Sacramento Valley, most notably Roseville, Chico, and Redding, have become nodes of settlement for relatively large numbers of retirees from throughout the state. Although most residents of new retirement communities in the area come from the North State, increasing numbers of people from the San Francisco Bay Area, Sacramento, and Southern California cities are retiring in the Sacramento Valley at the present time. One example of this new trend was reported in an interview with the marketing director at The Lodge, Sierra Sunrise Village. She reports that a large influx of new arrivals bought retirement property in Chico right after the Northridge earthquake in 1994 (Brimhall interview 1994).

Retirees are attracted here by many of the same factors that drew in other groups of newcomers including an appreciation of the safety and security often provided by smaller towns, nearness to family members who already live here, perceived climatic amenities, along with clean air and water, and the natural beauty of the surrounding area. The availability of medical and domestic services at military bases in the Sacramento area is also an important attraction for retired military couples. In addition, the increased number of new multi-use residential developments geared to the needs of people over the age of 55 are also significant reasons why many people are choosing selected communities in the Sacramento Valley for their retirement years.

Another vitally important reason why increasing numbers of people over 55 are choosing to retire in the Sacramento Valley is their longing for a sense of community not often found in large urban centers. Many seniors are interested in finding this in the smaller towns and rural areas of the North State. They are especially likely to connect with a community of like-minded neighbors in retirement "communities" like Sierra Sunrise in east Chico as described in Box 10.D.

Data collected from the 1950 through the 1990 census reveal that retirees form an increasingly important component of the Valley's population. This comparison of population data indicates that the counties of Butte, Glenn, Shasta, Sutter, and Yuba all showed a steady increase in the number of people over 55 years of age over time (from a 1 percent increase to an 8 percent increase!). The Valley will undoubtedly continue to attract large numbers of seniors into its communities in the twenty-first century as new and improved residential, medical, and commercial projects are developed to accommodate the special needs of this increasingly large piece of the demographic fabric of our state and nation.

Equity Immigrants

A less easily identified group of newcomers also are selecting Sacramento Valley towns and cities to find new and improved lifestyles for primarily economic reasons. Some of these "equity immigrants," as they are popularly called in local tabloids, were drawn into the region by sales pitches from real estate agents suggesting that "property goes down by $1000 every mile north of

---

Box 10.D
Sierra Sunrise Village: Wave of the Future?

In 1983, the Northern California Retirement Community, a group made up completely of seniors, realized that most of the retirement facilities in the area failed to meet their needs—and they decided to do something about it. Nearly eight years later, their dreams of creating a continuing care retirement community materialized into a 120 acre development at the eastern edge of Chico known as Sierra Sunrise Village. Many members of the original planning group now contentedly reside in the Village.

Every stage of a person's retirement needs has been accommodated in this development. Besides the 61 condominiums, 22 private lots, and 72 apartments, the Lodge at Sierra Sunrise offers 110 independent living units, 24 assisted living units, 25 skilled nursing beds, and adult day care and home health care. The needs of the older adults have been considered throughout the development of the project including shorter than average hallways, carpeting rather than slick floors, easy access to all facilities, a large community dining room, and ample lighting inside and out.

Sierra Sunrise goes beyond a concern for just the physical needs of its older residents. It also addresses their social concerns with the publication of a monthly newspaper announcing planned activities such as birthdays, anniversaries and other celebrations. In addition, transportation to medical appointments and other needs of residents is available 24 hours a day by vans owned and operated by the Village.

Sierra Sunrise provides one model of a Sacramento Valley "community of the future." Planned by seniors for seniors, it accommodates the needs of an increasingly large part of the population of the region with style and grace.

Source: Jeanette Betts, 1994, pp. 1-2.

---

the San Francisco Bay Area." While this expression may be slightly exaggerated, the Valley does boast considerably less expensive housing prices than those found in urban California.

Documenting the exact number of these new arrivals is difficult, although almost every local resident is familiar with the pattern. Professional-class families, disillusioned with life in the big city, sell their house in Los Angeles, San Diego, or the Bay Area for much more than the cost of a new house in the North State. They then move to Redding, Red Bluff, Chico, or Marysville/Yuba City, paying cash for their new property, some rapidly becoming *Nimbies* ("Not In My Backyard") in their new neighborhoods. Resisting future growth efforts brought on by other urban Californians (and incoming immigrant/refugee groups), these newcomers sometimes give lip service to preferring life in the Valley the way it was in the past—slow, safe, and quasi-rural. Many long-term residents believe these newcomers often fail to recognize their own contribution to change in the region, however, and react negatively to their impact on the already overextended infrastructure in some Valley communities. Equity immigrants are often blamed for the proliferation of new malls, overcrowded hospitals, impacted school classrooms, and environmental and social degradation.

Redding has experienced more growth from these equity immigrants than any other city in the North State. Entire housing developments have been constructed to accommodate the needs of this rapidly expanding group of new residents.

Economy

Improved Transportation Systems

In the mid-1980s, the California Department of Transportation conducted studies and public hearings to decide if Highway 99 or State Route 70 should be improved to full freeway status. Ten years later Highway 70 was selected for the improvements but by 1994 the state's financial condition was in such a poor situation that all major highway improvements were deferred indefinitely.

Improved rail (Amtrak) service has also been discussed for years, and again, there seems to be no funding source for high speed rail service or any other major transportation service in the 1990s although feasibility studies are being conducted at the present time.

Urban Sprawl and Renewal

Rapid growth in single and multiple family housing has had a major impact on agricultural areas in the counties surrounding the city of Sacramento such as Placer, El Dorado, Yolo, Solano, and Sutter counties. Likewise, parts of Butte and Shasta counties are experiencing urban *spread* if not sprawl. Most of the development has been along major highway corridors through agricultural lands. Suburban "ranchette" homes on relatively large parcels often surround urban areas and many historic small towns. Sometimes these projects convert non-irrigated lands to small irrigated pasture or orchards but usually they result in a net loss of agricultural output. In an attempt to accommodate future populations on a limited supply of urban land, as mentioned earlier in this chapter, the city of Chico initiated a new *General Plan Land Use Element* in 1994 that called for higher residential densities and a policy of not developing prime agricultural lands. Immediately, despite a lack of evidence, the neighbors of new projects claimed that their property values would decrease as higher density development takes place. A draft Butte County policy calling for minimum parcel sizes in agricultural lands was also hotly protested.

Suburban and rural development in the foothill regions adjacent to the Valley also have created issues related to water supply, suitability of septic disposal systems, response times for fire protection, and provision of adequate school facilities. Some county planning commissions have addressed these issues in recent years, but in a political climate of "government should leave us alone," any form of land use regulation has been resisted, even if the proposals had positive goals. Other contributing factors to urban expansion, especially at the expense of older downtowns, has been the entry of "big box" discount stores and regional shopping centers. Although appreciated by their tens of thousands of customers in search of a bargain, these commercial developments have had the effect, in some cases, of turning small downtowns into "ghost towns."

Attempts to address and plan for these processes have occurred in Butte, Yolo and Shasta counties with, as yet, limited success. One of the most dramatic examples of the pressure for new housing in the Sacramento Valley and an attempt to address it, was the proposal for the *New Town* of Sutter Bay. Located on approximately 4,000 acres of rice farm land near the community of Pleasant Grove, it proposed a mix of homes, schools, recreation areas, and employment centers. The project's first phase, proposed 3100 residences housing 8,000 people. Total build-out town would probably be four times this size after about 20 years. It was planned to incorporate advanced transportation and communication systems and to have an equitable jobs/housing balance. Although promoted as a self-sustaining community, Sutter Bay would undoubtedly absorb some of the demand for housing by those who work in Sacramento but might also slow immigration and growth of communities in the North Valley. The project is on hold at the time of this writing but promises to generate considerable debate about the nature and timing of growth that will almost assuredly occur in the late 1990s.

Another major development proposed for the Sacramento Valley is Celebrity City in Tehama County just north of Red Bluff. This project is designed to include a country-western entertainment center and 1,600 acres of residential development on a 3,278 acre site and is discussed in more detail in Chapter 11. Other, more tentative, large scale projects are proposed in Placer, Solano and Sutter Counties.

Part of the discussion of economic change throughout the country, especially in its rural areas, is the recent fact that most industries are no longer bound to resources and transportation centers. Improved transportation and communication systems, as well as the nature of industry itself, has created less of a place-based dependence. Employers, whether they be in the form of office, warehouse or factory, can more easily choose environment as a primary location factor. The very environmental resources that survived because they were remote from development such as farms, creeks, forests, and grasslands are now the target of *footloose industries* and their employees. The quality of life-related balance of economic security against environmental integrity will continue to be a fundamental consideration in decision making well into the next decade.

Agricultural Patterns

Agriculture is the largest industry in the Sacramento Valley region and it produces a significant amount of the overall tonnage of products in the area, especially rice, grain, tomatoes, field crops, fruit and nuts. About 1,847,000 acres are now irrigated on the Valley floor (Department of Water Resources, *California Water Plan Update* 1994, 122). Crop statistics show that irrigated agricultural acreage in the region peaked during the 1980s and has since declined. The primary reason for the decline is the conversion of irrigated agricultural lands to urban development. A comparison of 1980 and 1990 crop patterns shows that grain, field crops, rice, and pasture crops decreased by 137,000 acres. However, orchard crops, alfalfa, and tomatoes gained a total of 106,000 acres. The net decrease between 1980 and 1990 was 31,000 acres of irrigated crops.

Rice

The largest acreage devoted to any single crop is rice, which represents about 23 percent of total acreage in the region. After *wataribune* rice from Japan was planted experimentally by a Japanese farmer in Colusa County in the early part of the century, newly arriving immigrant farmers (mostly from Sweden by way of Nebraska!) began to plant rice with great enthusiasm and high hopes for its guarantee of future prosperity. The complete story of early rice production near Richvale and the founding of the Rice Experiment Station in Biggs was told in Chapter 6. Today, the Sacramento Valley's "Rice Belt" extends in a wide belt up the middle of the Valley north through the outskirts of Durham, Dayton, and Artois largely between Highway 99 and Interstate Route 5. The southern boundary extends south to Davis/Woodland and across northwest Sacramento

County. The biggest producer in the Valley is Colusa County, the same place where commercial rice growing began many decades ago.

Rice growing, like most other agricultural operations in the North State, is highly mechanized. Seeding, fertilizing, and pest control are all done by air; harvesting and threshing are accomplished in one complex operation with huge machinery. Fields are leveled by laser technology. Irrigated paddies are, in short, completely controlled throughout every step of the growing process. After the rice is harvested, fields are often burned since rice straw will not decompose when plowed under. In recent years, this step in rice production has led to enraged outcries from local urban residents who have demanded that state regulations and fees be imposed on rice burning to cut down on their allergic reactions and maintain cleaner air in the region.

Livestock

The raising of cattle and sheep also make an important contribution to agricultural production in the Sacramento Valley. Along with natural pastureland of seasonally nutritious bunch grasses, irrigated pastures, sugar beet tops, and grain stubble provide ample food for grazing animals. The proximity of foothill and high mountain pastures make feeding the animals flexible and less dependent on seasonal rainfall fluctuations. Some livestock kept on the Valley floor during the wet winter months are trucked or driven overland to greener pastures at higher elevations (see Mainwaring 1995).

Other Agricultural Products

Rice and livestock are not the only agricultural products in the region. The number and variety of crops grown in the Sacramento Valley is, in fact, almost unbelievable. The region's long and temperate growing season, fertile soils, extensive level land, available labor supply, and mechanization, along with its highly sophisticated water control systems make the Valley one of the most productive agricultural regions in the world. Some parts of the region have long been known for certain specialty crops. Olives in Corning, kiwifruit and hops in Gridley, almonds and walnuts in Durham, sugar beets in Hamilton City, and the region's "Peach Bowl" in Butte, Yuba, and Sutter counties represent only a few. These and a multitude of other agricultural products are grown in many parts of the fertile Sacramento Valley. Brief summaries of mid-1990s production levels in each county in the area follow. (All information was collected from county offices of the Department of Agriculture's annual *Crop and Livestock Reports*.)

Butte County

Estimated gross production in Butte County in 1993 totaled $325,899,000. This is a fifty million dollar increase over 1992 agricultural production and the highest ever reported for Butte County. Timber production showed the greatest percentage increase. Fruit and nut crops and nursery stock also helped produce the all-time record in crop values for the county. A decline was noted in livestock, apiary, and vegetable crops. Million dollar crops in Butte County include (in decreasing order of value) almonds, rice, timber, English walnuts, prunes, kiwi-fruit, peaches, nursery stock, olives, rice seed, cattle/calves, dryland pasture and range, miscellaneous fruit and nut crops, miscellaneous field crops, irrigated pasture, alfalfa hay, sugar beets, almond hulls, wheat, milk, apiary production, hogs, and beans.

Colusa County

Rice continues to be the county's leading crop with a total value of $98,737,000. It leads over all other crops in acreage, total value, and price over 1992. Almonds surpassed processing tomatoes as the county's second largest crop, with a value of $25,612,000. Colusa County's ten leading farm commodities include rice, almonds, processing tomatoes, wheat, seed rice, cattle/calves, cucumber seed, English walnuts, squash seed, and prunes.

Glenn County

Agriculture continues to be the leading industry in Glenn County with a gross value of $252,898,000 in 1993. This figure represents an increase from the 1992 record high which followed a decrease from earlier production levels primarily because of drought, the freeze, and bad weather during almond polli-nation season. Glenn County's ten leading agricultural commodities include rice, almonds, dairy products, prunes, cattle/calves, alfalfa hay, walnuts, wheat, corn, and sugar beets. Organic farmers in the county produced (in order of decreasing importance) almonds, citrus, miscellaneous fruits, dried beans and peas, rice, and vegetables.

Sacramento County

Milk continues to lead Sacramento County commodities with a value of $35,178,000. Pear production also remains strong with a total value for the crop of $33,720,000. Pears lead all other crops in Sacramento County and it continues to lead the state in pear production. Wine grape production suffered somewhat in 1993 by reduced yields due to disease problems brought on by the late rains. Field crop leaders continue to be corn and rice. Safflower acreage increased by 9,400 acres in response to a strong market demand. Sacramento County's ten leading farm commodities (in order of decreasing importance) include milk, Bartlett pears, cattle/calves, wine grapes, nursery stock, field corn, turkeys, processed tomatoes, safflower, and rice.

Shasta County

The dollar value of agricultural products did not change significantly between 1992 and 1993 in Shasta County. Livestock and livestock products held steady while the values of some field and orchard crops increased. Higher hay prices and higher walnut yields contributed to the increased value for these commodities. A 14 percent decline in nursery stock occurred due to a reduction in the number of acres of harvested strawberry nursery stock. The most important agricultural products in Shasta County in 1993 in decreasing order of importance included livestock, livestock products, apiary products, field crops, nursery stock, and orchard crops.

Solano County

The gross value of all agricultural production in Solano County in 1993 amounted to $177,705,000 which is an increase over the preceding year. Field crops increased most dramatically with strong prices for corn and increases in safflower, sugar beets, and non-irrigated wheat acreage. Fruit and nut prices were strong for almonds and prunes, although prune production was delayed due to spring rains. Walnuts continue to increase in acreage and, in fact, are now the county's largest acreage fruit and nut crop. Tomatoes grown for processing are Solano County's number one commodity. The county continues to be the state's number two county for sheep and lamb production as well.

Solano County's million dollar crops from most important to least important include processing tomatoes, sugar beets, cattle/calves, nursery stock, alfalfa hay, irrigated wheat, feeder lambs, field corn, pears, walnuts, grapes, sunflower seed, safflower oil, milk, edible beans, dryland wheat, pasture and rangeland, irrigated barley, apricots, prunes, irrigated pasture, almonds, sheep, seed and dry beans, and popcorn.

Sutter County

The gross value of all agricultural products in Sutter County in 1993 totaled $292,109,000, a 2.3 percent increase from the 1992 total. Fruit and nut crops continued to lead all commodity categories with a value of $119,990,900. Dried prunes experienced a major decline in yield per acre in 1993 because of brown rot disease. This resulted in a 33 percent crop value reduction. Almonds and walnuts, on the other hand, each increased by nearly 50 percent over the 1992 reported values.

Rice continues to be Sutter County's leading field crop and leads all other individual crops in acreage planted (79,896) and in value. Since 1910, rice has been in the top five commodities in Sutter County in gross value. The county's ten leading crops from most important to least important are rice, prunes, peaches, tomatoes, walnuts, melons, cattle/calves, nursery products, wheat, and dry beans.

Tehama County

Tehama County's total farm production increased 4.5 percent between 1992 and 1993 with a gross production of $100,365,200 reported in 1993. This sets a new all-time record for Tehama County agriculture. Significant increases in walnuts and almonds accounted for most of this increase. The only category that decreased significantly in total value was olives which decreased from a total of $9,756,000 in 1992 to $4,632,000 in 1993 due to an almost 30 percent drop in the price per ton. Livestock and poultry also showed a significant decrease in production from 1992 to 1993.

Tehama County's leading products (in decreasing order of value) include fruit and nut crops, livestock and poultry, field crops, pasture and rangelands, livestock and poultry products, seed crops, nursery products, apiary products, and vegetables.

Yolo County

Yolo County's million dollar crops in 1993 included (in order) tomatoes, alfalfa hay, rice, safflower, wheat, English walnuts, almonds, seed, sugar beets, corn, cattle/calves, melons. wine grapes, nursery stock, organic production, pears, dried prunes, irrigated pasture, dry beans, and milk. Yolo County is heavily involved in organic production and is a leader in the Valley in this type of agriculture. Examples of this include organic fruit and nut production which totaled 214 acres with a gross value of $610,200 in 1993. Organic vegetables and grains were raised on 1,028 acres that same year and produced $2,064,000 in total value.

Yuba County

Yuba County's agricultural gross crop value in 1993 was $124,902,400, an increase of 6.55 percent over 1992 production. Fruit (especially prunes) and nut values were down 5.1 percent as a result of adverse spring weather. The bad weather also reduced yields of early varieties of cling peaches, although almonds showed a significantly higher yield in 1993 because of higher prices and higher yields. Leading crops in Yuba County are rice, prunes, peaches, walnuts, cattle/calves, timber, milk, kiwi, almonds, and pasture land.

Regional agricultural production and location patterns for the entire Sacramento Valley may be discerned from an overview of these lists of gross values, acreages, and crops. In summary, the region's most important fruit and nut crops include almonds, apricots, grapes, kiwifruit, olives, peaches, pears, pistachios, prunes, and walnuts. Its leading field crops are alfalfa seed, corn, dry beans, alfalfa hay, hops, Ladino clover seed, rice, safflower, small grains, and sugar beets (*California Field Crop Statistics* 1982-1993, 1). These and other crops have played a pivotal role in the development and success of agriculture in the Sacramento Valley over the past several decades.

Several of the Valley's unique specialty crops are highlighted here as examples of the great diversity of agricultural products in the region. Sample selections include cotton, kiwifruit, olives, and finally, one of the Valley's newest economic activities, emu raising.

A Closer Look

Cotton

This crop was first brought into California by early Spanish settlers, although little record of their experiences with the crop exist today. Historically, cotton in the state has been grown in the southern San Joaquin valley and the lower desert valleys of Riverside and Imperial counties. As early as 1808, cotton was grown on an experimental basis in the southern part of the state. In 1862, the California legislature offered a reward of $3,000 for the first one hundred bales of cotton grown in the Palo Verde Valley. Thereafter, the majority of cotton produced in California was grown in the southern part of the state.

Then, on October 28, 1925, the first cotton planted in the Sacramento

Valley was harvested in Palermo in Butte County by the Sacramento Valley Cotton Gin Company. It remained an experimental crop until 1993 when a renewed interest in cotton growing began to be promoted in the northern Sacramento Valley. It met with stiff opposition from many orchardists, however. Their major concern is *verticillium wilt*, a soil-born fungus disease that could harm olive trees. Many olive growers believe that cotton residues will promote the establishment of this disease and that it could then spread aerobically.

Despite this opposition, Butte County granted a permit to a Glenn County farmer in 1994 to raise 100 acres of experimental cotton. His experiment was successful but the complex logistics involved did not make the venture profitable because cotton had to be trucked to the nearest cotton gin in Los Banos.

So far, there appears to be a mixed set of reactions to the possibility of raising cotton in the Sacramento Valley. Much depends on demand for the product and on market prices. But in 1995, high prices and high demand encouraged farmers like the Cook family to plant 1,000 new acres near Williams. Sixty acres were also been planted in Esparto in Yolo County by Frank Muller. But the need for a local ginning mill must be addressed before cotton can be made profitable in the region. Local farmers recently have stated that they might be willing to build a ginning facility in the Valley, perhaps in the Williams area (*Sacramento Bee,* December 20, 1994, D1-2).

Whatever the outcome of the ginning issues, many political and economic issues will also have to be addressed before local orchardists allow cotton to be grown on a large enough scale to make it profitable. But high prices and improved market access have promoted a renewed interest in cotton that will not go away for many Valley farmers. It seems at this point that the most important question is when and where cotton ginning facilities will be built to help prospective growers. Meanwhile, a real pioneer spirit has developed among these innovators in cotton planting and production. According to Judy Brown, experimental cotton farmer in Butte County (1994, D2):

> This was the first time I'd ever seen a cotton plant up close, but I'm real pleased. We learned a lot and had some fun. What more can you ask? And . . . maybe we even made a little money!

Kiwifruit

Anyone who has ever eaten in a restaurant specializing in *California cuisine* has undoubtedly experienced kiwifruit "up close and personal." But this crop, like most other popular California food products, is not native to North

America. The kiwifruit vine is native to China where it is called *yang tao*. The first commercial kiwifruit vineyard was planted in New Zealand about 1940. Fruit was exported from New Zealand to the United States as early as 1958 and was first called *Chinese gooseberries*. The name was later changed to kiwifruit (Beutel 1989, 1).

Kiwifruit is a relatively new crop in California. It was first planted here in 1967 and by 1971, at least one hundred acres were growing successfully in Butte and Kern counties. From the very beginning, Butte County was an important site for kiwifruit production because the original experimental vines were planted in 1934 at the Chico USDA Plant Introduction Station. These earliest plants are still growing and producing at the Chico US Forest Service Tree Nursery and are the source clone of almost all kiwi plants in the region. The area's first significant commercial crop was harvested and packed in 1977 At the present time, despite high production costs (including planting of vines, construction of trellises, and installation of drip irrigation systems) over eight million trays are packed every year. Kiwifruit has an average yield of 8000 pounds of packed fruit per acre. Butte County currently leads the state in kiwifruit production.

Olives

Early Spanish padres planted the first olives in California around 1770. Olive trees were planted throughout the state, especially in the Sacramento Valley with its ideal climate. Winters are not cold enough to kill the trees, yet they provide enough winter chilling hours to induce flowering. In addition, the Valley's long, hot, and dry summers allow olive fruit to mature correctly.

Despite these climatic amenities, until 1893, the quality of domestically-produced olives was considered to be inferior when compared to imported varieties. California olives had a short lifespan, which meant they were prone to botulism. Bucking these odds, Freda Ehmann, who inherited an olive orchard in Marysville, is credited with creating the North State's olive industry as it is known today. Ehmann produced the first truly successful packing of olives in 1893. Enlisting the expertise of E.W. Hilgard from the Agricultural College at the University of California, Davis, Ehmann and Hilgard experimented with various olive pickling methods. After many years of experimentation and perseverance, Ehmann's olives became quite well known and their cultivation spread throughout the Valley. Her Ehmann-Stow Company in Oroville won the highest award for olive oil at the 1900 Paris International Exposition. Today, California produces 100 percent of the nation's olives.

Emu Ranching

A 97 percent fat-free substitute for beef raised on small ranches typically
smaller than 10 acres without the trampling, grazing, grain consumption,
or methane production that makes the cattle industry the agricultural bane of
the globe. All that, and more, insist its proponents.

Chico News and Review, 1995

The national bird of Australia, the emu, has been gaining popularity on
ranches in the Sacramento Valley since the late 1980s. Emus provide a red meat
alternative for lovers of beef. The cost of emu meat ($13/lb), however, and the
limited number of the animals (roughly 6,000 in the entire United States), have
kept these huge birds from becoming instantly successful in regional markets.
These factors, along with the high cost of purchasing each animal have so far
limited economic gain from "emu ranching."

Future success may not be too far away, however, since the production of
emus has many strong selling points. First, their meat has less cholesterol than
chicken or turkey, a strong selling point for health-conscious consumers. In
addition, the hide can be used for leather goods and the oil, although not yet
verified by the FDA, is claimed to have therapeutic qualities. Many of the
animals are victims of the latest technology in marking for identification.
Tattoos and brands are no longer used. Instead, implanted micro-chips are used to
identify each animal. It is estimated that in order to capture one pound of the beef
market, 28 million birds will have to be raised.

Presently, over ten thousand families in the United States are pioneering the
raising of emu on their farms and emus are currently being raised in many parts
of the Sacramento Valley. They cope with the hot summers and wet winters of
the region quite well. Could emus be the wave of the future? Is emu ranching the
next step in promoting the Valley as a place for speculation by *dreamers*? The
American Emu Association thinks so. In a tone much like earlier promotional
statements by land developers creating agricultural colonies, their newest
brochure reports (1995, 4):

Emu ranching promises an opportunity to create a new family heritage and a
more desirable lifestyle that heralds a new century. Join a growing industry
that can be both financially rewarding and enjoyable. Join the new frontier
in ranching now Call today, and take the first step into tomorrow's lifestyle.

Environment

Resource Depletion

The process of human occupance on the land continues to make change on the landscape. Some of these changes are positive in human terms and turn out to have fairly benign impacts on the local and regional environment. Others, however, are more insidious and may produce harmful impacts at some time now or in the future. One blatant example of this is human activity as a geomorphic agent of change. We have created new landforms, hydrologic systems and plant cover, and have actually eliminated entire ecosystems. Some of these changes have created problems for planners, for law makers, and for concerned citizens. Many seem unsolvable at the present time.

Natural resources are found in a natural setting and used for economic purposes. In the Sacramento Valley they include soil, water, timber, rangelands, and wildlife habitat such as wetlands. Natural resources can also include minerals and recreational destinations such as wilderness areas. As in other parts of rural North America, the historical economy of the Valley has been based on the extraction and processing of natural resources. Examples are farming, mining, and logging. Other uses of the natural environment include recreation, power generation and provision of urban water supplies. As long as there is enough of the resource or it is renewable, there are few complaints. As competition and increased pressures for use appear (as they have in the Valley over the last two decades), major adjustments must be made. For example, the 500,000 acres of riparian forests in the Valley were reduced to 11,000 acres by 1979, about 2 percent if historic levels! Now, however, oak-dominated riparian lands have been increasing due to the fact that we no longer need wood to propel steam engines. Marginal farmlands have been abandoned and state and federal agencies have been acquiring river lands for habitat preservation (see McGill 1987). These and other examples of positive decision-making by Valley residents offer encouragement that the future may be better than the past in terms of our appreciation and protection of natural systems.

Generally speaking, the production of goods based on natural resources requires a lot of land and relatively few people. As populations increase, the economy becomes more involved with secondary and tertiary activities (manufacturing, services, and information processing) and is less mindful of resource management problems. Such is the case in the 1990s in the Sacramento Valley as in many other parts of the United States.

Habitat Protection

Much of the local economy and a great deal of the quality of life enjoyed in the Valley are based on natural ecosystems at work. Sport fishing, waterfowl hunting, and nature study are examples. But as populations increase and economic development occurs, natural areas have become threatened. For example, the Butte and Sutter Basins contain large wetland areas which serve as critical habitat for migratory waterfowl in the Pacific Flyway. There are about 13,000 acres of publicly owned and managed waterfowl habitat in the Butte Basin. In addition, private hunting clubs maintain more than 30,000 acres of habitat during normal years. The Sutter Basin has almost 2,600 acres of publicly owned waterfowl habitat, all located within the Sutter National Wildlife Refuge. Duck hunting clubs provide an additional 1,500 acres of waterfowl habitat. While this may sound like a huge acreage devoted to waterfowl habitat, it is only a fraction of what existed historically in the region.

Water-related problems of the Butte and Sutter basins include fish passage and habitat degradation, water quality, flooding and drainage problems and water rights (*California Water Plan Update* 1994, 146). The issues are complex because of competing uses and the maze-like pattern of water flow through the area. Both waterfowl and salmon habitats are particularly in need of more dependable water supplies. This area's greatest water management issue from a local perspective is the widely perceived need for local groundwater basin management. Local concern is motivated by fears that other areas of the state may try to purchase groundwater to the possible detriment of the local economy and rural lifestyle. New water user associations have been created to conduct research and to monitor political events related to these issues. In a similar manner, water users in the million acre Colusa Basin have been working on historical problems of flooding, drainage, water quality, subsidence and habitat problems.

Water Supply

The Sacramento River Region is the main water supply source for much of California's urban and agricultural land uses. Basin runoff averages 22,389,000 acre feet providing nearly one third of the state's total natural runoff (*California Water Plan Update* 1994, 124). Major water supplies in the region are provided through surface storage reservoirs and through groundwater pumping.

A major issue that is currently discussed by virtually all of the water delivery agencies is the long term supply of groundwater under the Valley floor.

In the past, most of the ground water was used by local farmers and municipal agencies, but recent demand combined with several years of drought have tempted some to sell their water to out-of-Valley users. Naturally, if many individuals or districts were to do this there would be a net deficit in total ground water supplies. In recognition of this possibility, the Butte Basin Water Users Association and other groups have placed this issue high on their agenda for future planning. At least in Butte County, primary water users have had a role in revising and updating the Conservation Element of the County General Plan. In most Valley agricultural areas, landowners are receptive to ongoing ground water modeling and computer-generated methods to help predict and enhance future water supplies.

Water Transfers

Individuals and water districts from several counties have recently sold or are considering selling surface water and groundwater to downstream users. As a result of this activity and the potential for much more of it, many North Valley water users are concerned about over-commitment to these obligations in drought years thereby causing net losses to local supplies. Organized groundwater management efforts are currently underway in Butte, Colusa, Glenn, Shasta, Solano, Sutter, Sacramento, Tehama, and Yolo counties.

At the same time, management and operations of the Central Valley Project and the California Water Project are being monitored. Some have suggested takeover of the CVP by the state of California in order to coordinate water distribution more efficiently. To date, nothing has been decided on this issue.

Endangered Species

Concern over implementation of federal and state Endangered Species Acts is like arranging deck chairs on the Titanic! The real issue is loss of wildlife habitat for which endangerment listing is an indicator. As habitat is reduced by pumping and irrigation, as in the case of the winter and spring run Chinook salmon, virtually all native aquatic life in the region will be threatened. Related to protection of riverine ecosystems is the need for preservation of their surrounding riparian vegetation corridors.

Protection of some endangered animals has affected the use of water in the Sacramento River basin such as increase of flows to protect smelt in the delta and winter-run Chinook salmon. The bank swallow, yellow-billed coo, and the long-horned elderberry beetle are all listed species that require protection along the riverine riparian forests of the Valley. All too often, habitat preservation and enhancement has been viewed as unnecessarily expensive, time consuming, and disruptive of farm operations and urban development.

The current approach to protection of rare and endangered plants and animals is through habitat improvement since habitat loss is the greatest single contributing factor in their losses. An example of such a plan now in its implementation stage is the *Sacramento River Fisheries and Riparian Habitat Management Plan*, authorized by Senate Bill 1086 (*Upper Sacramento River Fisheries and Riparian Habitat Management Plan* 1989).

The plan was adopted in recognition of the fact that the salmon and steelhead fishery in the upper Sacramento River has declined greatly in the last few decades. Contributing to this decline and perhaps the listing of the spring run salmon as "endangered," are problems on the river's main stem (e.g., unsuitable water temperatures, toxic heavy metals, degraded spawning gravels, obstructions to fish migration, fish losses from diversions, and riparian habitat loss). About one half of the twenty recommended actions in the plan are now underway while others await federal funding and participation.

Examples of projects that will help to restore the fisheries are screening or replacement of irrigation pumps that kill downstream migrating fish, replacement of the large Glenn-Colusa Irrigation District intake screen on the river which is now not functioning properly, installation of mechanisms to provide cold (lake bottom) water for the river below Shasta Dam, upgrade of fish ladders and screens at the Red Bluff diversion dam, and renovation or removal of various obstructions to fish migration on the river tributaries.

Toxic Wastes

Most water pollution in the Valley comes from herbicides, pesticides, heavy metals, chlorine, surfactants and ammonia (State Lands Commission 1994, 68). These pollutants come primarily from non-point sources such as agricultural operations and urban street runoff. Certain locations in the Valley have serious water pollution problems. The city of Chico, for example, has designated numerous places in the community as having poor water quality.

The Valley has been relatively free of large toxic waste problems because it did not support many heavy industries as was the case in the North American northeast and many other parts of the world. The exception is Sacramento

County which has fifteen toxic waste sites identified by the Environmental Protection Agency. These include military bases, oil companies, manufacturing plants, a state prison, and railroad facilities. Sacramento County toxic waste sites specifically include: Ace Oil Company, Aerojet General Corporation, Folsom State Prison, Howe Avenue PCB site, Jibboom Junk Yard, Chromalloy-Palm Iron and Bridge Works, Purity Oil Sales, Union Pacific Railroad, Pacific Gas and Electric, Southern Pacific Railroad, Mather Air Force base, McClelland Air Force Base, and the Sacramento Army Depot (see Wilson 1993). Mather AFB and the Army Depot were cleaned up and converted to civilian use in the mid-1990s. A final decision to close McClelland AFB was made in late 1995.

Three sites in the North Valley include heavy metal pollution into the Sacramento River drainage from the Iron Mountain Mine near Redding, the Simpson Paper Mill in Anderson, and the Koppers Inc. wood processing plant in Oroville which is contaminating local ground waters. The Koppers superfund site contains a 2.5 mile long groundwater plume containing pentachlorophenol (PCB) and some 15,000 cubic yards of dioxin tainted soil. The site is being cleaned up in 1995 by a new owner. The Anderson mill has been closed and clean up of dioxin there has begun. The Environmental Protection Agency continues its attempt to clean up acid and heavy metals drainage from the mine. So far, progress has been slow.

An even more challenging situation exists as less visible pollution in the Sacramento River from irrigation run-off. Nutrients from fertilizers can become poisonous when mixed with the chlorine used in municipal water treatment. This is especially an issue in the delta. In addition, pesticide pollution continues to be an ongoing problem.

Air Quality

Compliance with the federal and state clean air acts in the Sacramento Valley has been more of a success story in the last decade than is the case with other environmental issues. Enactment of emissions regulations for various transportation modes, particularly automobiles, has kept the urban areas mostly within state compliance standards, although many locals regularly complain about poor air quality and allergies. The major problem of seasonal field burning has been addressed with plans to phase out the practice and replace it with mulching or recycling of the rice straw.

Suggested solutions to other environmental issues that are introduced in this chapter are optimistically, yet cautiously, forecast in the next chapter. They form a vital part of the next generation's *Valley for Dreams.*

Chapter 11

Dreams Fulfilled?

Historical geography tells the story of a continuous process of change on the land. The Sacramento Valley has undergone monumental changes over the last two centuries and it is reasonable to expect that dramatic social, political, economic, and environmental changes will continue into the new century. Although the Valley will continue to be less isolated than ever before, it remains a unique place to live, work, play, and visit.

This final chapter speculates on potential changes this dynamic region may experience in the near future based on current trends. As in other chapters, we divide our discussion into four sections—economy, people, environment, and landscape.

Economy

Regional Urbanism

The city of Sacramento has remained the largest and most influential city in the Sacramento Valley since its founding over a century and a half ago. In recent years, growth in and around California's capital city has followed Highway 50 and Interstate 80 corridors to the east and Interstate 5 and Highway 99 to the south and north. Growth is now spilling over into the Highway 65 corridor through the urban area's sprawling northeast. Roseville and its neighbors, Rocklin, Loomis, and Lincoln, are both now emersed in the benefits and growing pains experienced throughout the last decade by such places as Orangevale, Citrus Heights, Folsom, Florin, Elk Grove, and North Natomas.

Unlike earlier patterns and processes of growth common to these Sacramento metropolitan area communities, urban development in the 1990s and beyond will be driven by a different set of economic forces. Rather than traditional residential subdivisions being followed by retail shopping centers, the newer developments of the 1990s focus on employment centers as their anchor points with residential development following close behind. Examples of this trend are found along Highway 65 and Interstate 80 east. For example, Wells Fargo Bank's headquarters moved to the Rocklin area as a refugee from the 1989 Santa Cruz/San Francisco Bay Area earthquake. Likewise, huge corporations such as Intel and Pacific Bell are typical electronic employers in the communications industry which could have located almost anywhere, but whose corporate executives chose this part of the Sacramento Valley

Other footloose industries are expected to follow. Signet Industries moved to Sacramento after conducting a nationwide search for the best location that combined environmental and economic advantages for its employees. Amenities of the Sacramento urban area included lower cost of living than other parts of metropolitan California, climatic benefits, and a generally favorable atmosphere for continued growth in the local area.

In anticipation of these employment magnets, the cities of Rocklin, Lincoln, Roseville, and Loomis are approving massive residential development projects bringing economic and population growth to the Placer County fringe of the Sacramento Urban Area. Service industries and institutions such as the massive new Kaiser Hospital under construction in Roseville are examples of the *Edge City* phenomenon described recently by journalist Joel Garreau in his best selling book of the same title (1992).

On the west side of the Valley, a slightly different but related growth trend is emerging in the late 1990s. Vacaville is currently the hub for several major grocery chains based on freeway location and time-distance considerations linking central and northern California and Nevada market areas. Similarly, communities such as Woodland are becoming distribution centers for mega-operations such as Target, Mazda, and Wal-Mart. Woodland and Dixon are also attracting young families in search of the perceived safety and security of life in "small town America."

Amidst these more mundane growth factors, a better defined sense of place for the formerly "invisible" Valley is emerging. This regional identity is maintained through such places as Old Town Sacramento with its restaurants, museums and annual entertainment events such as the Jazz Festival; the unique retail and restaurant complex on former ranch land at the Nut Tree in Vacaville; and the continuing historical attraction of Folsom's Gold Rush-era charm.

Many of these growth factors are also at work in the middle and northern portions of the Sacramento Valley. The westside Valley communities of Williams,

Willows, Orland, and Corning have long held policies encouraging retail and commercial development at the Interstate 5 interchanges. Corning boasts that the success of its two major truck stops lies in the fact that the city is exactly half-way between Portland and Los Angeles. The *General Plans* of these communities include various measures designed to bring more residents and visitors into the area. Economic development agencies such as Tri-County Economic Development Corporation, GEDCO (Glenn County Economic Development Corporation), Shasta County Economic Development Corporation, and the Tehama Local Development Corporation have replaced nineteenth century railroad land boomers in promising an affluent and pleasant lifestyle for potential new residents.

Larger development dreams are being debated among proposals for new multi-land use communities such as Sutter Bay in Sutter County and Celebrity City in Tehama County. The latter development proposal is being touted as a project that would bring 40 country music theaters, 20,000 hotel rooms and 800 new homes to thousands of acres of acres of undeveloped pasture land along Interstate 5 near Red Bluff. Developer and modern-day dreamer Leo Urbanski is currently trying to raise the needed $3 billion to build this 3,278 acre park. If he is successful, the returns to the local economy could be enormous. The enterprise would employ over 7,000 people (not including the construction workers hired to build it) and is projected to contribute at least 4,700 jobs to surrounding communities.

Many local residents, along with environmental organizations, remain unconvinced about the regional benefits of Celebrity City. The Sierra Club has demanded that developers rewrite the project's environmental impact report and asked that development be stopped until Tehama County's *General Plan* is revised to accommodate this type of massive growth. Meanwhile, concerned residents and some developers in both Tehama and Shasta counties cite concerns about the approval of Celebrity City because of potential traffic problems, air and water pollution, and loss of quality of life in the area. Others, particularly real estate developers, chambers of commerce, and development corporations, applaud Urbanski's planned "city." Whatever the outcome, as this book is going to press, as yet no ground had been broken for the project, no plans for construction have been approved, and no significant real estate deals have been struck (*Redding Record Searchlight* 1995, A4).

In the meantime, other somewhat less controversial growth incentives are occurring in communities far south of Red Bluff. In anticipation of the completion of freeway status for Highway 65 and 70 linking Sacramento with Oroville, for example, numerous new housing developments have sprung up in

Olivehurst, Linda, and Marysville. Promises of improvements to Highway 99 have likewise encouraged growth in Yuba City, Live Oak, and Gridley. The billboard advertisement shown in the photograph in Figure 11.1 symbolizes this new dream. There can be no doubt that completion of the planned freeway and other highway improvements will significantly shorten the daily commute between Chico and Sacramento. Improved transportation links between the Sacramento Valley's five urban nodes—Sacramento, Marysville/Yuba City, Chico, Red Bluff, and Redding—already make it possible for a person to live virtually anywhere in the region and work in an urban setting. Other smaller towns in the Sacramento Valley, for the most part, are strategically positioned to provide local services for nearby residents as well as performing their traditional agricultural service and processing function. Evidence that the North State has been heavily urbanized is the fact that now one can obtain the daily necessities—gasoline, food, and videos—almost anywhere.

Growth in the Sacramento Valley is summarized on Table 11.1. It tabulates recent population growth by county and city over a one year period. The percent change from January, 1993 through January, 1994 affords a relative indicator of the most rapidly growing communities in the region. On a percentage basis, the fastest growing counties include Butte, Colusa, and Sutter. The counties with the largest numerical increases are Sacramento, Placer, Butte, and Solano. Cities with more than a 5 percent growth rate in one year between the delta and Redding include Rocklin, Dixon, Galt, Live Oak, Williams, and Yuba City. The cities with the largest numerical increases during our representative year are Roseville, Rocklin, Chico, Redding, Sacramento, and Vacaville. Incredibly, these sometimes invisible Valley towns and cities all represent a net growth rate at least double the state average of 1.4 percent. A few places did lose population during this same time period. These included the newly incorporated city of West Sacramento and the unincorporated parts of Yolo and Sutter counties.

Census figures indicate that over the course of the last decade, the Sacramento Valley's population overall has increased by 30 percent. The city of Sacramento has the greatest total number of new residents, 93,600 people. More than half of the Valley population lives in the greater Sacramento metropolitan area. At the opposite end of the region is the second largest urban node, Redding. This rapidly developing city has emerged in the 1990s as a leader in attracting growth and economic development in the North State and is, therefore, profiled here as one example of the Sacramento Valley's increasingly urban landscape.

Figure 11.1. Real Estate Billboard Near Olivehurst.
Photo by Susan Wiley Hardwick.

A Closer Look: Redding

Why Redding? Like so many other communities in the emerging Sacramento Valley, this moderately sized city of 66,482 people is rapidly becoming a highly sophisticated urban place. Three freeways, highways 299 and 99 and Interstate 5, provide linkages both inside and outside the metropolitan area expanding

Table 11.1. Population and Percentage Growth Rates for Sacramento
Valley Counties and Cities, 1993-1994

County/City	Total Population		
	January 1, 1993	January 1, 1994	Percent Change
Butte	195,700	201,000	2.7
Biggs	1,660	1,680	1.2
Chico	45,400	46,750	3.0
Gridley	4,790	4,910	2.5
Oroville	12,350	12,650	2.4
Unincorproated	105,200	108,100	2.4
Colusa	17,400	17,750	2.0
Colusa	5,150	5,275	2.4
Williams	2,810	2,960	5.3
Unincorporated	9,425	9,525	1.1
Glenn	26,250	26,500	1.0
Orland	5,450	5,575	2.3
Willows	6,300	6,325	0.4
Unincorporated	14,450	14,600	1.0
Placer	194,300	201,600	3.8
Roseville	53,900	56,550	4.8
Lincoln	7,875	8,050	2.2

Table 11.1. Population and Percentage Growth Rates for Sacramento
Valley Counties and Cities, 1993-1994

County/City	Total Population		
	January 1, 1993	January 1, 1994	Percent Change
Rocklin	23,850	25,800	8.2
Loomis	6,000	6,200	3.3
Unincorporated	89,900	92,000	2.3
Sacramento	1,116,500	1,130,400	1.2
Folsom	38,350	39,850	3.9
Galt	12,900	13,900	7.8
Saramento	389,500	393,500	1.0
Unincorporated	675,000	682,300	1.1
Shasta	160,700	163,200	1.6
Anderson	8,700	8,775	0.9
Redding	75,400	76,800	1.9
Unincorporated	76,600	77,600	1.3
Solano	369,200	373,900	1.3
Dixon	11,800	12,450	5.5
Vacaville	80,900	82,500	2.0
Unincorporated	20,450	20,700	1.2
Sutter	71,200	73,100	2.7
Live Oak	4,830	5,100	5.6
Yuba City	31,500	33,600	6.7
Unincorporated	34,850	34,450	-1.1

Table 11.1. Population and Percentage Growth Rates for Sacramento
Valley Counties and Cities, 1993-1994

| County/City | Total Population | | |
	January 1, 1993	January 1, 1994	Percent Change
Tehama	53,900	54,700	1.5
Corning	6,150	6,200	0.8
Red Bluff	12,950	13,000	0.4
Tehama	420	420	0.0
Unincorporated	34,350	35,050	2.0
Yolo	149,600	150,800	0.8
Davis	50,400	51,400	2.0
West Sacramento	30,650	30,550	-0.3
Winters	4,900	4,980	1.6
Woodland	42,050	42,450	1.0
Unincorporated	21,550	21,450	-0.5
Yuba	62,900	63,500	1.0
Marysville	12,750	12,800	0.4
Wheatland	1,890	1,930	2.1
Unincorporated	48,250	48,800	1.1

Source: State of California Population Estimates for California Cities and
Counties, Report 94 E-1, May 1994.
Note: Totals may not equal sum due to independent rounding.

Redding's role as a historically important *gateway city* located at the extreme
northern terminus of the Valley at a jumping off point for the dramatic Klamath
Mountains to the north. Redding's longterm locational advantage has provided it
with ample opportunities for growth over the past century and a half. However,
since the mid-1980s, this Valley city has emerged as the fastest growing place
north of Rocklin and Sacramento as disillusioned Californians from southern

California, the San Francisco Bay Area, and even Sacramento move north. They come seeking safety and security for their families, a lower cost of living (and significantly lower cost of purchasing a home), and environmental amenities. As discussed in the previous chapter, these *equity immigrants* are rapidly changing the nature of life in cities such as Redding. Their expectations for a faster pace of life, consumer goods, and impacts on local services and institutions are stretching Redding's potential for growth to the limit. Medical facilities have tripled in size over the past ten years expanding Redding's role as a regional hub service city.

As urban newcomers settle in the Redding area, traditions are changing along with the more overt lifestyle changes mentioned above. Generally less conservative than local residents, new arrivals have changed the demographics of the formerly all male Redding City Council to include female members. The city has even had a woman mayor in recent years, something unheard of in the not-so-distant past. The new president of Shasta College currently is promoting his progressive *Redding 2000* program, an effort to link campus life with the needs of the local community. Shasta College, as well as nearby Simpson College, Shasta Bible College, and outreach courses and advanced degree programs offered by California State University, Chico provide educational opportunities for new-comers and longterm residents alike. Additionally, relatively new organizations such as *Women in Transition* and SCORE (*Shasta Corps of Retired Executives*) provide opportunities for networking with like-minded peers in the business community and serve as further evidence of Redding's pro-business mentality.

Meanwhile, selected establishments located in the city's older downtown have begun to gentrify along side streets near the downtown mall constructed with high hopes for reinvigorating a lagging downtown over twenty years ago. A large bookstore, several historic hotels, and authentic-looking restaurants like Jack's Grill persevere alongside the struggling downtown mall and the city's still beautiful old train station. Despite efforts to bring commercial life back to the downtown, however, the densely developed suburban commercial strip along Dana Drive (just east of the Hilltop Strip) boasts huge box outlet stores such as Target, Cosco, and Waremart and is the city's biggest and most profitable shopping district. These stores, along with numerous new schools, churches, retirement complexes, condominium projects, and sprawling single family sub-divisions seem to be fan out away from Redding's downtown in all directions. With so much growth, one wonders how long the area can hold onto its image as an "urban get-away" city. As one long time resident Irene Helzer put it (1995 interview):

We live in such a visually dramatic and stunning place. I just hope we can hold onto its beauty and work to preserve what we have always loved about this place.

People

Adjusting to Diversity

As Redding continues to grow, its population, as in other larger Valley cities, has become more ethnically and culturally diverse. Despite the long held image of places such as Redding and the North State in general as an Anglo-dominated region, as previous chapters have shown, most of the region's urban areas are becoming more ethnically and culturally diverse as the new century approaches (see Table 11.2). This demographic diversity is bringing new opportunities for cultural and social expression into the region. It is also bringing with it new challenges for increasingly overcrowded local institutions and infrastructure.

Education, health care, law enforcement, and county welfare offices have all been stretched to the limit by the increasing numbers of new arrivals from outside the state and nation in recent years. With cutbacks in both state and federal funding to these important community institutions in the 1990s, services have become impacted, especially in the most urban parts of the Sacramento Valley. As shown on Table 11.3, for example, there are a substantial number of students in Valley counties that are classified as Limited-English-Proficient. Their needs go well beyond typical classroom requirements for staffing and materials. Likewise, welfare offices throughout the region are facing cutbacks in funding along with dramatic increases in local needs.

Glenn County is one recent example of a county that has taken a pro-active and creative approach to solving economic and social problems brought on by new refugee populations. In Willows, City Police Chief Bob Shadley contacted local farmers about the availability of some of their land for use by newly arriving Hmong families from Southeast Asia. The city of Willows then submitted a grant to VISTA (Volunteers in Service to America) to help organize a cooperative project between Hmong families and local farmers (*Willows Journal* 1993, A1). This innovative project and others like it continue to gain momentum. Lee Family Produce, Inc, based at Glenn County's Cooperative Extension Office in Orland, is also flourishing. According to Kevin Secrist, Glenn County VISTA volunteer (*Orland Journal/Press Register* 1995, A6):

Table 11.2. Ancestry Groups, Sacramento Valley Counties, 1990

	Counties									
Ancestry	Butte	Colusa	Glenn	Sacramento	Shasta	Solano	Sutter	Tehama	Yolo	Yuba
Arab		27	0	2,601	83	561	37	47	377	58
Austrian		7	10	1,728	261	517	53	67	232	80
Belgian		8	6	603	48	133	29	30	115	47
Canadian		28	23	1,817	287	345	157	90	220	73
Czech	798	9	117	3,008	528	737	190	140	372	147
Danish	1,785	59	270	7,762	1,256	1,828	433	473	1,011	271
Dutch	3,429	333	626	12,711	2,691	3,474	843	961	2,085	957
English	25,170	1,152	2,389	105,468	22,326	27,004	6,608	6,347	13,834	5,612
Finnish	488	8	34	1,887	421	541	42	94	236	126
French (except Basque)	5,797	347	704	25,251	5,093	7,380	1,636	1,604	3,546	1,554
French Canadian	1,132	78	84	5,322	603	1,822	279	237	640	251
German	35,733	2,706	4,918	171,921	28,098	48,384	10,964	10,965	23,489	10,260
Greek	484	6	40	4,375	430	1,557	233	100	415	181

Table 11.2. Ancestry Groups, Sacramento Valley Counties, 1990

Ancestry	Butte	Colusa	Glenn	Sacramento	Shasta	Solano	Sutter	Tehama	Yolo	Yuba
					Counties					
Hungarian	491	18	59	2,879	457	522	50	19	305	116
Irish	18,890	1,264	1,959	84,974	16,587	25,360	5,437	5,580	10,442	5,278
Italian	7,150	563	697	40,228	5,044	12,922	1,612	1,463	4,940	1,397
Lithuanian	158	5	22	1,200	132	352	45	19	163	21
Norwegian	3,260	149	419	11,595	2,264	3,215	810	728	1,337	454
Polish	1,768	25	254	11,795	1,419	4,243	478	303	1,533	407
Portuguese	2,756	301	930	14,088	1,790	5,649	770	754	2,049	607
Romanian	252	0	0	1,523	69	177	39	0	92	12
Russian	814	29	62	6,855	474	1,259	211	26	1,440	118
Scotch-Irish	4,607	198	424	17,367	3,431	4,808	1,083	1,184	2,083	1,078
Scottish	3,758	211	229	15,915	3,081	4,655	993	998	2,378	787
Slovak	451	51	22	2,900	336	758	97	139	323	74
Subsaharan African	55	0	0	2,192	32	463	74	7	205	46
Swedish	3,667	72	315	16,719	3,038	4,365	945	956	1,857	733
Swiss	671	121	92	3,759	514	848	349	239	594	228

Table 11.2. Ancestry Groups, Sacramento Valley Counties, 1990

Ancestry	Counties									
	Butte	Colusa	Glenn	Sacramento	Shasta	Solano	Sutter	Tehama	Yolo	Yuba
Ukranian	150	10	11	1,555	38	358	105	53	211	34
Untied States/ American	7,439	627	1,066	28,693	6,925	8,038	2,907	2,198	3,813	3,694
Welsh	1,234	68	55	5,187	840	1,353	263	380	669	208
West Indian (excluding Hispanic origin groups)	40	16	0	1,165	41	409	18	16	140	109
Yugoslavian	254	0	0	2,360	285	456	98	5	200	57
Race or Hispanic Origin Groups	23,092	5,690		217,447	13,978	81,037	13,982	7,436	32,228	12,368
Other Groups	9,417	607		113,492	4,522	46,298	7,135	1,117	15,989	5,418
Unclassified or not reported	15,799	1,482		92,877	19,614	38,493	5,410	4,850	11,529	5,367

Source: 1990 Census of Population and Housing Summary, Tape File 3A.

Table 11.3. Trends in Number of Limited-English-Proficient Students in Sacramento Valley Public Schools by County, 1988-1992

County	1988	1989	1990	1991	1992
Butte	996	1,282	1,667	2,047	2,273
Colusa	293	421	506	644	695
Glenn	306	467	669	686	904
Sacramento	11,397	12,204	14,162	16,966	19,623
Shasta	416	519	576	738	843
Solano	3,095	3,511	4,079	5,013	4,963
Sutter	796	988	1,339	1,902	2,230
Tehama	278	441	470	619	679
Yolo	2,293	2,688	2,995	3,614	4,026
Yuba	1,093	1,284	1,687	1,962	2,204
State Totals	652,439	742,559	861,531	986,462	1,078,705

Source: Language Census Report for California Public Schools 1992, 1.

Now we have found a viable way to develop capable, productive and ambitious alternatives to public assistance. With the cooperative farm as a model, we are now looking for new ventures so we can create micro-businesses which will stimulate the economy of the region.

Environment

Previous chapters illustrated the close relationship between residents of the Valley and their natural environment. This human-environment interaction has resulted in the use and overuse of resources over the years. Many of today's Valley residents have begun to understand the importance of sustainable management of the resource base of water, soil, timber, minerals, and wildlife. Much remains to be done, however, to maintain a healthy balance of resource use and resource preservation in the coming years.

Resource Management and Protection

While more people are involved in service, communication, government, education, and other tertiary economic activities in the Sacramento Valley than in primary production, these jobs are only possible because of abundant natural resources in the area (e.g., fertile soils, clean water, timber, minerals). Water continues to be the single most important resource concern in the region and in the state. In 1990, annual net water use in the Sacramento River Region was 11.7 million acre feet; net use is forecasted to increase to 12 million acre feet in the year 2020 *(California Water Plan Update* 1994). Since 1980, urban use has increased while agricultural use has remained relatively stable except for the peak in irrigated acreage during the 1980s. Overall, agricultural water use in the region is expected to decline slightly during the next 30 years as irrigation efficiencies continue to improve. Environmental use is expected to increase by 143,000 acre feet by 2020 under existing fishery and wetland requirements.

The Sacramento River region contains the largest wetland areas in the state, totalling approximately 175,000 acres. Water for these wetlands originates in several places including the Central Valley Project, agricultural return flows, and groundwater. Forecasted needs for the year 2000 are expected to rise by 30 percent. Future urban water demand in the region is expected to rise from about 744,000 acre feet per year to 1,231,000 acre feet in the year 2020. Most of this demand will be to accommodate growth in the Sacramento urban area and will be supplied by groundwater.

No major additional water supply facilities are currently scheduled to come on line by the year 2020 in the Sacramento Valley region (*The California Water Plan Update* 1994, 127). Urban areas in the central part of the region generally have sufficient supplies to survive dry periods with only voluntary cutbacks. However, communities in Butte and Shasta counties and areas supplied by water from Folsom Lake have had to use rationing or water transfers during recent droughts to manage shortages.

The Redding Basin is fundamentally an area of abundant water supplies, but outlying areas are subject to severe shortages in dry years due to terms of U.S. Bureau of Reclamation contracts and the lack of alternative supplies. Small districts located virtually in the shadow of Shasta Dam face chronic water shortages. The most attractive surface water projects in the Sacramento Valley region have already been built. High construction costs and the increasing need for environmental considerations have greatly restricted remaining possibilities for additional surface water development. The construction of Auburn Dam or the Peripheral Canal remain as options for future generations. The Auburn Dam site remains in question, however, because its predicted cost exceeds the benefit provided by the additional capacity of its reservoir (2.3. million acre feet). Attention to more water storage rather than new impoundments or transfer facilities merits consideration by long term water facility planners. A reservoir at Sites, just west of Maxwell, the expansion of Shasta Lake, and increased use of groundwater recharge have also been suggested.

Cottonwood Creek in Shasta and Tehama counties is the largest uncontrolled tributary of the Sacramento River and a major contributor to flooding along the upper Sacramento River. Since 1970, the Corps of Engineers and the California Department of Water Resources have been considering a two dam project on the creek for flood protection and to provide additional water supplies for the State Water Project. Feasibility studies are ongoing. Financial considerations remain the most critical decision-making factors in all newly conceived water projects.

A proposal that may well bring more efficient use of water in California is a plan to purchase the federally-funded Central Valley Project by the state of California or a joint powers agency. A Central Valley Project Authority made up of 85 public water companies has been organized in hopes of purchasing the massive system of facilities. To date, no definite agreement has been reached.

Agricultural Issues

Intensive and extensive farming continue to be the single most important component of the North State economy. Many farm operations in the region are professionally run and environmentally sensitive. But issues relating to agricultural development and the environment still reach the newspapers on a regular basis. The first is the issue of field burning and its impact on air pollution. For decades, burning of the straw from rice and other grain fields was considered to be the only way to dispose of these leftovers after harvest of the grain. After passage of the California Clean Air Act of 1988, considerable progress has been made finding alternative ways to dispose of or recycle the surplus straw. Various processes are now being tried including energy co-generation plants, mulching the straw deep into the soil, or flooding fields in the wintertime so that the straw is decomposed. By 1997, it is expected that alternative straw disposal will completely replace field burning.

A second issue related to the success of agriculture in the Valley and protection of the environment is disposal of agricultural waste water from irrigated fields. New standards set by state and federal agencies are gradually insuring that agricultural run-off waters that enter aquatic wildlife habitats must be toxic free. A related issue is the question of clearance of streams to increase the removal of flood waters. Such clearance may be effective at flushing flood waters but is devastating to riparian wildlife. This issue has yet to be satisfactorily addressed by all concerned parties.

Other more positive relationships between farmers and environmentalists are exemplified in the use of conservation easements and land set-asides for construction of wildlife habitat on agricultural land. Wetland mitigation banking (construction of new wetlands to replace those filled in by development) is a similar plan now in operation for compliance with the Clean Water Act and other environmental laws while still allowing land development. The use of agricultural lands for recreational hunting and fishing has also augmented the local economy and created an incentive for preservation of wildlife habitat.

Urban land use has been impinging on Sacramento Valley farm land since the beginning of Euro-American settlement in the mid-nineteenth century. Beginning in 1965, however, the problem became increasingly pressing as towns and cities began to spread out and wave upon wave of new residential subdivisions began to move outward away from older commercial districts downtown. This devouring of farm land and concurrent demands for urban water, power, and new infrastructure continue to pose a challenge for Valley land use planners and local residents. The American Farmland Trust, a non-profit group that is working to stop the loss of productive farmland in the United States reports that California's Central Valley is the most threatened agricultural region in the country in terms of urban growth. According to Farmland Trust President Ralph E. Grossi, farmers in the Valley are "literally and figuratively living on the edge" (Weiss 1993, 6A). He reports that: (Doyle 1993, B1):

> There's nothing more fundamental to American agriculture than the land. But some of the nation's best land is being wasted by urban sprawl—low density patchwork development that uses much more land than necessary.

One example of this potential conflict is occurring on the large M and T Ranch in Butte County a few miles southwest of Chico. This huge operation specializes in the growing of prunes, rice, grain, beans, beets, alfalfa, almonds, and numerous other crops. According to Les Heringer, manager of the ranch, a housing development is being constructed on the ranch's northeast boundary on former orchard land. In 1995, 140 acres of walnut orchards belonging to an absentee owner have been divided into 10 acre parcels now up for sale as ranchettes. At the ranch's southside boundary, rice land is being converted into a proposed water ski lake to be surrounded by homesites. The county Planning

Commission has continually reviewed other "leapfrog" urban development proposals infringing on agricultural lands over the last decade. In response, Butte County planners have included a new Agricultural Element in its *General Plan*, developing policies that limit the division of large intensive agricultural parcels into smaller ones.

Other Resource Issues: Lumbering and Mining

Throughout its history, the Sacramento Valley has been economically tied to the Sierra, Cascade, and Klamath mountain ranges in the processing of minerals such as gold and harvesting and processing of timber products. In the early 1990s, timber production was significantly slowed for a variety of economic and political reasons throughout northern California and the Pacific Northwest. This not only impacted logging operations in the mountains but also affected employment in lumber mills in the Valley from Oroville to Anderson. The related decline in manufacturing employment in the wood products industry also affected other parts of the local economy. As of 1995, no political or scientific solution had been agreed upon to manage forest resources on a sustainable basis while protecting wildlife and still providing substantial employment.

Another as yet unresolved resource-related issue is the continuance of gravel mining and to a lesser extent suction dredge gold mining in Valley streams. Some jurisdictions such as Glenn County are coordinating plans for streambed habitat reconstruction after quarry operations have ceased. But no unified regional effort has yet been forthcoming. Suction dredge mining in Valley tributary streams is carefully regulated by state and federal agencies and enforcement is diligently being carried out by state agencies.

Landscape

Planning Issues

Local planning commissions spend most of their time reacting to proposals for land use change rather than initiating guidelines for how those changes should take place. The issues that citizens present to planning commissions usually involve concerns about property values, privacy, traffic, or the physical appearance of new developments. Standards that satisfy the wants and needs of the local community should be developed before decisions are made on development projects. Guidelines for land use density, design, transportation, and the creation of a jobs/housing balance should be included in every community's *General Plan* but oftentimes these issues are minimized due to lack of agreement on the definition of an ideal community. We suggest that with more informed and more committed citizen participation and guidance from professional planners, communities of the future should include:

- Development of urban land with mixed land uses so that homes are close to jobs, schools, entertainment, and shopping;
- Land use that is compacted with more people and activity per unit area to avoid wasting valuable open space;
- Transportation systems that include alternatives to the gasoline-powered automobile;
- A community design that is compatible with the local physical environment and cultural and social needs of its people.

In effect, it is recommended that the traditional single family residential subdivision of the 1950s and 1960s be replaced by a new and more compact "American small town" atmosphere as successfully created by land use planners and designers such as Peter Calthorpe and Andrus Duany. If the foregoing principles are carried out in Sacramento Valley towns and cities in the near future, the Valley landscape in the year 2050 could accommodate urban needs as well as maintain the small town/rural atmosphere that is the heritage of this expansive region.

Re-Visioning the Valley

In our introductory chapter, we asked you to visualize the Sacramento Valley before European and North American settlement when viewed from a high, free-floating balloon drifting northward from Sacramento. As a fitting conclusion to this book, we suggest that you once again imagine the Sacramento Valley, this time visualizing its landscape in the middle of the twenty-first century. We will travel in a hot air balloon once again, but this time our flight drifts southward from Redding toward the delta.

It is the year 2040. As on our first trip up the Valley, the view on this trip is magnificent. First in sight is the community of Redding, clearly seen below us as formed by distinct concentric circles of land use. In the center of these rings, we can see that the city's old downtown has been revitalized into a pedestrian-oriented shopping and service node. Businesses and stores surround the downtown, transitioning into tasteful garden apartments and condominiums with inspiring views of the river and the snow-peaked mountains beyond. More traditional suburban ranch-style living forms the next concentric ring. This zone is served by a series of radiating transportation ribbons carrying electric cars and trains. Orchards, grazing land, and open space beyond welcome bicyclists and others who have been drawn to the area because of its outdoor amenities.

Rich oak-studded grazing lands, pastures, and orchards dot the rural landscape on both sides of the Valley as we drift south over Anderson towards Red Bluff. The Sacramento River is buffered on both sides by wide *green belts* of forested land. On each side and parallel to the river run the Interstate 5 and Highway 99 corridors which accomodate various economic activities and connect urban nodes that string along both arterials. Neatly spaced rows of trees in orchards, bright green rice fields, field crops, and wildlife refugees exemplify the middle part of the Valley.

Father south, heading toward California's capital city, views and patterns change drastically. As we pass the Sutter Buttes and look toward the city of Sacramento and beyond, we see the area from the foothills of Placer County to the foothills of Vacaville are densely packed with new urban villages at the expense of agricultural land. Sacramento, in fact, is now one of the major metropolitan centers of the Pacific Rim, rivaling Portland, Seattle, and even San Francisco in size and economic and cultural importance.

The social and cultural context of the Sacramento Valley in the future will no doubt continue to reflect a fascinating mix of environments, economic activities, languages, foods, customs, and lifeways. Despite mega-growth in the Sacramento and Redding metropolitan areas, it is anticipated that the quality of life in the middle and northern Valley will continue to be based on enjoyment of this vast region's natural resources and appreciation of its rural and small town lifestyle.

The rest of the story of the "historical" geography of tomorrow's Sacramento Valley is left for your speculation and personal planning. Meanwhile, the region's future remains open and ready for the arrival of new dreamers who will hold onto its promise much like those who arrived before them.

Bibliography

Abajian, James. 1974. *Blacks and their Contributions to the American West.* Boston: G.K. Hall.

Abramson, David. "The Hmong: A Mountain Tribe Regroups in the Valley," *San Francisco Chronicle,* January 29, 1984, 9-12.

Adler, L.L. 1980. *Adjustments of the Yuba River, California: The Influx of Hydraulic Mining Debris, 1849-1979.* Unpub. M.S. Thesis, UCLA.

Allen, Kathryn Martin. 1945. "Hindoos in the Valley," *Westways,* V. 31, 8-9.

Allen, J.P. and Eugene Turner. 1988. *We the People: An Atlas of America's Ethnic Diversity.* New York: Macmillan.

Allen, Jimmy V. 1970. *Hugh Glenn.* Unpub. M.A. thesis, Sacramento State College.

Alt, David D. and Donald W. Hyndman. *Roadside Geology of Northern California.* Missoula, MT: Mountain Press, 1975.

Anderson, Kat, ed. 1994. *Before the Wilderness: Environmental Management by Native Americans.* Berkeley: University of California Press.

Anderson, Robert Allen. 1909. *Fighting the Mill Creeks.* Chico: The Chico Record Press.

Atherton, Gertrude. 1914. *California: An Intimate History.* New York & London: Harper and Brothers Publishers.

Bailey, Edgar H. 1966. *Geology of Northern California.* San Francisco: California Division of Mines and Geology.

Bakker, Elna. 1971. *An Island Called California.* Berkeley: University of California Press.

Bancroft, Hubert Howe. 1848-1890. *History of California* 7 volumes. San Francisco: The History Company.

Banerjee, Kalyan Kumar. 1964. "East Indian Immigration into America: Beginnings of Indian Revolutionary Activity," *Modern Review,* V. 116, 355-356.

Barry, W. James. 1972. *The Central Valley Prairie.* Sacramento: Department of Parks and Recreation.

Bauer, Margaret Cristy. 1970. *History of the Los Molinos Company and of Early Los Molinos.* Unpub. M.A. thesis, California State University, Chico.

Baumhoff, M.A. 1963. "Ecological Determinants of Aboriginal California Populations." *University of California Publications in American Archaeology and Ethnology,* V. 49, 155-236.

Bean, Walton and James L. Rawls. 1983. *California: An Interpretive History.* New York: McGraw-Hill.

Beck, Warren A. and Ynez D. Haase. 1974. *Historical Atlas of California.* Norman, OK: University of Oklahoma Press.

Belcher, Capt. Sir Edward. 1843. *Narrative of a Voyage Round the World Performed in Her Majesty's Ship Sulfer During the Years 1836-1842.* London: Henry Colburn.

Betts, Jeanette. 1994. *Sierra Sunrise Village.* Unpub. ms. prepared for Northern California Planning and Research, Chico, CA.

Beutel, James A. "Kiwifruit Production in California," *Family Farm Series,* Cooperative Extension, University of California, Davis, January, 1989, 1-7.

Bidwell, Annie E.K. 1891. *Rancho Chico Indians.* Unpub. ms. Sacramento: California State Library.

Bidwell, General John. 1842. A Journal to California With Observations About the Country, Climate and the Route to This Country. St. Louis: MO: n.p..

Bidwell, General John. 1987. "The First Emigrant Train to California," "Life in California Before the Gold Discovery," "Fremont in the Conquest of California" (in) *Echoes of the Past,* Sacramento: Department of Parks and Recreation.

Bidwell, John. 1845, 1869, 1883. *Bidwell Papers. Diaries of John Bidwell.* Chico: Meriam Library Special Collections, California State University, Chico.

Biggs and Richvale Chambers of Commerce. 1913. *Rice Culture at Biggs and Richvale.* Biggs and Richvale, CA: Chambers of Commerce.

Biggs, Robert O. 1954. *The Sacramento Valley Railroad, 1863-1865.* Unpub. M.A. Thesis, Sacramento State College.

Black, Michael. 1995. "Tragic Remedies: A Century of Failed Fishery Policy on California's Sacramento River." *Pacific Historical Review,* V. 64, 37-70.

Bleyhl, Norris Arthur. 1955. *A History of the Production and Marketing of Rice in California.* Unpub. Ph.D. diss., University of Minnesota.

Boggs, Mae Helene Bacon. 1942. *My Playhouse Was a Concord Coach.* Oakland: Howell-North Press.

Bogue, Donald J. 1957. "Streams of Migration Between Regions" (in) *Subregional Migration Streams in the United States, 1915-1940.* Miami, OH: Scripps Foundation Studies in Population Redistribution.

Book, Susan Wiley (aka Susan Wiley Hardwick). 1974. *Chinese Settlement in Butte County, 1860-1920.* San Francisco: R and E Research Associates.

Borthwick, J.D. 1975 (first ed. 1948). *Three Years in California.* Oakland: Biobooks.

Bosqui, E. 1904. *Memoirs.* San Francisco: n.p.

Bosworth, Allan R. 1967. *America's Concentration Camps.* New York: W.W. Norton and Company.

Brewer, William Henry. 1930. *Up and Down California in 1860-1864.* Francis P. Farquhar, ed. New Haven: Yale University Press. Also 1966, Berkeley: University of California Press.

Broughton, Jack M. 1988. *Archaeological Patterns of Prehistoric Fish Exploitation in the Sacramento Valley,* Unpub. Thesis, California State University, Chico.

Broughton, Jack M. 1994a. "Late Holocene Resource Intensification in the Sacramento Valley, California: The Vertebrate Evidence." *Journal of Archaeological Science,* V. 21, 501-514.

Broughton, Jack M. 1994b. "Declines in Mammalian Foraging Efficiency During the Late Holocene, San Francisco Bay, California," *Journal of Anthropological Archaeology,* V. 13, 371-401.

Brown, Patsi. "Native Americans Use Fire to Manage Their Land," *Chico Enterprise-Record,* July 7, 1994, 6C.

Brown, Patsi. "Willows Rice Farmers are Wildlife Friendly," *Chico Enterprise-Record,* December 8, 1994, 1F.

Brown, Randall J. 1973. *Colusa County During the Civil War.* Arbuckle, CA: the author.

Brown, Walton John. 1972. *Portuguese in California.* San Francisco: R and E Research.

Buck, Franklin A. 1930. *A Yankee Trader in the Gold Rush.* Boston & New York: Houghton-Mifflin Company.

Burrill, Richard. 1988. *River of Sorrows: Life History of the Maidu-Nisenan Indians.* Happy Camp, CA: Naturegraph Publishers.

Burrill, Richard. 1990. *Ishi: America's Last Stone Age Indian.* Sacramento: The Anthropology Company.

Buss, Shanahan and Co., Real Estate and Insurance Companies. 1885. *Notes on Shasta County Lands, Tributary to Anderson.* Sacramento, CA.

Butler, Eric. 1995. *Flood Update: California's Central Valley.* Unpub. ms. Sacramento: Department of Water Resources.

Butte County Board of Supervisors. 1991. *Butte County in the Sacramento Valley.* Oroville: Mercury Print.

Butte Remembers. 1973. Butte County Branch, The National League of American Pen Women. Chico, CA.

Cadwalader, C. *Map of the Town of Gridley*, Book of Maps, Number 1A, Butte County Recorder's Office, June 3, 1871, p. 66.

Calhoon, F.D. 1986. *Coolies, Kanakas, and Cousin Jacks*. Sacramento: Cal-Con Publishers.

California Agricultural Station Bulletins. 1920. 361-385. Bulletin 366. Berkeley: University of California Press.

California Department of Forestry and Fire Protection. 1986. *California Forests and Rangelands: Growing Conflict Over Changing Uses*. Sacramento.

California Department of Parks and Recreation. 1988. *Five Views: An Ethnic Sites Survey for California*. Sacramento: California Office of Historic Preservation.

California Department of Parks and Recreation. 1988. *California's Wetlands: An Element of the California Outdoor Recreation Plan*. Sacramento.

California Department of Water Resources. 1994. *California Water Plan Update*, Bulletin 160-93, V. 1- 3 (October).

California Governor's Office, Planning and Research. 1979. California Water Atlas. Sacramento.

California State Lands Commission. 1994. *California's Rivers: A Public Trust Report*. Sacramento: Department of Water Resources.

California: Irrigated Lands in the Sacramento Valley. n.d. Sacramento: Sacramento Valley Land Company.

California Mexican Fact-Finding Committee. 1930. *Mexicans in California Report of Governor C.C. Young's Mexican Fact-Finding Committee*. Sacramento: State Printing Office.

California Place Names. 1992. Sacramento: State of California Business, Transportation, and Housing Agency, Dept. of Transportation.

California Resources Agency. 1989. *Upper Sacramento River Fisheries and Riparian Habitat Management Plan*. Sacramento.

California State Department of Education. 1942. *The Central Valley Project*. Sacramento: State Department of Education.

Carter, Harold O. and George Goldman, 1992. *The Measure of California Agriculture: Its Impact on the State Economy*. Berkeley: University of California Division of Agriculture and Natural Resources.

Carter, Jane Foster. 1988. *If the Walls Could Talk: Colusa's Architectural Heritage*. Colusa: Heritage Preservation Committee.

Castro, Paulette. 1993. *Town Founding: Orangevale*. Unpub. M.A., Department of Geography and Planning. California State University, Chico.

Caughey, John. 1948. *Gold is the Cornerstone.* Berkeley University of California Press.

Caughey, John W. 1970. *California: A Remarkable State's Life History.* Englewood Cliffs, NJ: Prentice-Hall, Inc.

Caywood, Hal Dee. 1971. *The Chico Municipal Airport: Its History, Government, and Development.* Unpub. M.A. Thesis, California State University, Chico.

Chan, Sucheng. 1986. *This Bittersweet Soil: The Chinese in California Agriculture, 1860-1910.* Berkeley: University of California Press.

Chandresekhar, S. 1944. "Indian Immigration into America," *Far Eastern Survey,* V. 13, 138-143.

Chase, Don Marquis. 1945. *Pioneers: Sketches of Pioneer Days in Shasta, Tehama, Trinity, and Siskiyou Counties with Emphasis on the Beginnings of Religious Organizations.* Redding, CA: n.p.

Chico Cemetery 1852-1908. 1992. Paradise, CA: Paradise Genealogical Society.

City Directory of Chico and Oroville. 1922. Sacramento: R.L. Polk and Company.

City and County Directory of Yuba, Sutter, Colusa, Butte, and Tehama Counties. 1881. Sacramento: Polk and Company.

Cleary, Charles W. 1931. *Final Report.* Division of Land Settlement, Department of Agriculture, State of California. Sacramento: State Printing Office.

Cleland, Robert Glass. 1959. *From Wilderness to Empire: A History of California.* New York: Alfred A. Knopf.

Clewett, Ed. 1975. *The Reading Adobe Project: Phase I, Shasta County.* Redding: County Public Works.

Colusa County Board of Supervisors. 1909. *Colusa County and the Sacramento Valley, California* Colusa, CA: n.p.

Colby, W. Howard. 1982. *A Century of Transportation in Shasta County, 1821-1920.* Chico: Association for Northern California Records and Research.

Colman, Lois. 1972. *Tailings of Butte Creek Canyon.* Sacramento: Cal-Central Press (sponsored by Centerville Recreation and Historical Association, Inc).

Colton, Rev. Walter. 1850. *Three Years in California.* New York: A.S. Barns.

Cook, A.S. 1955. "The Epidemic of 1830-1833 in California and Oregon," *University of California Publications in American Archaeology and Ethnology,* V. 43.

Cook, Fred S., ed. 1976. *Historic Legends of Colusa County. Pioneer.* Sacramento: California Traveler, Inc.

Cook, Sherburne F. 1962. "Expeditions to the Interior of California's Central Valley, 1820-1840," *University of California Anthropological Records*, V. 20.

Cook, Sherburne F. 1970. "The California Indian and Anglo-American Culture" (in) *Ethnic Conflict in California History*, Charles Wollenberg, ed. Los Angeles: Tinnon-Brown, Inc.

Cook, Sherburne F. 1976a. *The Population of California Indians*. Berkeley: University of California Press.

Cook, Sherburne F. 1976b. *The Conflict Between the California Indians and White Civilization*. Berkeley: University of California Press.

Corning Centennial Committee. 1990. *Welcome to Corning: The Olive City Heritage Tour*, Corning, CA.

Corwin, Arthur. 1973. "Mexican-American History: An Assessment," *Pacific Historical Review*, V. 42 (August).

"Cotton Growers in North State Sowing Seeds of Hope," *Chico Enterprise-Record*, December 20, 1994, D1-D2.

Crampton, Beecher. 1974. *Grasses in California*. Berkeley: University of California Press.

Crawford, Melodye, ed. 1992. "Emu Farming in America," *The Ostrich News*, January, 1-4.

Creisler, Lillian. 1939. *Little Oklahoma or The Airport Community*. Unpub. Ph.D. Diss., University of California, Berkeley.

Cross, Wilma Jeanne. 1989. *Dayton: A Forgotten Town*. Unpub. ms., Department of Geography and Planning, California State University, Chico.

Crow, John A. 1953. *California as a Place to Live*. New York: Charles Scribner's Sons.

Crystal, Eric. 1992. "Iu-Mien: Highland Southeast Asian Community and Culture in California Context," (in) Judy Lewis, ed. *Minority Cultures in Laos: Kammu, Luà, Lahu, and Iu-Mien*. Rancho Cordova: Southeast Asian Community Resource Center, 327-401.

Cunningham, Julie. 1991. *Portrayal of the Sacramento River in 20th Century Booster Literature*. M.A. Thesis in Geography. California State University, Chico.

Currie, Anne H. 1963. *A Maidu Story*. Berkeley: Brandes Printing Company.

Cutter, Donald C. (trans and ed.). 1957. *The Diary of Ensign Gabrriel Moraga's Expedition of Discovery in the Sacramento Valley, 1808*. Los Angeles: Dawson.

D'Amico, Charlotte L. 1976. *A History of the Palermo-Honcut Area for Elementary School Students*. Unpub. M.A. Thesis, California State University, Chico.

Dadabhay, Yasuf. 1954. "Circuitous Assimilation among Rural Hindustas in California," *Social Forces*, V. 33, 139-141.

Dana, Julian. 1939. *The Sacramento; River of Gold*. New York: J. J. Little and Ives Company.

Daniel, Cletus E. 1981. *Bitter Harvest: A History of California's Farmworkers, 1870-1941*. Ithaca: Cornell University Press.

Daniels, Roger. 1962. *The Politics of Prejudice*. Berkeley: University California Press.

Daniels, Roger. 1971. *Concentration Camps USA: Japanese Americans and World War II*. New York: Holt, Rinehart and Winston, Inc.

Das, Rajani K. 1924. *Hindustani Workers on the Pacific Coast*. Berlin: Walter del Guyter.

Dasmann, Raymond. 1966. *The Destruction of California*. New York: Collier Books.

Davie, Michael. 1972. *California: The Vanishing Dream*. New York: Dodd, Mead.

Davis, Cynthia F. 1984. *Where Water is King: The Story of the Glenn-Colusa Irrigation District*. Willows: Glenn-Colusa Irrigation District.

Delay, Peter J. 1924. *History of Yuba and Sutter Counties*. Los Angeles: Historic Record Company.

Dennis, Nona B. 1984. *Status and Trends of California Wetlands: A Report to the California Assembly Resources Subcommittee*. Sacramento.

De Roos, Robert. 1948. *The Thirsty Land: The Story of the Central Valley Project*. Stanford: Stanford University Press.

Desbarats, Jacqueline. 1985. "Indochinese Resettlement in the United States," *Annals of the Association of American Geographers*, V. 75, 522-538.

Dieter, George D. 1963. *A Historical Survey of the Chico Airport and Its Impact Upon the City of Chico as a Military Installation*. Unpub. M.A. Thesis, California State University, Chico.

Dillon, Richard H. 1975. *Siskiyou Trail: The Hudson's Bay Company Route to California*. New York: McGraw-Hill.

Dixon, R.B. 1905. "The Northern Maidu," *Bulletin of the American Museum of Natural History*, V.17, 119-346.

Donley, Michael W, Stuart Allan, Patricia Caro, and Clyde P. Patton. 1979. *Atlas of California*. Culver City, CA: Pacific Book Center.

Doyle, Michael. 1993. "Central Valley Farmland Called Nation's Most Endangered," *Sacramento Bee*, July 15, 1993, B-1.

Dreyer, William Ray. 1984. *Prehistoric Settlement Strategies in a Portion of the Northern Sacramento Valley, California.* Unpub. M.A. Thesis, California State University, Chico.

Duffy, Jr., William J. 1972. *The Sutter Basin and Its People.* Sacramento: The Printer.

Dumke, Glenn. 1944. *The Boom of the Eighties.* San Marino, CA: Huntington Library.

Dunbar, Robert G. 1983. *Forging New Rights in Western Waters.* Lincoln: University of Nebraska Press.

Dunn, Forrest D. 1977. *Butte County Place Names: A Geographical and Historical Dictionary.* Chico: Assn. for Northern California Records and Research.

Durham State Land Colony Collection. Chico: Meriam Library Special Collections, California State University, Chico.

Eigenheer, Richard Allen. 1976. *Early Perceptions of Agricultural Resources in the Central Valley of California.* Unpub. Ph.D. Diss., University of California, Davis.

Eisen, Jonathon and Daid Fine, with Kim Eisen, eds. 1985. *Unknown California.* New York: Collier Books.

Ellen, Peter T. 1993. *Sander Christensen: Immigrant Entrepreneur.* Unpub. ms., Special Collections, Meriam Library, California State University, Chico.

Ellis, W.T. 1939. *Memories, My Seventy Years in the Romantic County of Yuba California.* Eugene: University of Oregon.

Englebert, Ernest A. with Ann Foley Scheuring, ed. 1982. *Competition for California Water; Alternative Solutions.* Berkeley: University of California Press.

"Ethnic Clash in the Central Valley," *San Francisco Chronicle*, September 30, 1991, A-1, A6-7.

Farley, Adriana. 1996. *Durham Land Colony: History of the State Land Settlement at Durham, 1917-1931.* Durham, CA: n.p.

Farquhar, Francis P. 1932. "The Topographic Reports of George H. Derby." *California Historical Society Quarterly,* V. 11, 114-117.

Fearis, Donald F. 1971. *The California Farm Worker, 1930-1942.* Unpub. Ph.D. Diss, University of California, Berkeley.

Federal Writer's Project of the Works Progress Administration for the State of California. 1939. *California: A Guide to the Golden State.* New York: Hastings House.

Felthouse, Patricia. 1980. Interview with Charles Mitchell. Red Bluff: Tehama County Library.

Figge, Pamela. 1993. *Gridley: The City Born Along the Tracks, Planned on the Grid and Lost to the Highway.* Unpub. ms., Department of Geography and Planning, California State University, Chico.

Finck, John. 1986. "Secondary Migration to California's Central Valley," (in) *The Hmong in Transition,* Glenn C. Hendricks, Bruce T. Downig, and Amos S. Deinard, eds. New York: Center for Migration Studies.

"First Rice Storage in California." 1922. *Pacific Rural Press,* V. CIII, 19.

Fisher, James. 1971. *A History of the Political and Social Development of the Black Community in California, 1850-1950.* Unpub. Ph.D. Diss., State University of New York.

Forbes, Jack. 1966. *Afro-Americans in the Far West.* Berkeley: Far West Laboratory.

Forbes, Jack D. 1969. *Native Americans of California and Nevada: A Handbook.* Healdsburg, CA: Naturegraph Publishers.

Forbes, Jack D. 1971. "The Native American Experience in California History," *California Historical Society Quaterly,* V. 50, 235-242.

Forbes, Kari. 1988. *Sacred Sites of the Konkow Maidu in Butte County.* Unpub. M.A. Thesis, California State University, Chico.

Frank, B.F. and H.W. Chappell. 1881. *The History and Business Directory of Shasta County: Comprising an Accurate Historical Sketch of the County From Its Earliest Settlement to the Present,* (1881-1978) (rep. 1978).

Frank, Ida W. 1988. *A Stonyford Pedigree: Compilation of Early Settlers Living in the Stonyford Area Prior to 1900.* Santa Rosa: C.M. Smith.

Frayer, W.E.. 1989. *Wetlands of the California Central Valley: Status and Trends, 1939-mid 1980s.* Portland, OR: U.S. Fish and Wildlife Service.

Freese, John R. 1983. *Redding, California; Origins and Development.* Unpub. M.A. Thesis, California State University, Chico.

Fremont, John Charles. 1848. *Geographical Memoir Upon Upper California.* Washington: Senate Document 148, 30th Congress.

French, H.A. 1901. *Needs and Commerce of the Sacramento River—A Memorial Submitted to the Commerce Committee on Rivers and Harbors, Hourse of Representatives, Sacramento.*

Gable, Elmer, ed. 1991. "Welcome to the Corning Museum." Corning: History Museum.

Gage, Helen Sommer. 1973. "The Role of the Chinese in Northern California," (in) *Butte County Remembers.* Butte County Branch of the National League of American Pen Women.

Galarza, Ernesto. 1964. *Merchants of Labor: The Mexican Bracero Story*. San Jose: Rosicrucian Press.

Galarza, Ernesto. 1971. *Barrio Boy*. South Bend, IN: Notre Dame University Press.

Garcia, Dawn and Michael McCabe. "Ethnic Clash in Central Valley: An Immigration Lab for US," *The San Francisco Chronicle*, Sept. 30, 1991, A1, A6.

Gardner, Michael. "Rice Farmers Fret Over State's Basin Plan Revision," *Chico Enterprise-Record*, February 2, 1995, 3A.

Garreau, Joel. 1991. *Edge City: Life on the New Frontier*. New York: Doubleday.

Gates, Paul W. 1967. *California's Ranchos and Farms*. Madison, WI: The State Historical Society of Wisconsin.

Gaut, David. 1971. *The Durham Land Colony: California's First Journey into State Land Settlement*. Unpub. M.A. Thesis, Sacramento State College.

Giffen, Helen S. 1985. *Man of Destiny: Pierson Barton Reading: Pioneer of Shasta County, California*. Redding: Shasta Historical Society.

Gilbert, E. W. 1966. *The Explorations of Western North America 1800-1850, An Historical Geography*. New York: Cooper Square Publishers.

Gilbert, Frank T. 1968. *Reproduction of Thompson and West's History of the San Joaquin Valley, California*. [Reprint of 1879 Edition] Berkeley: Howell-North Books.

Giles, Rosena A. 1949. *Shasta County, California; A History*. Oakland, CA: Biobooks.

Gillis, Michael J. 1995. "The Changing World of the Sacramento Valley During the 19th Century," *Wagon Wheels*, 45. Colusi County Historical Society.

Gittler, Joseph B., ed. 1981. *Jewish Life in the United States*. New York: New York University Press.

Glanz, Rudolf. 1960. *The Jews of California From the Discovery of Gold Until 1880*. New York: Waldon Press, Inc.

"Glenn's Asian-American Community Expands its Self-Help Business Plans," *Orland Journal/Press-Register*, March 15, 1995, A-6.

Godoy, Beatriz. 1992. *Oroville: After the Dam*. Unpub. ms. for Department of Geography and Planning, California State University, Chico.

Goldschmidt, W.R. 1951. "Nomlaki Ethnography," *University of California Publications in American Arcaeology and Ethnology*, V. 42, 211-241.

Gottesman, Jane. "Breakthrough Study of Indian Burial Site," *San Francisco Chronicle*, September 24, 1990, B-1.

Green, Will S. 1857. "The Upper Sacramento," *Hutching's California Magazine*, V. 1, 493-496.

Green, Will S. 1950 (rep.) *The History of Colusa County, California.* Sacramento: The Sacramento Lithograph Company.

Gregory, James N. 1989. *American Exodus: The Dust Bowl Migration and Okie Culture in California.* New York: Oxford University Press.

Gridley-Biggs Cemetery, 1874-1948. 1992. Paradise Genealogical Society.

Griffin, Paul F. and Robert N. Young. 1957. *California; The New Empire State.* San Francisco: Fearon Publishers.

Guinn, James Miller. 1904. *History of the State of California and Biographical Record of the Sacramento Valley.* Chicago: Chapman Publishing.

Hackett, George and Michael A. Lerner. "Discovering the 'Other' California." *Newsweek*, November 16, 1987, 68-69.

Haehn, James O. 1964. "Minorities in Northern California," *North State Review*, V. 1, 22-26.

Hall, Frank. 1972. *Farming in West Central Colusa County Including Rice Growing, Drainage Problems, and Hunting Clubs, 1915-1970.* Interview with local resident, Charles Dennis. Chico: Association for Northern California Records and Research.

Hall, Frank. 1973. *The History and Historical Geography of Portions of Glenn and Colusa Counties.* Six interviews with local residents. Chico: Association for Northern California Records and Research.

Hanson, Nick. 1953. "Colusa County: Waterfowls Paradise." *Wagon Wheels*, V. 3 (1953), 2.

Harbaugh, John W. 1974. *Geology Field Guide to Northern California.* Dubuque IA: Wm. C. Brown..

Harding, S.T. 1960. *Water in California.* Palo Alto, CA: N-P Publications.

Hardwick, Susan Wiley, 1986. *Ethnic Residential and Commercial Patterns in Sacramento with Special Reference to the Russian-American Experience.* Unpub. Ph.D. Diss., University of California, Davis.

Hardwick, Susan Wiley. 1986. *Ethnic Residential and Commercial Patterns in Sacramento with Special Reference to the Russian-American Experience.* Unpub. Ph.D. Diss., University of California, Davis.

Hardwick, Susan Wiley. 1989. "Rural Ethnicity in California's Heartland." Unpub. ms. presented to the Association of American Geographers, Baltimore, MD.

Hardwick, Susan Wiley. 1993. *Russian Refuge: Religion, Migration, and Settlement on the North American Pacific Rim.* Chicago: University of Chicago Press.

Hardwick, Susan Wiley. 1993. "Ethnic Settlement in the Sacramento Valley," Unpub. ms. presented to Shasta College Faculty, Redding, CA.

Hardwick, Susan Wiley and Donald G. Holtgrieve. 1995. *Geography for Educators.* Englewood Cliffs, NJ: Prentice Hall.

Hargis, Jay Jackson. 1979. *The History of Colusa County Politics, 1851-1865.* Unpub. M.A. Thesis, California State University, Chico.

Harney, P.J. 1905. "History of River Transportation," *The Sacramento Union,* November 26: 7.

Hart, John Fraser. 1975. *The Look of the Land.* Engelwood Cliffs, NJ: Prentice Hall.

Hartmann, HT, K.W. Opitz, and J.A. Beutel. 1990. *Olive Production in California.* Davis: Division of Agricultural Sciences, University of California.

Haslam, Gerald. 1987. *Voices of a Place: Social and Literary Essays from the Other California.* Walnut Creek: Devil Mountain Books.

Haslam, Gerald. "Californians From Everywhere." *Sacramento Bee,* July 5, 1987, 10-12.

Haslam, Gerald. 1994. *The Other California: The Great Central Valley in Life and Letters.* Reno: University of Nevada Press.

Haslam, Gerald and James D. Houston, eds. 1978. *California Heartland: Writing from the Great Central Valley.* Santa Barbara: Capra Press.

Heizer, Robert F. and Theodora Kroeber, eds. 1979. *Ishi: The Last Yahi: A Documentary History.* Berkeley: University of California Press.

Heizer, Robert F. 1978. *Handbook of North American Indians.* Washington, D.C.: Smithsonian Institution.

Heizer, Robert F., ed. 1974. *The Destruction of the California Indians.* Santa Barbara: Peregrine Smith.

Heizer, Robert F. and M.A. Whipple, eds. 1971. *The California Indians: A Source Book.* Berkeley: University of California Press.

Heizer, Robert F. and Thomas R. Hester. 1970. "Names and Locations of Some Ethnographic Patwin and Maidu Indian Villages," (in) *Contributions of the University of California Archaeological Research Faculty,* V. 9, 90-117.

Heizer, Robert F. 1966. *Territories and Names of California Indian Tribes.* New York: Garland Publishing.

Helzer, Jennifer Jill. 1993. *Maintenance of Ethnic Identity: Hmong and Mien Settlement and Survival in Northern California.* Unpub. M.A. Thesis, California State University, Chico.

Helzer, Jennifer J. 1994. "Continuity and Change: Hmong Settlement in California's Sacramento Valley," *The Journal of Cultural Geography*. V. 14, 51-64.

Hendrix, Chester E. 1994. *The Mormon Population of Northern California*. Unpub. ms., Department of Geography and Planning, California State University, Chico.

Hendrix, Louise Butts, ed. 1980. *Sutter Buttes: Land of Histum Yani*. Marysville: Normart Publishing Company.

Hess, Gary R. 1974. "The Forgotten Asian-Americans," *Pacific Historical Review*, V. 43, 590.

Highway Advisory Committee. 1925. *Report of a Study of the State Highway System of California*. Sacramento.

Hill, Dorothy. 1978. *The Indians of Chico Rancheria*. Sacramento: Department of Parks and Recreation.

Hill, Mary. 1984. *California Landscape: Origin and Evolution*. Berkeley: University of California Press.

Hine, Robert V. 1953. *California's Utopian Colonies*. San Marino: The Huntington Library.

Hilton, George Woodman and John F. Due. 1960. *The Electric Interurban Railways in America*. Stanford, CA: Stanford University Press.

Hirata, Lucie Cheng. 1979. "Chinese Immigrant Women in 19th Century California," (in) *Women of America: A History*. C.R. Berkin and M.B. Norton, eds. Boston: Houghton-Mifflin.

Hiskin, Clara. 1948. *Tehama: Little City of The Big Trees*. New York: Exposition Press.

Hislop, Donald L. 1978. *The Nome-Lackee Indian Reservation, 1854-1870*. Chico: Association of Northern California Records and Research.

History of the Latter Day Saint's Church in Gridley, California, 1906-1986. 1980. The Reunion Committee. Oroville, CA: McDowell Printing.

Hitchcock, Ruth Hughes. 1980. *Leaves of the Past: A Pioneer Register including an Overview of the History and Events of Early Tehama County*. Chico: Association for Northern California Records and Research.

Hittell, John S. 1863. *Resources of California*. San Francisco: A. Roman and Company.

Hodges, R.E. 1919. "Why We Have the Best Rice Conditions in the World," *Pacific Rural Press* V. XCVIII, 1.

Hodges, Terry. 1988. *Sabertooth: The Rip-Roaring Adventures of a Legendary Game Warden*. Boulder, CO: Paladin Press.

Hoffman, Abraham. 1974. *Unwanted Mexican-Americans in the Great Depression; Repatriation Pressures, 1929-1939*. Tucson: University of Arizona Press.

Hoiland, Scot. 1975. *Citrus Growing on the Northern Fringe: Butte County, A Case Study*. Unpub. M.A. Thesis, California State University, Chico.

Holland, Robert F. and F. Thomas Griggs. 1976. "A Unique Habitat— California's Vernal Pools," *Fremontia*, V. 4, 3-6.

Holliday. J.S. 1981. *The World Rushed In*. New York: Simon and Schuster.

Hornbeck, David, et. al. 1983. *California Patterns: A Geographical and Historical Atlas*. Palo Alto: Mayfield.

Houston, A.W. 1946. "Chinese Gold Diggers," *The Covered Wagon*. Shasta Historical Society, n.p.

Houston, James D. 1982. *Californians: Searching for the Golden State*. New York: Alfred Knopf.

Houston, James D. 1984. "Looking for the Great Central Valley," *Golden State*, V. 1, 38-41.

Hoy, Kirby. 1978. *The Swedes in Richvale*. Unpub. ms., Department of Social Science, California State University, Chico..

Hundley, Norris Jr. 1992. *The Great Thirst: Californians and Water—1770s-1990s*. Berkeley: University of California Press.

Hultgren, Ellen. 1982. *A Brief Early History of Corning and the Maywood Colony*. Corning Chamber of Commerce.

Hurtado, Albert L. 1980. *Ranchos, Gold Mines, and Rancherias: A Socioeconomic History of Indians and Whites in Northern California*. Ann Arbor, MI: University Microfilms.

Hunt, Rockwell 1942. *John Bidwell-Prince of California Pioneers*. Caldwell, Idaho: The Caxton Printers, Ltd.

Hust, Stephen G. 1956. *This is My Native Land*. Yuba City: Independent Press.

Hutchison, Claude B., ed. 1946. *California Agriculture*. Berkeley: University of California Press.

Hutchinson, W.H. 1980. *California: The Golden Shore by the Sundown Sea*. Belmont CA: Star Publishing Co.

Hutchinson, W.H. 1983. *When Chico Stole the College*. Chico, CA: Butte Savings and Loan Association.

Hutchinson, W.H. 1990. *Tales From 'Old Hutch'*. Chico: Association for Northern California Records and Research.

Hutchinson, W.H. and Clarence F. McIntosh et al. (developed by Pam Herman Bush). 1991. *A Precious Sense of Place: The Early Years of Chico State*. Chico: Friends of the Meriam Library.

Ichioka, Yuji. 1988. *The Issei: The World of the First Generation Japanese Immigrants, 1885-1924.* New York: The Free Press.

Itamura, Sadao Sud. 1971. *The Settlement Pattern of the Japanese in the Yuba-Sutter Area of California.* Unpub. M.A. Thesis, California State University, Chico.

Iwata, Masakazu. 1962. "Japanese Immigrants in California Agriculture," *Agricultural History,* V. 36, 25-37.

Jackson, William Turrentine. 1952. *Wagon Roads West.* Berkeley: University of California Press.

Jamieson, Stuart M. 1942. "A Settlement of Rural Migrant Families in the Sacramento Valley, California," *Rural Sociology,* V.VII, 50-58.

Japanese Association of Marysville. 1932. *History of the Japanese Big Four.*

Jensen, Joan M. 1976. *Outcasts in a Savage Land: The East Indians of North America.* Santa Barbara: Cleo Press.

Jensen, Joan M. 1988. *Passage from India: Asian Immigrants in North America.* New Haven: Yale University Press.

Jensen, Peter M. and Paul R. Reed. 1979, *An Anthropological Overview and Cultural Resources Inventory of the Northern Sacramento Valley and Southern Cascade Range.* Redding: Department of the Interior, Bureau of Land Management, District Office.

Johnson, Ladd, ed. 1979. *Northern California Atlas and Gazetteer: Including Origin of Place Names.* Chico: California State University, Chico.

Johnson, Lawrence E. 1969. *Negro Settlement in the Oroville Area, Middle Sacramento Valley,* Unpub. M.A. Thesis, Chico State College.

Johnson, Overton. 1846. *Winter Route Across the Rocky Mountains with a Description of Oregon and California.* Lafayette, IN: John B. Seemans Printer.

Johnson, Richard L. 1995. "Floods and Flood Control Along the Middle Sacramento River, 1850-1870." *Wagon Wheels,* V. 45, Colusi County Historical Society.

Johnson, Stephen and Robert Dawson. 1993. *The Great Central Valley: California's Heartland.* Text by Gerald Haslam. Berkeley: University of California Press.

Johnson, Wilmeth M. 1981. *The Town of Maxwell—From the Beginning, 1878 to Present.* Publisher unknown.

Johnston, Adam. *Letter to the Commissioner of Indian Affairs.* Chico: Meriam Library Special Collections, California State University, Chico, July 6, 1850.

Jones, William A., ed. 1982. *Register of the Palermo Land and Water Company.* Chico: Meriam Library Special Collections, California State University, Chico.

Jordan, Terry G. 1993. *North American Cattle Ranching Frontiers: Origins, Diffusions, and Differentiations.* Albuquerque: University of New Mexico Press.

"Journey to the Center of the State," *San Francisco Chronicle, California Magazine,* May, 1987, 58-62, 120.

Judah, H.W. *Letter to Major W.W. Mackall* (Ass't. Adj. General, Department of the Pacific). Written from Red Bluff. Chico: Meriam Library Special Collections, California State University, Chico, April 19, 1858.

Kackert, Kristine. 1995. *The Establishment of Hamilton City, California, 1905-1906, and Its Relation to the Beet Sugar Industry.* M.A. thesis, California State University, Chico.

Kahrl, William L, William A. Bowen, Stewart Brand, Marlyn L. Shelton, David L. Fuller, and Donald A. Ryan. 1978-79. *The California Water Atlas.* Sacramento: Governor's Office of Planning and Research.

Katibah, Edwin F. 1984. "A Brief History of Riparian Forests in the Central Valley of California," (in) Richard E. Warner and Kathleen Hendrix, eds. *California Riparian Systems.* Berkeley: University of Califonia Press.

Kearney, Michael and Carole Nagengast. 1989. "Anthropological Perspectives on Transnational Communities in Northern California," (in) *Working Group on Farm Labor and Rural Poverty,* Working Paper #3, Davis: California Institute for Rural Studies.

Kelley, Robert L. 1956. "The Mining Controversy in the Sacramento Valley," *Pacific Historical Review,* V.25, 331-346.

Kelley, Robert L. 1959. *Gold vs. Grain: The Hydraulic Mining Controversy in California's Sacramento Valley.* Glendale, CA: The Arthur H. Clark Company.

Kelly, Robert L. 1965. "Taming the Sacramento: Hamiltonianism in Action." *Pacific Historical Review,* V. 34, 21-49.

Kelly, Robert L. 1989. *Battling the Inland Sea: American Political Culture, Public Policy, and the Sacramento Valley, 1850-1986.* Berkeley: University of California Press.

Kelley, Robert L. and Ronald L. Nye. 1984. "Historical Perspective on Salinity and Drainage Problems in California," *California Agriculture,* V. 30, 4-6.

Kelly, Joan. 1950. "The Chinese in Chico." *California Folklore,* V. 6, 282-319.

Kilcollins, Sandra. 1993. *Early Butte County History: Hamilton.* Unpub. ms. for Department of Geography and Planning, California State University, Chico.

Kilcollins, Sandra. 1994. *A Survey of the Chicano Presence in Early Chico History*, Unpub. ms. for Department of Geography and Planning, California State University, Chico.

Kirk, Robin. "The Paving of the Central Valley." *San Francisco Chronicle*, Feb. 28, 1988, Image Section, 10-17.

Kirsch, Robert and William S. Murphy. 1967. *West of the West.* New York: E.P. Dutton and Company.

Kluger, James R. 1992. *Turning on Water With a Shovel: The Career of Elwood Mead.* Albuquerque: University of New Mexico Press.

Knowlton, A.L. 1877. *Butte County, California: Illustrations.* Oakland: Smith and Elliott.

Kreiger, John. "Still Waging the Vietnam War," *US News and World Report*, September, 1992, 48-49.

Kreissman, Bern and Barbara Lekisch. 1991. *California: An Environmental Atlas and Guide.* Davis, CA: Bear Klaw Press.

Kroeber, Alfred. 1967. *Handbook of the Indians of California.* Berkeley: California Book Company.

Kroeber, Alfred L. 1925. *Handbook of the California Indians.* Washington: Smithsonian Institution.

Kroeber, Alfred L. 1932. "The Patwin and their Neighbors." *University of California Publications in Arcaeology and Ethnology*, V. 29, 253-423.

Kroeber, Alfred L. 1939. *Cultural and Natural Areas of Native North America.* Berkeley: University of California Press.

Kroeber, Theodora. 1961. *Ishi in Two Worlds: A Biography of the Last Wild Indian in North America.* Berkeley: University of California Press.

Kurtz, Carol Cameron. 1984. *The Sikhs of Yuba City.* Unpub. M.A. Thesis, California State University, Hayward.

Kutras, Christopher George. 1984. *Who Owns Shasta County: A Critical Analysis.* Unpub. M.A. Thesis, California State University, Chico.

Kutras, George C. 1956. *Shasta County: A History, 1849-1888.* Unpub. M.A. Thesis, Chico State College.

LaBrack, Bruce. 1970. "The Growth of the Sikh Community in the Sacramento Valley," *Sikh Sansar*, V. 3, 48-50.

LaBrack, Bruce. 1982. "Occupational Specialization Among Rural California Sikhs: The Interplay of Culture and Economics." *Amerasia*, V. 9, 29-56.

LaBrack, Bruce. 1988. *The Sikhs of Northern California: A Socio-Historical Study.* New York: AMS Press.

Lantis, David W., Rodney Steiner, and Arthur E. Karinen. 1963. *California: Land of Contrast.* Belmont, CA: Wadsworth Publishing Company, Inc.

Lantis, David W., Rodney Steiner, and Arthur E. Karinen. 1989. *California: The Pacific Connection.* Chico: Creekside Press.

Lantis, David with Rodney Steiner and Arthur F. Karinen. 1981. *California: Land of Contrast.* Dubuque, IA: Kendall/Hunt.

"Laos Hill People Try Yet Again in Central Valley," *The New York Times,* June 17, 1983, N7, L-A10.

Lapp, Rudolph. 1977. *Blacks in Gold Rush California.* New Haven: Yale University Press.

Larkey, Joann L. and Shipley Walters. 1987. *Yolo County: Land of Changing Patterns.* Northridge, CA: Windsor Publications, Inc.

Latour, Ira H., ed. 1993. *Silver Shadows: A Directory and History of Early Photography in Chico and Twelve Counties of Northern California.* Chico: Chico Museum Association, Chico Art Center.

Lawson, John S. 1986. *Redding and Shasta County: Gateway to the Cascades: An Illustrated History.* Northridge: Windsor Publications.

Leader, Herman Alexander. 1928. *The Hudson's Bay Company in California.* Unpub. Ph.D. Diss., University of California, Berkeley.

Lemos, Judi. "Celebrity City: Will It Play?" *Redding Record-Searchlight,* January 22, 1995: A-5-A-6 and January 23, 1995, A-4-A-5.

Levinson, Robert E. 1978. *The Jews in the California Gold Rush.* New York: KTAV Publishing House.

Levinson, Rosaline. 1985. "Jewish Communities Of Butte County: Rise and Development in the 19th Century." *Diggins,* V. 29, 51-99.

Lewis, E.J. 1880. *Tehama County, California.* San Francisco: n.p.

List of Active Annual Workplan Sites, FY 1994-1995. 1995. Sacramento: California Environmental Protection Agency, Department of Toxic Substances.

Lundberg Family Farms. 1994. *A Partnership with Nature.* Richvale, CA.

Lutheran Immigration and Refugee Service. n.d. *The Hmong: History and Culture.* New York: Lutheran Council in the USA.

Lydon, Philip A. and J.C. O'Brien. 1974. *Shasta County, California Mines and Mineral Resources.* California Division of Mines and Geology.

MacCannell, Dean. 1986. "Agribusiness and the Small Community," *Technology, Public Policy, and the Changing Structure of American*

Agriculture. Background Papers, V.2. Washington, D.C: Office of Technology Assessment.

MacMullen, Jerry. 1944. *Paddle-Wheel Days in California.* Stanford: Stanford University Press.

Magliari, Michael. 1989. "Populism, Steamboats, and the Octopus: Transportation Rates and Monopoly in California's Wheat Regions, 1890-1896," *Pacific Historical Review,* V. 58, 449-469.

Mainwaring, Laura. 1995. *Geography of Mennonite Settlement: From Europe to a Holdeman Mennonite Community in Glenn County, California.* Unpub. M.A. Thesis, California State University, Chico.

Mainwaring, Philip. 1995. *Transhumance in Northern California: Geography of Seasonal Livestock Movement in the Sierra Nevada.* Unpub. M.A. Thesis, California State University, Chico.

Maloney, Alice B. 1845. "Shasta was Shastala in 1814," *California Historical Society Quarterly,* V. 24, 230-234.

Maloney, Alice Bay. 1945. *Fur Brigade to the Buenaventure: John Work's California Expedition 1832-1833 for the Hudson's Bay Company.* San Francisco: California Historical Society.

Mansfield, George C. 1918. *History of Butte County.* Los Angeles: Historic Record Company.

Mansfield, George C. 1919. *Butte: The Story of a California County.* Oroville: Oroville Register.

Margolin, Malcolm. 1981. *The Way We Lived.* Berkeley: Heyday Books.

Marshall, Robert Bradford. 1919. *Irrigation of Twelve Million Acres in the Valley of California.* Sacramento: California State Irrigation Association.

Martin, Ilse. 1981. *Overview of the Cultural Historic Resources of Euro-American and Other Immigrant Groups in the Shasta-Trinity National Forest.* Playa Del Rey, CA: Geoscientific Systems and Consulting.

Martin, Joe. "Clinically Speaking: Groundbreaking Study Helps Immigrant Patients," *Chico News and Review,* September 2, 1993, 29.

Marysville Buddhist Church. 1982. *Marysville Buddhist Church 75th Anniversary.* Marysville, CA.

Matsumoto, David Mas. 1987. *Country Voices: The Oral History of a Japanese American Family Farm Community.* Del Rey, CA: Inaka Countryside Publications.

Mayne, Alicia Ann Alves. 1992. *Azorean Portuguese-Americans: Immigration and Settlement Patterns: The Factors that Influenced the Community in California.* Unpub. ms., Department of Social Science, California State University, Chico.

McComish, Charles D. and Rebecca T. Lambert. 1918. *History of Colusa and Glenn Counties*. Los Angeles: Historic Record Company.

McDonald, Archie. 1993. *The Japanese Experience in Butte County*. Chico: Association for Northern California Records and Research.

McDonald, Lois Halliday. 1989. *Elsie Hamburger: I Never Look Back*. Paradise: Paradise Fact and Folklore, Inc.

McDonald, Lois Halliday, ed. 1992. *Ripples along Chico Creek: Perspectives on People and Times*. Chico, CA: Butte County Branch, National League of American Pen Women.

McEvoy, Arthur. 1986. *The Fisherman's Problem: Ecology and Law in the California Fisheries, 1850-1980*. Cambridge, MA: Cambridge University Press.

McGee, Phil. 1994. *Certified Organic Membership Directory*. Santa Cruz, CA: California Certified Organic Farmers.

McGie, Joseph F. 1957. "The Gridley Story," *Diggins*, V. 1, n.p.

McGie, Joseph F. 1970. *Gridley Centennial Pictorial-History Book*. Oroville: Mercury Printers.

McGie, Joseph F. 1982. *History of Butte County*. 2 vol. Oroville: Butte County Board of Education.

McGill, Robert R. 1987. *Land Use Changes in the Sacramento River Riparian Zone, Redding to Colusa, 1982-1987*. Sacramento: Department of Water Resources.

McGowan, Joseph A. 1961. *History of the Sacramento Valley*. V. 1-3. New York: Lewis Historical Publishing Company.

McGowan, Joseph A. 1967. *History of the Sacramento Valley: A Student's Guide to Localized History*. New York: Teacher's College Press, Columbia University.

McGowan, Joseph A. and Terry R. Willis. 1983. *Sacramento: Heart of the Golden State*. Woodland Hills, CA: Windsor Publications, Inc.

McIntosh, Clarence F. 1962. "The Chico and Red Bluff Route," *The Quaterly Journal of the Idaho Historical Society*, V. 6.

McKinstry, George. 1872. *Documents for the History of California, 1846-49*. Berkeley: University of California, Bancroft Library Manuscript.

McLeod, Alexander Roderick. 1968. *The Hudson Bay Company's First Fur Brigade to the Sacramento Valley: Alexander Mcleod's 1829 Hunt*. Sacramento: Sacramento Book Collector's Club.

McNamar, Myrtle. n.d. *Way Back When*. Cottonwood, CA: n.p.

McWilliams, Carey. 1939. *Ill Fares the Land*. Boston: Little, Brown, and Company.

McWilliams, Carey. 1939. *Factories in the Field.* Boston: Little, Brown, and Company.

McWilliams, Carey. 1944. *Prejudice: Japanese-Americans: Symbol of Racial Intolerance.* Boston: Little, Brown, and Company.

McWilliams, Carey. 1948. *North From Mexico: The Spanish-Speaking People of the United States.* New York: Greenwood Press.

McWilliams, Carey. 1949. *California: The Great Exception.* New York: A.A. Wyn Publishers.

McWilliams, Carey. 1976. "And the People Came." *Westways,* 38-49.

Medeiros, Joseph L. 1976. "The Future of the Great Valley Pools," *Fremontia,* V. 4, 24-27.

Memorial and Biographical History of Northern California. 1891. Chicago: Lewis Publishing Company.

Merriam, C. Hart. 1905. "The Indian Population of California," *American Anthropologist,* V. 7, 594-606.

Milich, Nick. "Nigger Heaven," *The Davis Enterprise,* September 20, 1987, 25, 29.

Miller, Allan P. 1950. *An Ethnographic Report on the Sikh (East) Indians of the Sacramento Valley,* Unpub. ms, South/Southeast Asia Library, University of California, Berkeley.

Miller, Crane S. and Richard S. Hyslop. 1983. *California: The Geography of Diversity.* Palo Alto, CA: Mayfield Publishing Company.

Moak, Sim. 1923. *Last of the Mill Creeks and Early Life in Northern California.* Chico: n.p.

Moles, Jerry A. 1979. "Who Tills the Soil? Mexican-American Workers Replace the Small Farmer in California: An Example From Colusa, County." *Human Organization,* V. 38, 20-27.

Monaco, James Edward. 1986. *The Changing Ethnic Character of a California Gold Mining Community: Butte County, California.* Unpub. M.A. Thesis, California State University, Chico.

Morgan, Dale L. 1943. *The Humboldt: Highroad of the West.* New York: Farrar and Rinehart.

Morgan, Dale L. 1953. *Jedediah Smith and the Opening of the West.* New York, Bobbs-Merrill, 1953.

Moulton, Larry E. 1969. *The Vina District, Tehama County, California: Evolution of Land Utilization in a Small Segment of the Middle Sacramento Valley.* Unpub. M.A. Thesis, California State University, Chico.

Muller, Thomas. 1985. *The Fourth Wave: California's Newest Immigrants.* Washington, D.C: Urban Institute Press.

Nadeau, Remi. 1965. *Ghost Towns and Mining Camps of California*. Los
   Angeles: The Ward Richie Press.
Newberry, J.S. 1857. *Report Upon the Mammals. Reports of Explorations and
   Surveys to Ascertain the Most Practical and Economical Route for a Railroad
   from the Mississippi River to the Pacific Ocean*. Washington, D.C.: U.S.
   War Department, V. 6, 35-72.
Nielsen, Valentina. 1956. "Living Towns in Tehama County," and
   "Geographical Features of Tehama County," *Wagon Wheels*, V. 1, 1-8.
Nordhoff, Charles. 1875. *California: For Health, Pleasure, and Residence: A
   Book for Travelers and Settlers*. New York: Harper and Brothers.
Norris, Robert M. and Robert W. Webb. 1990. *Geology of California*. New
   York: Wiley and Sons.
Nostrand, Richard L. 1992. *The Hispano Homeland*. Norman and Lincoln:
   University of Oklahoma Press.
Nunis, Doyce B. Jr. and Gloria Ricci Lothrup. 1989. *A Guide to the History of
   California*. New York: Greenwood Press.
Oakeshott, Gordon B. 1978. *California's Changing Landscapes: A Guide to the
   Geology of the State*. New York: McGraw-Hill.
O'Connell, Agnes Catherine. 1930. *The Historical Development of the
   Sacramento Valley Before 1848*. Unpub. M.A. Thesis, University of
   California, Berkeley.
Old Oroville Cemetery. 1992. Oroville: The Paradise Genealogical Society.
Ornduff, Robert. 1974. *Introduction to California Plant Life*. Berkeley:
   University of California Press.
Oroville Park Department. n.d. *Chinese Temple*. Oroville, California.
Orsi, Richard J. 1974. *A List of References for the History of Agriculture in
   California*. Davis: Agricultural History Center, University of California.
Orsi, Richard J. 1975. "The Octopus Reconsidered: The Southern Pacific and
   Agricultural Modernization in California, 1865-1915." *California Historical
   Quarterly*, V. 2, 197-220.
Osborn, Arthur D. 1953. *A History of the Biggs, Butte County Area*. Unpub.
   M.A. Thesis, California State University, Chico.
Osborne, Andrew J. 1985. *J. Granville Doll and the Formative Years of Red
   Bluff*. Chico: Association for Northern California Records and Research.
Ostrander, Daniel Lee. 1968. *The Steamboat: Catalytic Element in the
   Development of Red Bluff, California, 1850-1862*. Unpub. M.A. Thesis,
   California State University, Chico.
Owens, Kenneth N., ed. 1994. *John Sutter and a Wider West*. Lincoln:
   University of Nebraska Press.

Pacific Coast Business Directory. 1967. San Francisco: Henry F. Langley.

Pacific Constructor, Inc. 1945. *Shasta Dam and Its Builders.* San Francisco, Pacific Constructors.

Packard, Walter. *Statement Prepared for Walter Packard to be forwarded to Washington,* August 3, 1935. Harry E. Dobrisch Papers, Bancroft Library. Paul S. Taylor Collection, University of California, Berkeley.

Palermo Land and Water Company (Register). 1982. Chico: William A. Jones, compiler. California State University, Chico Meriam Library.

Palmquist, Peter E. 1987. *Once Upon a Dam Site: Howard Colby's Shasta Dam Photographs, 1838-1950.* Redding: The Redding Museum and Art Center.

Peck, James E. 1966. *The Durham Land Colony: California's Noble Experiment.* Unpub. M.A. Thesis, Chico State College.

Peck, William C. 1969. *The County Seat Struggle of 1914.* Unpub. M.A. Thesis, California State University, Chico.

Petersen, Dan, AIA and Assoc. Inc. 1980. *Colusa Historic Survey.* Santa Rosa, CA.

Petersen, Edward. 1972. *Redding, 1872-1972: A Centennial History.* Redding: Nor-Cal Printing and Litho.

Phay, Wilbert L. 1986. *John Brown's Family in Red Bluff, 1864-1870.* Chico: Association for Northern California Records and Research. Occasional Publication #12.

Pinkerton, Robert E. 1931. *Hudson's Bay Company.* New York: Henry Holt and Company.

Pisani, Donald J. 1984. *From Family Farm to Agribusness.* Berkeley: University of California Press.

Pitt, Leonard. 1966. *The Decline of the Californios: A Social History of the Spanish-Speaking Californias, 1846-1890.* Berkeley: University of California Press.

Powers, Stephen. 1976. *Tribes of California.* Berkeley: University of California Press.

Price, Charles K. 1980. *History of Monroeville Cemetery 1851-1910.* Colusa, CA: Colusi County Historical Society.

Pryor, Frank. 1915. *Colusa County in the Sacramento Valley, California: Back to the Farm, Why?* Colusa County Chamber of Commerce.

Ramey, Earl. 1935. "The Beginnings of Marysville," *California Historical Society Quarterly,* V. 14.

Ransome, F. Leslie. 1896. *The Great Valley of California, a Criticism of the Theory of Isostasy.* Bulletin of the Department of Geology, V. 1. Berkeley: University of California.

Reading, Alice M. n.d. *Collection of Materials Relating to Her Father, Person B. Reading*. Unpub. ms. Berkeley: Bancroft Library Collection.

Reager, Frank S. 1951. "Monroeville," *Colusi County Historical Society, Wagon Wheels*, V. I.

Redmond, Judith. 1989. *Troubled Waters, Troubled Lands*. Davis, CA: Institute for Rural Studies.

Reed, Karen Lea. 1977. *The Chinese in Tehama County: With Attention to the Anti-Chinese Sentiment*. Unpub. M.A. Thesis, California State University, Chico.

Reed, Karen Lea. 1980. *The Chinese in Tehama County, 1860-1890*. Chico: Association for Northern California Records and Research.

"Regional Rice at a Glance," *Chico Enterprise-Record*, May 11, 1994, 7A.

Reid, Robert Lee, Jr. 1969. *The Study of Minorities in Shasta County, 1850-1880*. Unpub. M.A. Thesis, Chico State College.

Reisler, Mark. 1976. *By the Sweat of their Brow: Mexican Immigrant Labor in the United States: 1900-1940*.Westport, CN: Greenwood Press.

Reisner, Marc. 1986. *Cadillac Desert*. New York: Viking Press.

Rensch, H.E., E.G. Rensch, and Mildred Brooke Hoover. 1948. *Historic Spots in California: Valley and Sierra Counties*. Stanford, CA: Stanford University Press.

Reports of Explorations and Survey to Ascertain the Most Practicable and Economical Routes for a Railroad from the Mississippi River to the Pacific Ocean, Made According to the Acts of Congrss of March 3, 1853, May 31, 1854, and August 5, 1854. 1857. United States Senate, 33rd Congress. Ex. Doc. 78, V. 6, Geological Report. Washington, 20-21.

Resources of the Sacramento Valley and Tributary Country. 1883. Sacramento: Immigration Association of California.

Reynolds, Forrest et al. 1993. *Restoring Central Valley Streams: A Plan for Action*. Sacramento: California Department of Fish and Game.

Rice, Richard, William Bullough and Richard Orsi. 1988. *The Illusive Eden: A New History of California*. New York: Alfred A. Knopf.

"Rice: The New Crop in the Sacramento Valley." 1914. *Sacramento Valley Monthly*, V. 4, 1.

Robertson, Joan A. 1988. *Career Aspirations and Life Themes of the Hmong in Butte County*. Unpub. M.A. Thesis, California State University, Chico.

Robinson, Clarence Cromwell. 1951. *Ranching In the Gay 90's*. Stockton, CA: n.p.

Robinson, W.W. 1948. *Land in California*. Berkeley: University of California Press.

Rocca, Al M. 1993. *The Shasta Dam Boomtowns: A Community Building in the New Deal Era*. Redding, CA: Redding Museum of Art and History.

Rochlin, Harriet and Fred. 1984. *Pioneer Jews: A New Life in the Far West*. Boston: Houghton-Mifflin.

Rodriquez, Richard. "Reflections on the Flatland," *California Magazine. The San Francisco Chronicle,* May, 1987, 63, 113.

Rogers, Justus H. 1891. *Colusa County*. Orland: n.p.

Root, Riley. 1955. *Journal of Travels from St. Josephs to Oregon*. Oakland, CA: Biobooks. [Originally Published in 1850]

Roske, Ralph J. 1968. *Everyman's Eden: A History of California*. New York: The Macmillan Company.

Rouse, Roger. n.d. *Migration and the Politics of Family Life: Divergent Projects and Rhetorical Strategies in a Mexican Transnational Community*. Unpub. ms., University of California, Davis.

Royce, Josiah. 1886. *California*. Cambridge, MA: The Riverside Press.

Sacramento County and Its Resources. 1894. Sacramento: H.S. Crocker Company.

Sacramento Development Association. 1914. *1915: Opportunities for the Sacramento Valley: a Great Plan for Taking the Fullest Advantage of the Presence in this Next Year of Two Great Expositions*. Sacramento.

Sacramento River, Sloughs, and Tributaries, California: 1991 Aerial Atlas— Collinsville to Shasta Dam. 1991. Sacramento: U.S.Army Corps Engineers.

Sacramento Valley Development Association. n.d. *Sacramento Valley, California*. San Francisco: Sunset Magazine Homeseeker's Bureau.

Samora, Julian, ed. 1966. La Raza: *Forgotten Americans*. Notre Dame: University of Notre Dame Press./

Sands, Anne E., ed. 1980. *Riparian Forests in California: Their Ecology and Conservation*. Berkeley: University of California Press.

Santa Clara County Schools. n.d. *Vietnamese Guidance Project*. Santa Clara, CA.

Satorius, Veronica. 1978. *Between the Lines: The Catholic Church in Shasta County, California, 1853-1977*. Portland, OR: Graphic Arts Center.

Savage, W. Sherman. 1946. "Early Negro Education in the Pacific Coast States," *Journal of Negro Education*, V. 15, 134-139.

Scheuring, Ann Foley, ed. 1983. *A Guidebook to California Agriculture*. Berkeley: University of California Press.

Scheuring, Ann Foley. "From Many Lands," *California Farmer*, November 21, 1987, 16-18, 35-36; December 12, 1987, 34-36, 52; and January 2, 1988, 26-28.

Schleff, Nancy. 1991. "Oroville Maidu," *Diggins*, V. 35, 75-81.

Schoener, Allon. 1981. *The American Jewish Experience: From 1654 to the Present*. Philadelphia: Museum of Jewish History.

Scott, Edwin. 1976. *California to Oregon by Trail, Steamboat, Stagecoach, and Train, 1850-1887*. Unpub. ms., Pasadena City College.

Scott, Lauren and Sandra Marquiss. 1984. "An Historical Overview of the Sacramento River," (in) Richard E. Warner and Kathleen Hendrix, eds. *California Riparian Systems*. Berkeley: University of California Press.

Shasta County Advertising Fund. 1935. *Facts about Shasta County*. Redding: Shasta County Chamber of Commerce.

Shasta County Scrapbook. n.d. Sacramento: California State Library.

Shaw, George A. 1963. *A History of Steamboating on the Upper Sacramento, 1850-1862*. Unpub. M.A. Thesis, Chico State College.

Shepherd, Sandra Brubaker. 1993. *California Heartland: A Pictorial History and Tour Guide of Eight Northern California Counties*. San Francisco: Scottwall Associates.

Shover, Michele. 1981. *Chico's Little Chapman Mansion: The House and its People*. Chico: Association for Northern Californian Records and Research.

Shover, Michele. 1988. "Chico Women: Nemesis of a Rural Town's Anti-Chinese Campaigns, 1876-1888," *California History*, V. 68, 228-243.

Shover, Michele. 1991. *Blacks in Chico: Climbing the Slippery Slope*. Chico: Association for Northern California Records and Research.

Shover, Michele. 1996. "Fighting Back: The Chinese Influence on Chico Law and Politics, 1880-1886." *California History*, V. 74, 408-421.

Simpson, George Sir. 1847. *Narrative of a Journey Around the World During the Years 1841 and 1842*. London: H. Colburn.

Simmons, Paul. 1993. *California Water: The Inland Surface Waters Plan Litigation; Revisiting Basic Issues in Water Quality Regulation*. New York: McGraw-Hill.

Singh, Gurdial. 1946. "East Indians in the United States," *Sociology and Social Work*, V. 30, 208-216.

Smith, Betty. 1987. *Jewish Ethnic Patterns in Shasta County, California*. Unpub. ms., Department of Geography and Planning, California State University, Chico.

Smith, D. 1991. *The Dictionary of Early Shasta County History*. Cottonwood: D. Smith.

Smith, Jesse M., ed. 1976. *Sketches of Old Sacramento: A Tribute to Joseph A. McGowan*. Sacramento: Sacramento County Historical Society.

Smith, Roy James. 1937. *An Economic Analysis of the State Land Settlements at Delhi and Durham*. Unpub. Ph.D. Diss., University of California, Berkeley.

Sommarston, Allan. 1963. *Hamilton City*. Unpub. ms., Department of Geography and Planning, California State University, Chico.

Southern, May Hazel. 1942. *Our Storied Landmarks: Shasta County, California*. San Francisco: P. Balakshin Printing.

Starr, Kevin. 1973. *Americans and the California Dream, 1850-1915*. New York: Oxford University Press.

Starr, Kevin. 1985. *Inventing the Dream: California Through the Progressive Era*. New York: Oxford University Press.

Stebbins, G. Ledyard. 1976. "Ecological Islands and Vernal Pools," *Fremontia*, V. 4, 12-18.

Stegner, Wallace. 1992. *Living and Writing in the West*. New York: Penguin Books.

Stein, Walter. 1973. *California and the Dust Bowl Migration*. Westport, CT: Greenwood Press.

Steinbeck, John. 1939. *Grapes of Wrath*. New York: Viking Press.

Steinbeck, John. 1952. *East of Eden*. New York: The Viking Press.

Steinhart, Peter. 1987. "A River of Birds," *Pacific Discovery*, V. 2, 16-33.

Stern, Norton B. 1966. *Log of California Jewish History Trip*. Unpub. ms. at the Western History Jewish History Center of Judah L. Magnes Memorial Museum, Berkeley.

Stewart, George R. 1962. *The California Trail: An Epic with Many Heroes*. New York: McGraw-Hill.

Sudahl, Elaine. 1986. *Archaeological Investigations in the Jones Valley Area of Shasta Lake*. Washington, D.C.: U.S. Dept of Agriculture, Forest Service.

Sullivan, Janet and Maryjane Zall. 1974. *The Survivors: Existing Homes and Buildings of Yuba and Sutter Counties' Past*, n.p.

Sullivan, Maurice S. 1934. *The Travels of Jedediah Smith*. Santa Ana, CA: The Fine Arts Press.

Takaki, Ronald. 1989. *Strangers From A Different Shore: A History Of Asian Americans*. Boston: Little, Brown.

Talbitzer, Bill. 1963. *Lost Beneath the Feather*. Oroville, CA: Bill Talbitzer Publishers.

Talbitzer, Bill. 1967. *The Gandydancers*. Oroville, CA: Las Plumas Publications.

Talbitzer, Bill. 1987. *Butte County: An Illustrated History*. Northridge, CA: Windsor Books, Inc.

Taylor, Paul S. 1928-1934. *Mexican Labor in the United States*. 6 volumes. Berkeley: University of California Press.

Taylor, Paul S. 1935. "Again the Covered Wagon," *Survey*, V. 24, 351-355.

Teets, Bob and Shelby Young. 1986. *Rivers of Fear: The Great California Flood of 1986*. Terra Alta, WV: C.R. Publications, Inc.

Tenbroek, Jacobus, Edward N. Barnhart, and Floyd W. Matson. 1954. *Prejudice, War, and the Constitution*. Berkeley: University of California Press.

The Dam. 1907. Advertisements to Attract Settlers to Colusa County.

"The Last Chinatown," *Sacramento Bee*, "Scene Section," V.1, October 13, 1993, 1-2.

The Reunion Committee. 1980. *History of the LDS Church, Gridley, California, 1906-1980*. Gridley: McDowell Printing.

The Sacramento River Basin. 1931. Sacramento: State of California Dept. of Water Resources.

Thomas, Dorothy Swine. 1952. *The Salvage*. Berkeley: University of California Press.

Thompson, John. 1957. *The Settlement Geography of the Sacramento-San Joaquin Delta, California*. Unpub. Ph.D. Diss., Stanford University.

Thompson, Kenneth. 1960. "Historic Flooding in the Sacramento Valley," *Pacific Historical Review*, V. 24, 349-360.

Thompson, Kenneth. 1961. "Riparian Forests of the Sacramento Valley, California," *Annals of the Association of American Geographers*, V. 51, 294-315.

Thompson T.H. and A.A. West. 1880. *History of Sacramento County. History of Yuba County* (1879). Oakland: Pacific Press.

Thompson and West. 1879, rep. 1974. *History of Sutter County, California with Illustrations*. Berkeley: Howell-North Books.

Tincher, Phillip Anthony. 1972. *A Morphological Study of the City of Redding*. Unpub. M.A. Thesis, California State University, Chico.

Tolan Committee. 1940. United States Congress. House of Representatives. Select Committee to Investigate the Interstate Migration of Destitute Citizens. Pursuant to House Resolution 63 and House Resolution 491, 76th Congress.

Tordoff, Judith D. 1987. *Dutch Gulch Lake Excavation at Thirteen Historic Sites in the Cottonwood Mining District*. Sacramento: U.S. Army Corps of Engineers.

Trevino, Manuel O. 1966. *Floods of the Sacramento Valley, 1849-1907*. Unpub. ms., Dept. of History, California State University, Chico.

Trevino, Manuel O. 1970. *The History of Oroville, 1849-1857*. Unpub. M.A. Thesis, California State University, Chico.

Trussell, Margaret Edith. 1969. *Land Choice by Pioneer Farmers: Western Butte County Through 1877*. Unpub. Ph.D. Diss., University of Oregon.

Tsuji, Eugene. 1967. *The Federal Government and the Japanese Evacuation from Yuba-Sutter Counties*. Unpub. ms., Report for History 200, Chico State College.

Turner B.L. II and Stephen B. Brush. 1987. *Comparative Farming Systems*. New York: The Guilford Press.

Upper Sacramento River Fisheries and Riparian Habitat Management Plan. 1989. Sacramento: California Resources Agency.

Urbhans, T.D. n.d. *History of Agriculture in Sutter County*. Yuba City: Sutter County Library.

Urseny, Laura. "North State is Mending But Growth will be Slow," *Chico Enterprise-Record*, February 16, 1995, 3A.

U.S. Census of Shasta County, California. 1983. Redding: Shasta County Genealogical Society.

U.S. Department of Agriculture. 1993. *California Field Crops Statistics, 1982-92* (published cooperatively with the CA Department of Food and Agriculture).

U.S. Department of Agriculture. 1993. *Agricultural Crop and Livestock Reports for Counties of Butte, Colusa, Glenn, Sacramento, Shasta, Solano, Sutter, Tehama, Yolo, and Yuba*.

Usdansky, Margaret. "California's Mix Offers a Look at the Future," *USA Today*, December 4, 1992, 8A.

Usdansky, Margaret. "Minorities Are Headed Toward the Majority," *USA Today*, December 4, 1992, 1A.

Vang, Za and Judy Lewis. 1984. *Grandmother's Path, Grandfather's Way*. San Francisco: Zellerback Family Fund.

Vaughn, Trudy. 1986. *Ecological Investigations at a Sacramento River Mining Camp*. Redding: n.p.

Vieira, Richard J. 1968. *Gridley, California: The Evolution of a Mid-Sacramento Valley Farm Community*. Unpub. M.A. Thesis, Chico State College.

Voorhis, Jerry to Jonathon Garst. 1938. *U.S. Department of Agriculture Collection* V. 36. Berkeley: Bancroft Library, University of California.

Walter, Dan. "New Pilgrims Come to State," *Sacramento Bee*, November 24, 1988, A-3.

Warner, Richard C. and Kathleen Hendrix. eds. 1984. *California's Riparian Systems*. Berkeley: University of California Press.

Waterland, John S. Untitled collection of newspaper clippings of historical articles published in the Chico Record, 1934-40. V. I. Available in Meriam Library Special Collections, California State University, Chico.

Waxman, Tressa J. 1961. *History of County Division in Colusa County, California.* Unpub. M.A. Thesis, Sacramento State College.

Weaver, Nancy. "Proud Sikhs Often Find the U.S. Dream Only Dust," *Sacramento Bee*, September 29, 1986, A1,14.

Webster, Virginia. "Farm Cooperative Idea Moves to Grant Stage." *Willows Journal,* November 22, 1993, A-1.

Weir, Walter Wallace. 1929. *Drainage in the Sacramento Valley Rice Fields.* Bulletin: California Agricultural Experiment Station, No. 464.

Weiss, Clyde. "America's Vanishing Farms," *Chico Enterprise Record,* July 19, 1993, 6A.

Weissberg, Al. 1985. "Congregation Beth Israel of Redding." Unpub. ms., Redding, California.

Weston, Joshua Francis. 1953. "Monroeville as I Remember It," *Wagon Wheels,* V. I.

White, Thelma. 1953. "Geese Hunting." *Wagon Wheels,* V. 3, 1-3.

White, Thelma Buckley. 1995. *Glenn County Sketchbook.* Chico: Butte County Branch, National League of American Pen Women.

"Why We Have the Best Rice Conditions in the World," *Pacific Rural Press,* July 19, 1919, 6-7.

Wildman, Esther Theresa. 1924. *The Settlement and Resources of the Sacramento Valley.* Unpub. M.A. Thesis, University of California, Berkeley.

Wiley, Walt. "Tiny Zamora Finally Has A 'Business District' Again," *Sacramento Bee*, April 21, 1993, B1, B4.

Wilkes, Charles. 1845. *Narrative of the United States Exploring Expedition During the Years 1838, 1839, 1840, 1841, 1842.* 5 Vols. and Atlas. Philadelphia: Lea & Blanchard.

Williams, Jerry. 1982. *And Yet They Come.* New York: Center for Migration Studies.

Williams, Robert Earl. 1992. *Durham Mutual Water Company: A Microcosm of the Agricultural Waterscape in Butte County, California.* Unpub. M.A. Thesis, California State University, Chico.

Willson, Jack H. 1979. *Rice in California.* Butte County Rice Grower's Association.

Wilson, Robert A. and Bill Hosokawa. 1980. *East to America: A History of the Japanese in the United States.* New York: William Morrow and Company.

Winther, Oscar O. 1938. *Via Western Express and Stagecoach.* Palo Alto, CA: Stanford University Press.

Withers, Carl. 1945. *Plainville, USA.* New York: Columbia University Press.

Wollenberg, Charles, ed. 1970. *Ethnic Conflict in California History.* Los Angeles: Tinnon-Brown.

Wood, Rev. Jesse. Reprint of 1886 edition. *Butte County, California. Its Resources and Advantages for Home Seekers.* Chico: Association for Northern California Records and Research.

Wood, Ruth Kedzie. 1915. *The Tourist's California.* New York: Dodd, Mead, and Company.

Woolridge, Major Jesse Walton. 1931. *History of the Sacramento Valley.*V 1-3. Chicago: The Pioneer Historical Publishing Company.

Worcester, Hugh. 1955. *Hunting the Lawless.* Berkeley: American Wildlife Associates.

Worster, Donald. 1986. *Rivers of Empire: Water, Aridity, amid the Growth of the American West.* New York: Pantheon.

Wright, George Vandergriff. 1969. *The Legal Status of the Negro in California: 1849-1865.* Unpub. Thesis, California State University, Chico.

Wyant, William K. 1982. *Westward in Eden.* Berkeley: University of California Press.

Wyman, Christie. 1994. *Organic Farming Directory.* Family Farm Series, Cooperative Extension, University of California, Davis.

Yates, John. 1971. *A Sailor's Sketch of the Sacramento Valley in 1842.* Berkeley: Friends of the Bancroft Library.

Yeadon, David. 1973. *Exploring Small Towns 2. Northern California.* Los Angeles: The Ward Richie Press.

Young, Helen D. 1978. *Arbuckle and College City.* Fresno, CA: Pioneer Publishing.

Interviews

Betts, Jeanette. November 12, 1994, Chico.

Boulware, Mary. January 14, 1974, Sacramento.

Brimhall, Brenda. November 5, 1994, Chico.

Chao, Pahin. June 1, 1993, Redding.

Crown, Christine. October 23, 1994, Chico.

Gage, Helen. April 2, 1973, Chico.

Helzer, Irene. December 5, 1994, Redding.

Helzer, Jennifer. September 10, 1993, Chico.

Hill, Dorothy. September 12, 1973, Chico.
Hom, George. October 14 and 23, 1974, Chico.
Jones, Sadhana. August 2, 1994, Chico.
Kelly, Candace. November 8, 1993, Oroville.
Lantis, David. 1972 through 1996, Chico.
Leppard, Misty. July 19, 1994, Chico.
Luvas, Jon. September 29, 1994, Chico.
Luvas, Tanha. September 29, 1994, Chico.
Meriam, Ted. March 26, 1996, Chico.
Morehead, Mrs. J.F. September 12, 1973, Chico.
Morris, Angela, January 28, 1995, Chico.
Selene, Dawn. August 17, 1994, Chico.
Struthers, John. July 17, 1994, Chico.
Tochterman, Mendel. January 2, 1974, Chico.
Vang, May. December 11, 1994, Chico.

Index

About the Authors

Susan Wiley Hardwick is professor of geography at California State University, Chico. Her primary areas of research and teaching focus on immigrant settlement and survival in the American West, especially in the Sacramento Valley. Dr. Hardwick's most recent book on the immigrant experience is *Russian Refuge: Religion, Migration, and Settlement on the North American Pacific Rim* (University of Chicago Press, 1993). She earned her Ph.D. in geography at the University of California, Davis. Dr. Hardwick was awarded the Outstanding Professor Award for the nineteen-campus California State University system in 1995 and is active in state and national professional geography organizations. She is best known at the national level for her publications and presentations on geographic education and is, most recently, the coauthor of *Geography for Educators: Standards, Themes, and Concepts* published by Prentice Hall in 1996. Dr. Hardwick has worked as an educational consultant for the National Geographic Society, the California and Florida Departments of Education, the College Board, and a wide variety of other educational and publishing projects.

Donald Gordon Holtgrieve is professor of geography and planning at California State University, Chico. His responsibilities there involve teaching courses in historical geography, rural and town planning, and environmental planning. Both of these programs allow him to be "in the field" in the Sacramento Valley as often as possible. Dr. Holtgrieve received his Ph.D. in geography at the University of Oregon. He is a former police officer, high school teacher, and corporate executive. Dr. Holtgrieve is a frequent consultant to state and local agencies in the preparation of environmental impact reports, community plans, and historical-geographic studies. In addition to more than one hundred environmental studies and planning documents, he is the coauthor of *Geography for Educators: Standards,Themes, and Concepts*, the *California Wine Atlas*, and a poster-size map, *Vineyards and Wineries of California*, published by Allan Cartography in Medford, Oregon.

Susan Hardwick and Donald Holtgrieve are the parents of four grown sons who proudly proclaim they are "geographers by assimilation."

DATE DUE

GAYLORD			PRINTED IN U.S.A.